CHILDREN'S LITERATURE IN THE CLASSROOM

SOLVING PROBLEMS IN THE TEACHING OF LITERACY
Cathy Collins Block, Series Editor

RECENT VOLUMES

Reading More, Reading Better
Edited by Elfrieda H. Hiebert

The Reading Specialist, Second Edition:
Leadership for the Classroom, School, and Community
Rita M. Bean

Teaching New Literacies in Grades K–3:
Resources for 21st-Century Classrooms
Edited by Barbara Moss and Diane Lapp

Teaching New Literacies in Grades 4–6:
Resources for 21st-Century Classrooms
Edited by Barbara Moss and Diane Lapp

Teaching Reading: Strategies and Resources for Grades K–6
Rachel L. McCormack and Susan Lee Pasquarelli

Comprehension Across the Curriculum: Perspectives and Practices K–12
Edited by Kathy Ganske and Douglas Fisher

Best Practices in ELL Instruction
Edited by Guofang Li and Patricia A. Edwards

Responsive Guided Reading in Grades K–5:
Simplifying Small-Group Instruction
Jennifer Berne and Sophie C. Degener

Early Intervention for Reading Difficulties:
The Interactive Strategies Approach
Donna M. Scanlon, Kimberly L. Anderson, and Joan M. Sweeney

Matching Books and Readers: Helping English Learners in Grades K–6
Nancy L. Hadaway and Terrell A. Young

Children's Literature in the Classroom: Engaging Lifelong Readers
Diane M. Barone

Children's Literature in the Classroom

ENGAGING LIFELONG READERS

Diane M. Barone

THE GUILFORD PRESS
New York London

A Division of Guilford Publications, Inc.
72 Spring Street, New York, NY 10012
www.guilford.com

Printed in the United States of America

This book is printed on acid-free paper.

Last digit is print number: 9 8 7 6 5 4 3 2 1

Library of Congress Cataloging-in-Publication Data

Barone, Diane M.
Children's literature in the classroom : engaging lifelong readers / Diane M. Barone.
p. cm. — (Solving problems in the teaching of literacy)
Includes bibliographical references and index.
ISBN 978-1-60623-938-4 (pbk.: alk. paper) — ISBN 978-1-60623-939-1 (hardcover: alk. paper)
1. Language arts (Elementary) 2. Reading (Elementary) 3. English language—Composition and exercises—Study and teaching (Elementary) I. Title.
LB1573.B3586 2011
372.64—dc22

2010027457

About the Author

Diane M. Barone, EdD, is Foundation Professor of Literacy at the University of Nevada, Reno. Her research focuses predominantly on young children's literacy development and instruction in high-poverty schools. She has conducted two longitudinal studies of literacy development: a 4-year study of children prenatally exposed to crack/cocaine and a 7-year study of children, primarily English language learners, in a high-poverty school. Dr. Barone has had articles published in journals such as *Reading Research Quarterly, Journal of Literacy Research, Elementary School Journal, The Reading Teacher, Gifted Childhood Quarterly*, and *Research in the Teaching of English*. She has written several books, including *Resilient Children, Literacy and Young Children, Narrowing the Literacy Gap*, and *Your Core Reading Program and Children's Literature K–3* and *4–6*. She works daily in public schools to enhance student learning in literacy and has mentored teachers seeking National Board Certification. Dr. Barone served as the Editor of *Reading Research Quarterly* and was a board member of the International Reading Association and the National Reading Conference. She has received the Albert J. Kingston Award from the National Reading Conference for distinguished service to the organization and the John Chorlton Manning Public School Service Award from the International Reading Association for her work in public schools.

Preface

Today's teachers are often stressed beyond belief. They are expected to bring each student in their classrooms to grade-level standards in reading, math, and other subjects, and they get one academic year to do this. What a challenge! Schools, districts, and states are evaluated based on a single test that determines how well teachers did in reaching this goal. Because of these pressures, enjoyment has seeped out of many classrooms as teachers try to squeeze in every moment possible to prepare students for ongoing assessments.

Most teachers focus on the cognitive parts of reading—teaching reading strategies or skills. The selections in their anthology (most often, quality children's literature) are used to teach comprehension, decoding, vocabulary, and fluency. In these situations, the literature becomes a vehicle for an instructional strategy or skill. Children infrequently have the opportunity to emotionally or intellectually respond to books as works of art. For instance, students are expected to decide on single answers to comprehension questions rather than to pursue multiple or critical perspectives of a book.

Although teaching children strategies and skills is important to developing readers, I don't see it as sufficient in creating lifelong, engaged readers. My hope is that this book will encourage and help teachers to provide time for the emotional and intellectual connections to literature—the real reason that most of us pick up a book.

As I share amazing children's literature in this book, the pragmatics of classroom situations, such as time and attention to curriculum, are also considered throughout. I write directly to teachers, addressing their concerns and trying to alleviate them as they ponder how to engage with children's literature beyond the expectations of their literacy block. Within the book I provide units of instruction that teachers can immediately bring to the classroom, often connected to units they are expected to teach. Chapters 1–8 also include a "Student Voices" section, in which students share their favorite books, to further spark interest in children's literature.

When I was a teacher, I frequently would hear of a wonderful children's book and then search for it, only to find it was out of print, so I could not use it. When I wrote this book, I made sure all the books mentioned were available, but they may not be that way forever. In this book, I share children's books for instructional purposes, but the unit of instruction does not rely on a single text. Through this more organic instructional planning, teachers are able to switch to an available text if a book mentioned in this book goes out of print.

I also share more familiar books—those that have been used by teachers and parents for a long time. Balanced with these more comfortable books are newer ones that teachers may not be familiar with. I have also included genres that may be new for teachers, such as graphic and postmodern books. These books stretch teachers' current understandings of children's literature to newer perspectives.

The book is organized as follows: Chapter 1 identifies and discusses the issues that arise in defining children's literature. I also present an abbreviated history of children's literature with attention to current trends. In Chapter 2, I try to convince teachers that reading aloud and independent reading are important. I suggest ways to find small moments of time within an academic day for these activities. Chapter 3 provides an overview of narrative genres. Many book examples are shared to make these descriptions come to life. Chapter 4 provides descriptions of informational texts. As in Chapter 3, many examples are shared. Writer's craft is the focus of Chapter 5. Attention is paid to plot, characters, setting, theme, style, and point of view. I share examples of each to facilitate teachers' awareness of these characteristics in the books they read and in those read independently by students.

Parallel to the focus of Chapter 5, Chapter 6 considers the visual qualities of illustrated narrative and nonfiction picturebooks. Teachers learn about line, shape, color, texture, and perspective. I forewarn teachers that after reading this chapter, they may find it takes longer to explore picturebooks with students because the illustrations will have taken on deeper, more important meanings for them. Chapter 7 ponders students' views about reading. I explore book selections and genres that appeal to boys and girls. Chapters 8 and 9 are full of text sets to enjoy with students. I support teachers in creating small to larger text sets. I included an Epilogue because I kept finding more books that I wanted to share and that I thought were just too good to miss.

Throughout my writing of this book, I constantly read and reread children's books. I also explored websites and found information and videos featuring authors and illustrators. As I read, I left my *teacher* expectations aside and just enjoyed the books for themselves. This was hard to do but necessary when making a shift from using literature as a means to teach reading to using it as a source of information and enjoyment. I suggest that you, too, try to leave aside your teacher questions and consideration of books based solely on what they can teach and then just simply enjoy children's books yourself and with your students. I think you will be very pleased at what you discover.

Acknowledgments

Permission to reproduce covers from the following books has been granted by their publishers:

Buffalo Before Breakfast by Mary Pope Osborne, copyright 1999 by Random House Children's Books. Used by permission of Random House Children's Books, a division of Random House, Inc.

The Poky Little Puppy by Janette Sebring Lowrey, illustrated by Gustaf Tenggren, copyright 1942, renewed 1970 by Random House, Inc. The Poky Little Puppy is a registered trademark of Random House, Inc. Used by permission of Golden Books, an imprint of Random House Children's Books, a division of Random House, Inc.

Richard Scarry's Best Little Word Book Ever by Richard Scarry, copyright 2001 by Random House Children's Books. Used by permission of Random House Children's Books, a division of Random House, Inc.

Moxy Maxwell Does Not Love Stuart Little by Peggy Gifford (2008). Used by permission of Yearling, a division of Random House, Inc.

The Shape Game by Anthony Browne, copyright 2003 by A. E. T. Browne & Partners. Reprinted by permission of Farrar, Straus and Giroux, LLC.

Aesop's Fables by John Cech, copyright 2009 by John Cech. Illustrations copyright 2009 by Martin Jarrie. Used with permission from Sterling Publishing Co., Inc.

Goldilocks and the Three Bears by Lauren Child, copyright 2009 by Lauren Child. Reprinted by permission of Disney·Hyperion, an imprint of Disney Book Group LLC. All rights reserved.

Crispin: The Cross of Lead by Avi, copyright 2002 by Avi. Reprinted by permission of Disney·Hyperion, an imprint of Disney Book Group LLC. All rights reserved.

Don't Let the Pigeon Drive the Bus by Mo Willems, copyright 2003 by Mo Willems. Reprinted by permission of Disney·Hyperion, an imprint of Disney Book Group LLC. All rights reserved.

My Friend Rabbit by Eric Rohmann, copyright 2002 by Eric Rohmann. Roaring Brook Press. Reprinted by permission of Henry Holt and Company, LLC.

Bad Kitty by Nick Bruel, copyright 2005 by Nick Bruel. Roaring Brook Press. Reprinted by permission of Henry Holt and Company, LLC.

Alphabeasties by Sharon Werner and Sarah Forss (2009). Reprinted by permission of Blue Apple Books.

Tracking Trash: Flotsam, Jetsam, and the Science of Ocean Motion by Loree Griffin Burns, copyright 2007 by Loree Griffin Burns. Used by permission of Houghton Mifflin Harcourt Publishing Company. All rights reserved.

Flotsam by David Wiesner (2006). Jacket illustrations copyright by David Wiesner. Used by permission of Clarion Books, an imprint of Houghton Mifflin Harcourt Publishing Company. All rights reserved.

Golem by David Wisniewski. Copyright 1996 by David Wisniewski. Used by permission of Clarion Books, an imprint of Houghton Mifflin Harcourt Publishing Company. All rights reserved.

The Graveyard Book by Neil Gaiman (2008). Used by permission of HarperCollins.

Free Fall by David Wiesner (1988). Used by permission of HarperCollins.

All the Places to Love by Patricia MacLachlan (1994). Used by permission of HarperCollins.

The Paper Crane by Molly Bang (1987). Used by permission of HarperCollins.

Kitten's Full Moon by Kevin Henkes (2004). Used by permission of HarperCollins.

Once I Ate a Pie by Patricia MacLachlan (2006). Used by permission of HarperCollins.

Trail by David Pelham, copyright 2007 by David Pelham. Reprinted with the permission of Little Simon, an imprint of Simon & Schuster Children's Publishing Division.

Oh, Yikes!: History's Grossest, Wackiest Moments by Joy Masoff, copyright 2006 by Joy Masoff. Used by permission of Workman Publishing Co., Inc., New York. All rights reserved.

Dawn by Molly Bang, copyright 2002 by Molly Bang. Used with permission from Chronicle Books LLC, San Francisco.

Chester's Back by Melanie Watt, copyright 2008 by Melanie Watt. Used with permission of Kids Can Press Ltd., Toronto, Canada.

Willy the Dreamer by Anthony Browne, copyright 1997, 2000 by A. E. T. Browne & Partners. Reproduced by permission of the publisher, Candlewick Press on behalf of Walker Books, London.

Little Beauty by Anthony Browne, copyright 2008 by Anthony Browne. Reproduced by permission of the publisher, Candlewick Press on behalf of Walker Books, London.

Evangeline Mudd and the Golden-Haired Apes of the Ikkinasti Jungle by David Elliott. Text copyright 2004 by David Elliott. Illustrations copyright Andrea Wesson. Reproduced by permission of the publisher, Candlewick Press, Somerville, MA.

Wabi Sabi by Mark Reibstein, illustrated by Ed Young. Text copyright 2008 by Mark Reibstein. Illustrations copyright by Ed Young. Reprinted by permission of Little, Brown and Company.

Letters Home from—Italy, 1E by Lisa Halvorsen, copyright 2000 GALE, a part of Cengage Learning, Inc. Reproduced by permission. www.cengage.com/permissions.

Out of the Dust by Karen Hesse. Jacket copyright 1997 by Scholastic Inc. Used by permission.

Jacket photograph courtesy of the Library of Congress Prints and Photographs division, Farm Security Administration collection.

My Light by Molly Bang, copyright 2004 by Molly Bang. Reprinted by permission of Scholastic, Inc.

Wolf by Becky Bloom, illustrated by Pascal Biet, copyright 1999 by Siphano, Montpellier. Reprinted by permission of Orchard Books, an imprint of Scholastic, Inc.

The Lemonade Club by Patricia Polacco (2007). Reprinted by permission of the Penguin Group.

The Art Lesson by Tomie dePaola (1997). Reprinted by permission of the Penguin Group.

Skippyjon Jones by Judy Schachner (2003). Reprinted by permission of the Penguin Group.

Seen Art? by Jon Scieszka, illustrated by Lane Smith (2005). Reprinted by permission of the Penguin Group.

Marvin the Ape by Caralyn Buehner, illustrated by Mark Buehner (1999). Reprinted by permission of the Penguin Group.

The Witches by Roald Dahl (1983). Reprinted by permission of the Penguin Group.

Poppy by Avi (1995), illustrated by Brian Floca. Reprinted by permission of HarperCollins Publishers.

Can You Hear It? by William Lach (2006). Cover painting "Circus Sideshow" by Georges-Pierre Seurat. Image copyright The Metropolitan Museum of Art, Art Resource NY. Reprinted by permission.

Extinct Alphabet by Jerry Pallotta (1993). Illustrated by Ralph Masiello. Reprinted by permission from Jerry Pallotta.

Permission to reproduce text material from the following books has been granted by their publishers:

Extreme Weather by Glen Phelan, pp. 20–21, copyright 2004 by National Geographic School. Reprinted by permission of Hampton-Brown and National Geographic School Publishing. All rights reserved.

Butterflies by Emily Neye, p. 7, illustrated by Ron Broada. Text copyright 2000 by Emily Neye. Illustration copyright 2000 by Ron Broda. Used by permission of Grosset & Dunlap, A Division of Penguin Young Readers Group, A Member of Penguin Group (USA) Inc., 345 Hudson Street, New York, NY 10014. All rights reserved.

Contents

CHAPTER 1

Engaging Teachers and Their Use of Children's Literature

When I first read *Wolf!* (Bloom, 1999), I enjoyed a story about a wolf learning to read with the help of farm animals. I giggled when the animals complained that the wolf was interrupting their reading with his noises. I have shared annoying times similar to the animals when someone, especially at an airport, has interrupted my reading by making noise. I noticed that when the wolf went to school to learn to read so that he could become *educated*, the classroom looked like rooms of old where children sat in isolated seats. Then I enjoyed how the wolf developed as a reader, similar to first graders whom I taught. So, on my first reading, I was most concerned with the text and the story being told. But then I went back to the book on numerous occasions as I shared it with teachers and students and discovered other interesting aspects.

Before rereading, I noticed that the opening and closing pages of the book illustrated two different viewpoints. In the opening, everyone is bored, except for one young child, as the wolf is marching through town with a knapsack over his shoulder. On the closing page, everyone is active and the wolf is reading to young children and a duck. So, I wondered, do the author and illustrator share their view about reading and the excitement it brings? Then I considered the title page, where the wolf is engaged in writing practice. He looks bored and exhausted from this repeated writing of letters.

Is this a commentary of school-based practices by the author and the illustrator? The first page shows the wolf seated with his knapsack and children nervously looking at him. The wolf is front and center and captures the viewer's eye. Several illustrations of the farm are not framed, indicating an openness to them. However, when the wolf is in school, the library, and other places where he is learning to read, the illustrations are framed, seeming to indicate a confined space. The use of framing continues until the wolf becomes a proficient reader. I wondered what the illustrator wanted me to think about this framing, because I know it is purposeful.

On a third reading of this book, I noticed that all of the illustrations are watercolors and, for the most part, bright. Some pages are complete in that there is a setting for the animals, whereas on others the animals are silhouetted against a white background. I also saw a congruency between the illustrations and the text. The illustrator created images that replicate the text rather than deviating from it. Although it took me three readings to make these visual observations, I wondered whether this is what children would notice first.

After numerous readings of this one picturebook, I discovered an interesting story of a wolf learning to read, I learned about the way the illustrator visualized this story, I pondered the meanings shared in the illustrations, and I appreciated the connections between illustrations and text. However, it took multiple readings of this single book to absorb these nuances. Now I think I better understand why young children want to hear a book over and over again. The real appreciation for the story happens after you know what is happening. Once the plot is resolved, attention can be given to other details.

Perhaps you are wondering why I would begin a book about children's literature reflecting on my readings of a single picturebook. When I thought about my discoveries over several readings of this book, I wondered about children and their experiences with children's literature. Are they similar to mine in that they can return to a single text for the pleasure of multiple readings? Unfortunately, I think these opportunities are rare in schools today, where teachers are concerned with bringing children to grade-level expectations in reading. There is a much more hurried pace from kindergarten on as teachers quickly move children through text to develop skills and strategies (Keene & Zimmermann, 2007; Lehr, 2008). Frustrating to teachers is finding time to engage in read-aloud sessions with children where they can read and reread books for pleasure and then additional time for students to read independently (Lehman, 2009). Although time is always an issue in classrooms, I hope that this book convinces teachers that reading aloud and providing space for students to read independently is as important in developing exemplary skills as are direct lessons in learning *how* to read. It is worth the effort to squeeze these moments from ongoing classroom routines and expectations so that children develop a love of reading as well as skill.

In my recent work in schools, the focus for reading has been on the cognitive elements, where children learn to decode, comprehend, and read fluently. The cognitive focus requires that literature move to the background of instruction, because it is a means or the material to develop skillful readers (National Reading Panel, 2001; Snow, Burns, & Griffin, 1998). For instance, core reading anthologies contain previously published children's literature. The difference for children is that the selection is used to teach a comprehension strategy, vocabulary, decoding, and so on. Unless there is a visual literacy element, children are not asked to consider the illustrations and how they further develop a story's meaning. Moreover, because a selection is repurposed in an anthology, the peritextual elements are missing (e.g., front and back covers and flaps, beginning and end pages). Only if a teacher brought a hardbound copy of the book to the classroom would children experience the book in the way the author and the illustrator planned.

I don't want readers to leap to the conclusion that I am opposed to cognitive-based instruction in reading. I believe that children need scaffolded instructional support to become proficient readers, as the wolf did in *Wolf!* Teachers and their strategies for providing direct instruction and opportunities to practice reading and writing are critical to children's success in developing as readers and writers (Barone, 2006; Wharton-McDonald, 2006). However, there is another part to reading that moves beyond the skill element: that is the emotional or intellectual drive that makes a reader want to read more. Emotional or intellectual connections are why we continue to read even when no one expects us to. We want to find out what happens or know more about a character, event, or animal, for instance.

Maryanne Wolf (2007) writes about the cognitive and emotional aspects of reading, with emphasis on the cognitive aspects as she shows how a child develops to become a proficient reader.

> As every teacher knows, emotional engagement is often the tipping point between leaping into the reading life or remaining in a childhood bog where reading is endured only as a means to other ends. An enormously important influence on the development of comprehension in childhood is what happens after we remember, predict, and infer: We feel, we identify, and in the process we understand more fully and can't wait to turn the page. (p. 132)

Her focus on emotional engagement continues as she writes:

> After all the letters and decoding rules are learned, after the subterranean life of words is grasped, after various comprehension processes are beginning to be deployed, the elicitation of feelings can bring children into a lifelong, head-on love affair with reading and develop their ability to become fluent comprehending readers. (p. 133)

Wolf (2007) helped me once again understand that children require opportunities to explore books emotionally and intellectually, not just use them to learn to read. A particular book may be the trigger for a child to move beyond reading as a learning expectation to reading as an intrinsically pleasurable act. The intertwining of emotion and intellect are, in essence, what drive literary engagement.

This book is the result of that rediscovery of the importance of emotional and intellectual connections to literature. It is a book that shares children's literature with a significant focus on picturebooks, because they are most often read aloud by teachers and include the intertwining of textual and visual elements. This book also offers teachers ways of exploring and understanding children's books that support both the emotional and the cognitive aspects of reading.

REEXAMINING WHY WE READ

As a primary teacher I stressed about developing my students into competent readers. I supported them as they learned to decode and independently read text. I engaged in written and oral conversations with them as they explored text in reading club groups to deepen and clarify comprehension (Barone, 1989, 1990). In all of these activities, I was clearly grounded in the cognitive side of reading. Even today as I work with teachers and schools to improve the reading achievement of students, I often focus more on the cognitive aspects of reading. However, in the last few years in my work with teachers, we have thoughtfully planned to include time for read-aloud events and time for children to just read. Although we have not conducted a systematic study of these practices, we are noticing that children talk more easily about books and return to books for repeated readings. We are seeing joyful reading reenter these classrooms for both teachers and students. In these rooms, children and adults are engaging in a wider repertoire of reading purposes; in some circumstances, literature is used as a tool for strategy or skill learning, and in others literature is being appreciated for its story, art, information, and so on.

For most of us, away from school settings, we read for pleasure or escape or to find information. We choose books by a favorite author and read everything that he or she has written. Or we choose a genre such as mysteries or romances and read work by multiple authors. Alternatively, we may skip books altogether and search the Internet for information or read in an electronic format such as on a Kindle. Although readers are diverse in their personal choices, they do share common reasons for reading:

- *Reading to learn to read.* Young children and adults alike engage in reading in order to learn to read. Teachers, parents, or tutors carefully select books that are just right for independent reading or a bit challenging for reading supported by a competent reader.

- *Reading for pleasure.* Adults and children read just for the joy of entering an imaginative world. Or they read just for the pleasure and satisfaction of learning something.

- *Reading to enjoy vicarious experiences.* Some books allow readers to discover what it was like to participate in a historical event, live in a different environment, or survive hardships. Readers are able to take on the persona of a character to better understand an event beyond their personal realm.

- *Reading to develop background knowledge.* Frequently, readers pursue topics that inform them about the world and important events. It is not possible for adults and children to experience everything directly; books offer these opportunities.

- *Reading to understand.* Adults and children often read biographies and historical fiction to understand an event or person. Others read to better understand an aspect of science or a scientist and the motivation behind a discovery.

- *Reading to understand who we are.* By exploring how characters solve dilemmas, readers can reflect how they might respond to similar circumstances and thus come to know themselves better.

- *Reading to ponder.* Adults and children read to explore ideas and beliefs—for instance, the beliefs of a culture or community—to compare them with their own.

- *Reading to appreciate.* Adults and children read to appreciate the quality of a book or the art within. They reread a favorite phrase or explore an illustration for the pleasure they derive from it.

- *Reading to engage in conversation.* Reading opens opportunities for adults and children to exchange ideas. They argue about a character and why he or she did something. They disagree about whether they both liked the same book or author. Importantly, this exchange allows readers to enjoy and appreciate a book more fully.

- *Reading to solve problems.* Books can help readers solve a current problem they are facing.

When teachers cultivate these reasons for reading, children move beyond the single focus of deciphering print. Their interactions with the literary language and images in books support creativity, connections, and certainly criticism as they participate in conversation centered on them.

Shelby Wolf (2004) writes about classrooms where literature is valued rather than seen just as material to develop readers:

> Moments of art occur in the classrooms of exemplary teachers who recognize the powerful combination of literature and children, and these moments come in many forms. They come in a variety of critical stances as children learn about authors and close readings, investigating the intersection of the narrative components (genre, theme, character, setting, plot, point of view, style, and tone) and the life of the author behind it. They come when children learn to make connections in an ever-widening net—connections to other written texts, to personal life experience, and to the cultural, political, and social-historical issues of the larger world. (p. 285)

In classrooms described by Wolf, children laugh, cry, or shiver as they connect with the story. They fully enter the books they read rather than just hoping the end is in sight (Fox, 2008). These are the kinds of classrooms that build lifelong passionate readers, not just people who can read, preferring any activity that does not result in reading.

Esquith (2007), an educator known for motivating students to read, described the test that his fifth graders developed to show reading proficiency. I believe this test also recognizes when children have moved from learning to read to reading for purpose, as discussed previously, and are on their way to becoming lifelong readers. Interestingly, the test only has three questions, very different from many of the tests that students currently take to document reading proficiency:

1. Have you ever secretly read under your desk in school because the teacher was boring and you were dying to finish the book you were reading?
2. Have you ever been scolded for reading at the dinner table?
3. Have you ever read secretly under the covers after being told to go to bed? (p. 33)

As you engage with this book on children's literature, keep this quiz in mind. At the end of this book, I hope that you personally answer yes to the last question, especially if you have never had this experience before. I know that you will be moved to read many of the books identified in these pages, books that will keep you up at night. Then, through your sharing of children's literature with your students, I hope that each of them also passes this quiz with three positive responses. Enjoy!

WHAT IS CHILDREN'S LITERATURE, ANYWAY?

It seems like defining children's literature should be easy: It is literature written for children. That definition is certainly a beginning; however, what do you do with books that are appealing to adults *and* children like *Harry Potter* (Rowling, 2007)? Would you consider this an adult book taken over by children or a children's book loved by adults? What appears to be a simple definition is a bit more complicated.

Tomlinson and Lynch-Brown (2002) define children's literature by age range: infancy to adolescence. Further, they suggest that it includes "good quality trade books" that "cover topics of relevance and interest to children of those ages, through prose and poetry, fiction and nonfiction" (p. 2). Although their definition is somewhat helpful, it's details are vague.

For instance, I wonder about the qualifier "good." Does that mean that much of what I enjoyed as a child was bad? I can remember reading Golden Books, those books my parents bought in the grocery store. I loved *The Poky Little Puppy* (Lowrey, 1942/1996), and I clearly wasn't the only one because it is still in print. Golden Books were economically successful—*Pat the Bunny* (Kunhardt, 1940) was even a Golden Book—but they were never part of library collections (Marcus, 2008). So would they count as "good"? Then I considered other marginalized literature: the book series. Series books such as *Nancy Drew* (Keene) have long been criticized for their lack of sophistication. For example, Tunnell and Jacobs (2008) share the experience of Maria, a fifth grader who, much like myself at her age, loved *Nancy Drew* mysteries and couldn't put them down once she began reading. Her school librarian, however, told her, "*Nancy Drew* books lack quality and merit. This series is predictable and weak" (p. 11). Would *Nancy Drew* books be considered good literature?

Perhaps then, when considering children's literature, "good" can have two interpretations, the first being that the book holds up to expert critical analysis. These books often win awards like the Newbery Medal for writing or the Caldecott Medal for illustrations. The second interpretation is based on readers' appreciation. Readers may like a book that is considered "good" or not, or they may like a more popular book that is not necessarily considered "good." Hunt (2005) argues that critics should focus on books as being "good for" instead of being "good" (p. 10). A book may be good because it answered a question or because it filled time, or it may be good because it excited the imagination or helped solve a problem. For Hunt, the quality of a book is subjective, depending on each reader's expectation and what he or she derived from it.

Building on these ideas about the quality of a book, Tunnell and Jacobs (2008) argue that a good book is "one of respect" (p. 17). The reader has respect for the craftsmanship of the author and the illustrator, who have created a book that has lasting value. Likewise, there is respect for the reader who connects to the book. Tunnell and Jacobs also note that when people's personal "library" favorites include a range, from the simple, like *The Poky Little Puppy*, to the more refined, the quality titles are more satisfying and result in deeper pleasure or clearer understanding. For most adults and children, a good book is one that at a particular moment caused them to feel and to think. These experiences don't end when the book is returned to the shelf; rather, readers internalize them, applying them to personal experiences and other reading events.

Tomlinson and Lynch-Brown (2002) note that children's books should be interesting and have relevance for the intended audience. Today more books are published for children than ever before, and authors and illustrators are pushing creativity beyond what has been comfortable in form and content. Lurie (1990) writes that the three main topics of adult writers—sex, money, and death—are prominent in children's books. Fairy tales, in particular, frequently carry these themes: for instance, romance between a prince and a commoner; a pauper seeking treasure; and evil witches. Books of other genres, like *Taste of Blackberries* (Smith, 2004), *Bridge to Terabithia* (Paterson, 2004), and *Charlotte's Web* (White, 1952/2001) deal with death in a more substantial way.

Appropriateness of topic or language in children's books has been an issue for some adults since at least the time of Mark Twain. Lurie (1990) writes that *The Adventures of Tom Sawyer* (1876) did not run into criticism because the preface highlighted that its purpose was enjoyment. In contrast, *The Adventures of Huckleberry Finn* (Twain, 1884), perhaps because it did not have similar text in its preface, was considered vulgar and faced banning in Massachusetts as well as other states. Between World Wars I and II, Leaf (1936/2001) wrote about a pacifist bull in *The Story of Ferdinand*, not exactly a popular topic at this time for adults. Later, in 1964, Fitzhugh's *Harriet the Spy* met with criticism because Harriet secretly observed and recorded adult behavior. Another book written in the 1960s, *Where the Wild Things Are* (Sendak, 1963/1988), caused quite a stir because adults thought the wild things were just too scary for children (Marcus, 2008). Interestingly, fairytales, which can typically have similar fearsome creatures, have not been subject to such criticism (Lurie, 1990).

Today, there are many groups of adults—parents, teachers, district administrators, librarians, the general public, and publishers—who attempt to protect children from the perceived inappropriate content of some books (Lehr, 2008; see *www.trelease-on-reading.com* for further information on censorship). Historically, however, it has been librarians who assumed this responsibility (Marcus, 2008). They created areas in libraries just for children to explore, isolating them from books that might be considered harmful. For readers who would like to know more about challenged or banned books, the American Library Association (*www.ala.org*) maintains lists of books that have been challenged and the reasons why. Most recently, books dealing with sex and homosexuality and those containing offensive language have been scrutinized.

Clearly, children's books are different from adults' books in that they are written for a specific audience—children—by adults. They are influenced by what cultures believe about children and thus change with the times. Ray (2004) notes that when books were first printed there were few targeted to children. Children basically read adult books. Gradually, more stories were written for children and the topics expanded. Children's books, therefore, are written with the current view of childhood in mind and include topics that authors perceive as relevant to them.

Returning to a working definition for children's literature, I found one that encapsulates many critical elements of children's literature. Hunt (2005) writes:

> Children's books are different from adults' books: They are written for a different audience, with different skills, different needs, and different ways of reading: Equally, children experience texts in ways which are often unknowable, but which many of us strongly suspect to be very rich and complex. (p. 3)

Within this book, I challenge readers to think about children's books and children's responses to them so that the emotional and intellectual qualities of reading become transparent. For teachers, this means putting away thoughts about how a certain book might be used to teach vocabulary, science, or some other curricular area. This will be difficult to do! I encourage readers to just engage with children's books and notice whether the joy and intellectual challenge of reading them returns.

A BRIEF HISTORY OF CHILDREN'S LITERATURE

I share a brief overview of children's literature so that teachers understand the historical underpinnings of today's children's books. In particular, two significant phenomena have dramatically altered the course and the pace of children's literature. First, the child audience has gained significantly in stature compared with earlier times, where the only reading material for children was borrowed from adults. Second, technology has advanced the possibilities for illustration and, with the Internet, redefined what a book is.

Early Beginnings

The evolution of children's literature is the subject of debate as to whether it began with books directly written for children or, instead, literature written for adults but usurped by children. Lerer's view (2008) is that children's literature began with the Greeks and Romans, who valued reciting poetry and drama. During this time, children listened to Aesop's fables and other adult texts. There were no books directly written for children; rather, adult texts became familiar to children. It is interesting that fables are still a part of children's literature, and many readers may have thought they were written with children in mind. Counter to Lerer's opinion, Nikolajeva (2005) argues that it is impossible to think about children's literature as existing before the 18th or 19th century, when books were targeted to children and not written for adults and appreciated by children. Identifying the beginning of children's literature is as complicated as deciding what exactly qualifies as children's literature. In what follows, I share literature that, although written for adults, was enjoyed by children and later rewritten with them as the primary audience.

During medieval times in Europe, children also heard lullabies that became familiar as the family structure developed. There was also print material that consisted of primers and prayer books that also contained alphabet instruction (Lerer, 2008). Children learned to read from these books, although their primary audience was still adults. Many of these books focused on expectations for children's behavior. Children were not limited to these didactic writings; they also experienced storytelling targeted to adults in the form of fairytales, myths, and legends, among others (Tunnell & Jacobs, 2008). Eventually, these tales changed their audience and became popular in children's books.

With Caxton's invention of the printing press, children's literature began to thrive as a separate entity, at first mostly in the form of manner books and stories of Robin Hood, although many adults thought that the latter might be too damaging to child readers (Lerer, 2008).

From these beginnings, the Puritans, in both England and America, recognized children's literature and pursued it as a separate form of literature. Many families taught their children to read before school entrance (Marcus, 2008). Not surprisingly, their narratives were filled with life lessons, often targeting the virtue of living a good life before death, not exactly the topics that parents today would think appropriate for their children. *The New England Primer* became popular during this time (1689) and served to teach children the alphabet and morals for an extensive period (see

In Adam's fall
We sinned all,

Thy life to mend,
This Book attend.

The Cat doth play,
And after slay.

A Dog will bite
A thief at night

An Eagle's flight
Is out of sight

The idle Fool
Is whipt at school.

image from Wikipedia), for example "Time cuts down all—both great and small." The primer was still popular into the 1800s and is thought to have sold between 6 and 8 million copies (Ford, 1897). (For more information on the *New England Primer*, see *www.encyclopedia.com/doc/1E1-NewEngPrm.html.*)

During this same time period, Perrault published his collection of French fairytales, which included stories of Cinderella and Sleeping Beauty (Kiefer, 2007; Tunnell & Jacobs, 2008). Children read books for enjoyment rather than just to learn a lesson, although lessons were embedded in many fairytales. In addition to traditional tales, authors wrote books for adults about adventures to strange lands (e.g., Robinson Crusoe, by Defoe, 1719). These books, as occurred in the past, were taken over by children, who although they enjoyed the plot, likely failed to understand the satire (Kiefer, 2007).

There were also popular texts available to adults and children known as chapbooks. Not very sophisticated in their creation, these books were sold by street peddlers for pennies. These books were not didactic; they could be read for enjoyment rather than for a lesson. The Puritans criticized them (Tunnell & Jacobs, 2008) for their lack of quality and for their topics.

Like Caxton with the printing press, John Newbery changed the world of children's books when he published *A Little Pretty Pocket-Book* (1744), which was written and illustrated for children. On the title pages, Newbery wrote that this story and others in the collection were meant to instruct and amuse. Newbery moved beyond the use of woodcuts for illustration and drew black and white or color illustrations (Kiefer, 2007, 2008; Lerer, 2008). Newbery is credited with being the first to recognize that children deserved literature written specifically for them, and not just literature usurped from adults. When I reviewed Newbery's version of the *Mother Goose* rhyme *Hey Diddle Diddle*, I noticed that, unlike most illustrators, Newbery did not have the cow jumping into the air; he was much more literal and creative in his interpretation. Rather, he placed the cow on a hill with the moon low in the horizon. The cow appears to move or jump, but it is on land, not in the air. (For other illustrations by Newbery, see *www.mothergoose.com* or *books.google.com/books?idj8&hl* [once at this page type in John Newbery].)

During the shift in the focus of literature—from adult literature appropriated for children to literature specifically intended for children—several other significant changes were also occurring. Children's literature, in its early stages, transitioned from mainly oral presentation to written form. Illustrations went from woodcuts to drawn illustrations with color. And, importantly, children's literature no longer was primarily didactic, it was now being written for sheer enjoyment.

Transitions: 1800s and Early 1900s

During the 1800s, fairytales became popular as the Grimms tailored their tales for the newly developing middle class (Lerer, 2008). These stories were filled with stepfamilies and evil stepmothers. Lurie (1990) discussed how fairytales were women's literature, in that women were most often the central characters and maintained power. However, as these tales were rewritten, women ceased to be as dominant or powerful. She also wrote that the Grimms changed the original tales and targeted them to children. Whereas the Grimms created stories from retold German folk- and fairytales, Andersen wrote original tales like *The Ugly Duckling* (1906), often based on his own life. His tales were meant to be read, because they did not come from the oral tradition (Lurie, 1990). His stories were very different from oral tales, in that there were not necessarily evil stepmothers or enemies at all, and they rarely had happy endings. When thinking about *The Ugly Duckling*, the issues were with the ugly duckling itself. Although there were bullies in the story, there was no physical threat to the duckling; rather, it was a story of identity.

In addition to fairytales, there were two other major changes to children's literature during this time. First, publishing moved from England to the United States. Similar to the *New England Primer*, Webster produced the *Blue Backed Speller*, a school text (Kiefer, 2007; to see pages of this book, see *www.mcguffeyreaders.com*). Although the majority of this book targeted sound–symbol instruction, a portion contained stories of American patriotism.

The second change was the expansion of genres written for children. There were family stories like *Little Women* (Alcott, 1868/1997) and adventures such as *Ivanhoe* (Scott, 1820/2000). Kipling wrote animal stories—*The Jungle Book* (1894/1950). Verne wrote science fiction—*Twenty Thousand Leagues Under the Sea* (1869/2000); and Carroll wrote fantasy—*Alice's Adventures in Wonderland* (1865/2008). Poetry—Stevenson's (1885/1985) *A Child's Garden of Verses*, for example—filled out this huge expansion of possibilities to delight children.

Not surprising, with so many children's books being published, Caldecott, an illustrator himself, created standards for illustration. Later, picturebooks were recognized with a yearly prize for their illustrations named after Caldecott. The first Caldecott Medal award was granted in 1938 to *Animals of the Bible, A Picture Book* by Fish (1937) and illustrated by Dorothy Lathrop (Kiefer, 2007; Lerer, 2008; Tunnell & Jacobs, 2008).

During this time, color printing was expensive until Evans mastered multiblock wood engraving in the 1860s. This technique allowed for higher quality color printing at lower costs. This development led the way to the production of picturebooks for children (Kiefer, 2008).

This time in history witnessed huge changes in children's literature. Didactic books, although still present, did not dominate. Many authors and illustrators created works for children that were expected to result in joy rather than just lessons learned. With the growth of children's book publishing in the United States, American patriotism became a burgeoning theme, and leading to an even richer variety of genres available to children.

Another interesting result of this increase in children's literature was that public libraries, and librarians, became the guardians of children's reading. They created children's rooms in the library and ushered children into these private spaces where children could escape to the private world of the books within. They decided what was appropriate for children to read and were responsible for the major awards given to children's books (Lerer, 2008).

Moving to More Current Times

Publishing houses saw huge changes during the early 1900s, with the publication of more children's books and the creation of separate divisions focused solely on children's literature. Seaman, at Macmillan, noted that there were two audiences for children's books: those who could easily afford high-quality books and those who could not. She chose to expand into literature for poorer children with the Little Library, where each book sold for approximately $1.00 (Marcus, 2008). Massee, at Doubleday, found that the picturebook was her area of interest and wanted to match the quality of European illustrations with American illustrators. An interesting tidbit is that Massee rejected *Madeline* (Bemelmans, 1939/1967) because she believed it was too sophisticated for young children to appreciate (Marcus, 2007a). Ogle, at Simon & Schuster, led the way with Golden Books, marketed to the masses, including the tactile book *Pat the Bunny*, by Kunhardt (1940; see Marcus, 2007a).

Marcus (2008) wrote that in 1919 "433 new books for children were published in the United States" (p. 104), a number that increased to more than 900 just 10 years later. A large-scale survey of children conducted by librarians to learn about their reading preferences, revealed, as many teachers and parents had discovered, that what children prefer isn't always what one hopes. Most children identified Stratemeyer, author of series books like the *Hardy Boys*, as their favorite author. In years before this survey, New York public libraries had banished all series fiction from their shelves. Those books most dear to children were not available in the library, thus demonstrating the power of young children to convince their parents to buy books they favor (Marcus, 2008).

With the increased focus on children's literature, Melcher, an owner of Macmillan, created the Newbery Medal award to honor quality writing in children's books. The first winner of this award, chosen by a board of librarians, was *The Story of Mankind* (Van Loon, 1921/2007), which had as its primary audience adults and was seen as a gift book for children. Many years later, Melcher also created the Caldecott Medal award to recognize illustrations in children's books (Marcus, 2008).

The Great Depression affected children's literature in negative but predictable ways. Fewer children's books were published, and librarians reduced the number of books they purchased. With economic recovery, by the 1940s, this trend shifted as more books were produced and added to library collections. Although librarians were pleased with these changes, they worried about the latest trend targeting children: comic books, which were introduced in 1934. With their increasing popularity, comic books were selling much more successfully than children's books, *Superman* leading the pack (Marcus,

2008). Game-type books were also appearing on the market, like crossword puzzle books (Marcus, 2008).

Other influential books that appeared during this time included Potter's (1902/2002) *The Tale of Peter Rabbit*, which was one of the first to tell a story through the interaction of pictures and words; Baum's (1900) *The Wonderful Wizard of Oz*, the first American fantasy; Gág's (1928) *Millions of Cats*, the first American picturebook; Brown's (1939) *Goodnight Moon*, now a classic read-aloud story for parents and young children; and Dr. Seuss's (1937) first book, *And to Think That I Saw It on Mulberry Street* (Tunnell & Jacobs, 2008).

What is especially notable about the early 1900s is that publishers recognized the potential of the children's literature market and created juvenile divisions. Librarians also created reading rooms just for children. Series books and comics became immensely popular, to the disappointment of librarians among others. Firsts in American children's publishing occurred with the first picturebook and fantasy written by American authors.

Literature for the Masses

Although many publishing houses began small children's literature ventures to capture the expanding middle class market, the story of Golden Books represents the most successful move in this direction. Marcus (2007a) wrote, "Golden Books began with the tale of two cities, two industries, and two largely compatible visions of the American dream" (p. 2). The two cities were Racine, Wisconsin and Chicago. In 1916, Racine's Western Printing and Lithographing Company entered into an agreement with the Hamming-Whitman Publishing Company of Chicago to print a huge order of children's books. When the work was completed, the publishing house could not pay its bill, so Western decided to find buyers for the books. Marcus (2008) wrote that Western, under the leadership of Sam Lowe, entered into an agreement with Kresge, an inexpensive retail store, to sell the books during the Christmas season. The books sold well enough that Lowe distributed children's books to similar stores for sale year-round. In the late 1920s, with children's books costing approximately $2.00, most adults could only afford to purchase them for special occasions. Seeing an opportunity for market expansion, Simon & Schuster developed an inexpensive line of children's books, soon to be known as Golden Books. When Simon & Schuster marketed the first 12 books, which cost $0.25 each, they found that the established department stores did not want them, believing the books to be inferior because of the price. In response, Simon & Schuster offered Golden Books and display racks to any store that wanted them. Golden Books sold well in grocery stores, where children shopped with their parents. Because of their affordability, rather than just buying one title, parents often bought multiple titles. To address the issue of quality, Golden Books gained the endorsement of Dr. Mary Reed from Teachers College (Marcus, 2007a). (To learn more about Golden Books, see *www.randomhouse.com/golden/lgb.*)

Golden Books, unlike others, were known by their logo rather than a specific author or illustrator. They were often distributed in sets, with new books always being published. Authors and illustrators who signed on were expected to produce each book quickly. Most Golden Book covers did not carry the names of their creators, which included many now well-known and respected authors and illustrators, among them Margaret Wise Brown, Richard Scarry, Trina Schart Hyman, Jack Kent, Garth Williams, and Ruth Krauss. Richard Scarry was one of the first to have his name placed prominently on a cover.

The entrepreneurship behind Golden Books is one factor in their longevity. Some of the novel ideas supported by Golden Books included their entry into publishing arrangements with producers of popular culture. There were books about Disneyland and its cartoon characters such as Goofy. There were books about TV cartoons (e.g., *The Jetsons* and personalities from TV shows (e.g., *Donny and Marie*). Golden Books also produced traditional literature like *The Little Red Hen* and anthologies of tales. There were *Mother Goose* books, alphabet books, and nursery rhymes. Some books were published in different formats such as tall or oversized shapes. The Golden Book line included almanacs and encyclopedias (sold one volume at a time at grocery stores). There were books targeting occupations, such as postmen, firemen, and policemen, an early social studies curriculum. Innovative books like *Dr. Dan the Bandage Man* included BAND-AID bandages in the book. Golden Books also created the first scratch-and-sniff books and the first audio recordings, so that children could listen to the stories as well as read them. Golden Books also published many informational books like *Birds: A Guide to the Most Familiar American Birds* and *Dinosaurs*.

In the 1960s, Golden Books and other publishers faced criticism regarding the lack of racial diversity among their book characters. In response, Golden Books not only began including children of color in their publications, but they also revised books to include more gender-neutral language (e.g., "fireman" became "firefighter") and more culturally sensitive and accurate illustrations.

Although criticism regarding the quality of Golden Books never waned, their support by the media thrived. For instance, one widely circulated photograph showed Koko, the world-famous "talking" gorilla, being read to from the 1976 Golden Book version of *Three Little Kittens*. Another iconic photo published in a 1961 issue of *Parade* Magazine featured U.S. First Lady Jacqueline Kennedy with her young daughter, Caroline, clutching a Golden Book. In the early 2000s, Random House bought the company and launched several exhibitions honoring the many illustrators of its books. Golden Books, still in print and widely read today, tend to evoke strong nostalgic emotions among the older generations, particularly as they have come full circle, now reading these books to their children and grandchildren (Marcus, 2007a).

CURRENT TRENDS

With currently more than 50,000 titles in print in the United States, and approximately 5,000 new books being added each year, children's literature is certainly a healthy business (Temple, Martinez, & Yokota, 2006). Unlike earlier periods in history, children's divisions are often the most successful parts of publishing institutions. Newspapers and magazines also tend to provide as much coverage—reviewing and promoting—of children's books as they do adult books.

With the whole-language movement of the late 1990s and early 2000s, children's literature assumed a major role in the classroom (Pressley, 2006). The whole-language approach promoted the use of children's literature for all literacy instruction, thus requiring an extensive inventory of books in the classroom in order to meet the needs of all students. However, as this movement came under attack, the focus shifted to a reliance primarily on core reading programs for the majority of instruction. Children's books, although still essential, lost their place of prominence in literacy instruction. Today's classrooms have libraries for students' independent reading and core reading program anthologies and leveled text for instruction.

Since the evolution of children's literature, several books have come to be considered classics. E. B. White's *Charlotte's Web* (1952/2001), C. S. Lewis's *The Lion, the Witch and the Wardrobe* (1950/2005), Maurice Sendak's *Where the Wild Things Are* (1963/1988), and Ezra Jack Keats's *The Snowy Day* (1962/1976) are certainly among this group. *Charlotte's Web* allowed the reader to understand about characters and the nuanced relationships among them. *The Lion, the Witch and the Wardrobe* engaged children in fantasy where a wardrobe was the border between fantasy and reality. *Where the Wild Things Are* is an adventure where the young boy is in charge of all the events. This book, discussed more thoroughly later, is widely considered to be an exemplary picturebook for the ways the text and illustrations support and extend each other. Finally, in *The Snowy Day*, the central character, a young Black child, engages in a typical day playing with snow (Temple, Martinez, & Yokota, 2006; Tunnell & Jacobs, 2008).

Current children's literature is more than just an extension of what has been written or illustrated previously. Nodelman (2008) notes that each new book is just a bit more creative than the last, with authors and illustrators always pushing the limits of what was. Building on this idea, several new trends are evident in today's children's books.

- *The development of the picture storybook.* Whereas early picture storybooks often presented text and illustrations that supported one another and told one story, newer versions may have text that is in conflict with illustrations (see Anthony Browne's work) or text and illustrations that present multiple stories (Macaulay's 1990, *Black and White*).

- *New media for illustration.* Because of technological advances in color reproduction, illustrators are making greater use of color. They are also using computer-generated art (Kiefer, 2008).

- *Expansion of topic and issue.* Current writers are including sensitive topics such as death, divorce, and alcoholism, previously considered inappropriate, in their narrative books. For example, the 1996 Newbery Medal winner, *The Midwife's Apprentice* (Cushman, 1996), openly discussed childbirth. Informational books also are more explicit and deal with critical topics like the AIDS virus.

- *Complexity with genre.* For many books, it is easy to identify the genre, whether it is a fantasy, a mystery, or other. However, some current books are less identifiable because the authors are incorporating multiple genres within. For instance, *The Jolly Postman* (Ahlberg & Ahlberg, 2006) and *Chasing Vermeer* (Balliett, 2004) include narrative, letters, monologues, poems, and puzzles. Other books, like *Out of the Dust* (Hesse, 1997), are complete stories written in poetic form.

- *Acknowledgment of racial diversity.* Although many books continue to feature Caucasian characters, more and more are including children and adults of color and from other cultures, such as Asian American, Hispanic, Native American, Amish, and Jewish. Along these lines, awards are also being endowed to honor distinguished minority writers and illustrators. Notable among these is the Coretta Scott King Award (started in 1974) for African American writers and illustrators.

- *Growth of informational text.* From baby board books onward, there has been an explosion in quality informational text. Books are simultaneously entertaining children and teaching them about presidents, dinosaurs, planets, natural disorders, and world wars. They are bringing to life sports heroes and war heroes, artists and musicians. Books are available on virtually every real-life topic.

- *Accessibility to international books.* Increasingly. books from other countries are being translated and offered to children in the United States: for example, from Canada, the picturebooks of Robert Munsch, and from Australia, the work of Mem Fox. Works from renown authors from other countries, such as China, France, and Germany, are also being made available.

- *Appearance of graphic novels.* Books that include comic-like graphics and text are rapidly entering the marketplace. The *Bone* series (Smith), for example, is a collection of graphic novels. Even traditional children's literature, such as *The Adventures of Tom Sawyer*, is being rewritten in graphic novel format.

- *A return of didacticism.* More children's books, unfortunately many written by celebrities, are intending to deliver heavy-handed messages. Actress Jamie Lee Curtis writes about self-control and self-esteem, and TV journalist Katie Couric pontificates about tolerance. Other authors have also written somewhat preachy books; see Van Allsburg's *Just a Dream* (1990), for example.

- *The success of book series.* The *Harry Potter* series is probably the most vivid example of the popular book series, with children and adults clamoring to read the next newest story written by J. K. Rowling. So successful was this format that millions of copies of each book in the series were sold even before publication. Other successful book series include *The Magic Tree House Series* (Osborne), which combines fiction and information; the humorous *The Wimpy Kid* books (Kinney); and *Twilight* (Meyer), the vampire romance collection.

- *A new division within children's literature.* The marketplace determined a new category of consumers of books: tweens, which include children in the 8- to 12-year age range (Marcus, 2008), the largest demographic group to purchase *Harry Potter* books and to participate in late-night promotional events at bookstores on the eve of release.
- *Books that have multimedia components.* Many children's books have Internet connections, where the content of the book is expanded through games and other extensions. For example, each book in the series *39 Clues: The Maze of Bones* (Riordan, 2008) is extended at the 39 Clues website (*www.the39clues.com*). The website allows readers to play the game, collect clue cards, and potentially win prizes.
- *Books written on the Internet.* Jon Scieszka has teamed with other notable authors such as Natalie Babbitt, Steven Kellogg, and Katherine Paterson to write *The Exquisite Corpse Adventure*, which debuted at the 2009 Library of Congress Book Festival (*read.gov*). The story starts with one author's ideas and then, at the end of a sentence or paragraph, is continued by another author until its conclusion. The story is offered at the Library of Congress website (*www.loc.gov*). Other websites, such as *www.magickeys.com/books*, offer books that are available for reading on the Internet only. Readers can turn pages with a click to read text, view images (often animated), and hear sounds.

Although the preceding list includes many positive changes in children's literature, Zipes (2009) shares the worries about today's market: Will the new digital technologies dull children's senses so that they no longer are capable of being reflective or engaging in prolonged reading events? With children being increasingly seen as consumers, will literature be produced solely to encourage their buying without regard for quality and craft? With the new dominance of design, will images become more salient than words? Zipes notes that today's children do not read as their parents or grandparents did. Likewise, books are no longer viewed as "sacred" commodities (p. 24). He elaborates:

> Children are not as literate as their parents were in the domain of literature, but their parents are also not as literate in the new technologies that are pivotal for their children's acquiring a distinct and distinguished habitus under present cultural and economic conditions. If children are being reconfigured to act primarily as savvy consumers and supporters of globalized capitalism, alphabetic literature, as we have understood it, is incidental to their major interests. (pp. 24–25)

Zipes's worries are particularly interesting to reflect upon, especially with the rapid development of graphic novels and the dominance of image within them. With Zipes's commentary in mind, I returned to my favorite bookstore to assess the children's area, particularly how books were displayed. What I gained was a strong lesson in marketing:

Books and related paraphernalia, such as CDs, DVDs, games, stuffed animals, and other gimmicks, were strategically placed and displayed to maximize their selling potential among young consumers.

Perhaps more reflective of Zipes's observations, other significant transformations in children's literature include the changing nature of publishing and marketing. The 1980s were volatile years for publishing houses, with numerous mergers and corporate takeovers. For instance, Macmillan purchased Atheneum in 1985. Later, Macmillan was purchased by Simon & Schuster (Nodelman, 2008; Tunnell & Jacobs, 2008), which was then absorbed by Paramount Communications, which was later taken over by Viacom (Marcus, 2008). These types of transactions were not limited to domestic companies. International companies also purchased American publishers and consolidated them; for example, when Bertelsmann, a German company that also owned Bantam, Doubleday, and Dell, purchased Random House, they merged all four publishers into one (Marcus, 2008). As Kiefer (2007) writes, there are few independent publishing houses still in existence. The end result is that fewer individuals decide what children's books might be published. Smaller houses that may have taken risks with new writers or illustrators just don't exist anymore.

Simultaneous with the changes in the publishing industry were adjustments in the marketplace. Schools, libraries, and big booksellers (e.g., Amazon, Barnes and Noble, Borders) now purchase most children's books. Because these entities buy in large quantities, they are able to do so at lower prices, making it more difficult for small booksellers to compete and succeed. Schools and libraries also tailor their purchases to more closely match the academic curricula. As an example, schools and libraries have increased their purchases of historical fiction that matches their social studies curriculum content, bypassing other historical novels that do not. Additionally, because of their limited budgets, they do not purchase books that might be considered risky (Nodelman & Reimer, 2003). Large bookstores and Internet sellers purchase books they believe will sell, books they believe will be appealing to adults, the buyers, and to children (Nodelman & Reimer, 2003; Nodelman, 2008). They typically buy reprints or new editions of favorite books, movie or TV tie-ins, and books that come in a series (Nodelman & Reimer, 2003). Lamenting the demise of small bookstores, Avi (1999b) in *Ragweed* had mice form a club in a vacated building that was called The Last Independent Bookstore. I am not sure that many children understand this satiric comment, but adult readers cannot miss its message.

Kiefer (2007) shared other interesting publishing tidbits. Although many children's books go out of print each year, others are successfully sold over time. The all-time five best selling picturebooks are *The Poky Little Puppy* (Lowrey, 1942/1996; approximately 15 million); *The Tale of Peter Rabbit* (Potter, 1940; approximately 9 million); *Harry Potter and the Goblet of Fire* (Rowling, 2002; approximately 8 million); *Tootle* (Crampton, 1973; approximately 9 million); and *Green Eggs and Ham* (Dr. Seuss, 1988; 8 million). The best selling paperbacks are *Charlotte's Web* (White, 2001; approximately 20 million); *The Outsiders* (Hinton, 1997; 10 million); and *Tales of a Fourth Grade Nothing* (Blume, 1972; 7 million).

When reflecting on the history of children's literature, a few significant ideas provide a synthesis of this development. First, children's books vary from time period to time period mainly because of adult views of childhood. If children were expected to learn from books and were seen as naive, then books like the *Blue Backed Speller* or fables were the result. If children were thought to have freedom to engage in enjoyment, then books like *Peter Rabbit* resulted.

Today's authors appear to believe that children are more sophisticated than before, especially with the influence of the Internet, and thus create more complex picturebooks, novels, and informational text (Lewis, 2001). For instance, these books may combine genres, have unusual illustrations, or share especially complex plot lines.

Second, children's books often have both didactic and enjoyment elements (Nodelman, 2008). For instance, fairytales are meant for enjoyment but there is always a lesson: for example, it is dangerous to go into the woods alone. Nodelman writes, "Children's literature as we know it thus emerged as a combination of these two different and even opposite forms of story [didactic and pleasure], implying two different and opposite needs in their readers" (p. 270). It is interesting to reread many children's book classics and note the intersection of these elements.

ENGAGING STUDENTS

Teachers can engage students with the content of this chapter in several ways:

1. *Rereading a picturebook*
   a. *Preparing.* Select enough picturebooks for your class of students. Make sure that the picturebooks are not ones that most students have encountered previously.
   b. *Day 1.* Students select a picturebook they have not read before and read this book independently. Once the book is completed, they write about what they noticed during this reading event. Typically, students focus on the plot during this first reading.
   c. *Day 2.* Students independently reread the same picturebook. Once completed, they write what they noticed on this second read.
   d. *Day 3.* Students independently reread the same picturebook. Once completed, they write about what they noticed on this third read. Then students reflect on their reading journey and share with a partner or small group.
   e. *Optional.* Teachers may create a chart highlighting the typical patterns of reading noted by students.
2. *Rereading an informational picturebook.* The process just described for rereading a picturebook is replicated. It is important that informational picturebooks include maps, charts, tables, glossaries, and indexes.

3. *Sharing older children's literature*
   a. Comparison of children from different time periods. Teachers choose a page from the *New England Primer* (*www.encyclopedia.com/topic/New_England_Primer.aspx#1E1-NewEngPrm*), *Baby's Own Aesop* (*www.loc.gov/rr/rarebook/coll/046.html*), and *Where the Wild Things Are*. Students talk about what the authors and illustrators thought about children. Teachers might view each source with students. Students can talk with a partner about how children were viewed, with one student in the partnership taking notes. The process is repeated for other sources, with the notetaker responsibility rotating. Students will notice that in older books children are well behaved and dress extravagantly. They never look like they play or get dirty. In newer books, children get into trouble and wear more relaxed clothing.
   b. Teachers share older children's literature and engage students in discussion about the issue of didacticism: Should all children's stories teach a lesson? Students create charts highlighting the pros and cons of stories containing lessons.
4. *Comparing older and newer children's informational literature*
   a. Students visit *www.loc.gov/rr/rarebook/digitalcoll/digitalcoll-children.html* where they can access *The Children's Object Book*, a book that shares images of a family, their home, their neighborhood, and so on. As students view the pages, they jot observational notes. Their notes can be structured into a three-column table, with the first column representing a topic, such as Family, House, and Bedroom. In the second column, students note what they view within this book on the specific topic (e.g., family: the members of the family, how they relate to each other, how they are dressed). The final column can include characteristics more typical of families today. Students might refer to *The Knuffle Bunny, Bigmama's, The Hello Goodbye Window*, or Scarry's (1968) *What Do People Do all Day?* for more current images of families and their surroundings for their comparisons.
5. *Comparing Internet and traditional book formats*
   a. Students visit *www.magickeys.com/books* to view *ABC Online* and then compare it with a print-based alphabet book. Students compare the format and illustrations between the two.
   b. Students visit *www.magickeys.com/books* to view *Animals You Can See at the Zoo* and then read a traditional book about animals. They can compare the cartoon-like illustrations in the online book with the illustrations in their animal book. They may chat about the sounds the animals make, which are available online but not in the traditional book format.

At the end of this chapter, it is time to take a few moments to reflect:

1. What are your experiences with children's literature?
2. What are some of your favorites books from childhood? Why do you believe they are favorites?
3. Visit The Horn Book website (*www.hbook.com*), Children's Books Online: The Rosetta Project (*www.childrensbooksonline.org*), Library of Congress (*www.loc.gov/rr/rarebook/digitalcoll/digitalcoll-children.html*), or *www.library.uiuc.edu/edx/history.htm* and explore the history of children's literature there. You can view historical children's books at these sites. What new discoveries did you make?
4. Learn more about Golden Books at *www.randomhouse.com/golden*.
5. If you are a teacher, make a list of the last five books you read to your students. Keep this list in a safe place, and return to it as we explore children's literature throughout this book. What did you discover about the choices you made for read-aloud?

RECOMMENDED READING

For readers who would like to know about some of the topics in this chapter, the following books provide additional information.

Marcus, L. (2007). *Golden legacy*. New York: Golden Books.

This book is rich in information about the history of Golden Books. Once I started paging through the text and perusing the illustrations, I couldn't put it down, reading it from cover to cover. A fascinating book, I know I will return to it for reading. Readers not only learn about the franchise itself but also gain insight into a slice of U.S. history, the world of publishing and marketing, and the early careers of numerous authors and illustrators.

Lurie, A. (1990). *Don't tell the grown-ups: The subversive power of children's literature*. Boston: Little, Brown.

Just the title of this book makes you want to read it. I read this book almost like a novel, it was that pleasurable from beginning to end. I will never think about folktales in the same way again.

Lerer, S. (2008). *Children's literature: A reader's history from Aesop to Harry Potter.* Chicago: University of Chicago Press.

Unlike the previous two books, this one is more challenging to read. It reveals the intricate history of children's literature in America.

Student Voices

Schooled (Korman, 2007)

"There is no best part to this book. It's all so good. You just can't pick one part. I enjoyed it. I love realistic fiction. It shows that I can do what this kid has done. He is a hippie, and he came from his life to the real world. He learned about violence in middle school. He had never seen it before. He didn't even know it existed. He became the eighth-grade president and overcame the horror of being the geekiest kid in the school. (That is how you get picked to be president.) He was responsible for the Halloween party, and he was given checks; he just wrote them out because he didn't know about money. Kids thought he died when he got punched and went to the hospital in an ambulance. Then he memorized everyone's name in the school. He said 1,100 kids' names. He thinks it is a good thing that he knows all the names. The kids were amazed."

—Noah, a fifth grader

CHAPTER 2

Reading Aloud, Independent Reading, and Response in the Classroom

It was Kitten's first full moon. When she saw it, she thought, there's a little bowl of milk in the sky. And she wanted it.

—KEVIN HENKES, *Kitten's First Full Moon* (2004, unpaged)

Not so long ago, before she could even speak words, Trixie went on an errand with her daddy. . . .

—MO WILLEMS, *Knuffle Bunny* (2004, unpaged)

She wasn't always a bad kitty. She used to be a good kitty, until one day. . . .

—NICK BRUEL, *Bad Kitty* (2005, unpaged)

Wabi Sabi was a cat who lived in Kyoto, Japan. One day, visitors from another country asked Wabi Sabi's master what her name meant. It had never occurred to her before that Wabi Sabi was anything more than her name. Wabi Sabi watched as her master drew breath through her teeth, shook her head, and said, "That's hard to explain."

—MARK REIBSTEIN, *Wabi Sabi* (2008, unpaged)

"Cluck, cluck," the thing rumbled in a deep voice. "Is that thing talking to us?" said Fred. I looked around the small playground. Fred, Sam, and I stood at one end against a chain-link fence. A very large, white, feathered thing stood next to the swing set at the other end. It had yellow, scaly legs as big as baseball bats, little red eyes, and a dog collar.

—JON SCIESZKA, *Summer Reading Is Killing Me* (1998, 73 pages)

If an experienced reader had read you any of these opening sentences from books, how could you not want to continue? Would it be possible not to encourage the reader to keep reading to discover what Kitten learns about the moon, or what happens on Trixie's errand, or why the kitten is bad, or what Wabi Sabi means, or what really is on the playground? Even as an adult I am drawn into these books just through their opening sentences. I know that children will want the reader to continue, not being satisfied until the end is reached.

This wanting to hear more is the magic that comes from reading aloud to students. Students have the opportunity to imagine a wealth of experiences through the support of a more experienced reader. And some very fortunate children are able to share in an enchanted reading moment where "the story is read aloud, but unfettered by anything before, during, or after that resembles a skills or strategy lesson" (Cooper, 2009, p. 178). Cooper writes further that perhaps the strength of the read-aloud, when not connected to a comprehension strategy, has attracted little attention because its direct relationship to comprehension has not been evident in current research. She further hypothesizes that read-alouds have drifted from classrooms because universities are cutting children's literature classes, where teachers and future teachers learn about the value of the read-aloud as they learn about children's books.

As a teacher, even if you are convinced that reading aloud is important to students, you are most likely preoccupied by the expectations for children to develop reading competencies (visit any state standard list to view the numerous expectations) and the dismal awareness that there is little time for reading aloud in today's assessment-driven classrooms. Because of these dominant worries, I first discuss ways to find opportunities for reading aloud and independent reading before delving into the benefits of reading aloud and independent reading. I doubt that you would care about the benefits if you believe you don't have time for these reading activities. For this planning, I ask you to write down your daily schedule and to think about daily block transitions and activities that students might accomplish independently, like writing in a journal.

I based this planning on a typical elementary schoolday that starts at 9:00 A.M. and ends at 3:00 P.M. I assumed that most teachers have a mandated 90-minute literacy block, a writing block, literacy intervention time, a math block, a science and social studies block, and specials. Because districts and states vary on special classes, I planned one half-hour daily block for these. In some classrooms, teachers may have an hour of special classes one day and no special class the next. In others, teachers only have music and technology specials or art and physical education or some other combination of specials. I also planned 45 minutes for lunch and one 15-minute recess. As you go over the schedule template in Figure 2.1, think about your own circumstances and revise accordingly. The goal of this exercise is to find time for a read-aloud and independent reading. Read-alouds require a separate block of time, whereas independent reading can be a part of other literacy blocks, as an activity completed while the teacher works with small groups of students.

In this simple example, 15 minutes were found for a stand-alone, daily read-aloud. What is important is that the period repeats at the same time each day so that students understand and are prepared for this routine in their instructional day, and no time is lost in getting ready. The key to finding even this much time is that transitions have to be tight and all preparation for teaching must be accomplished before students are present. If reading aloud is planned for right after recess, the allocated time needs to be a bit

9:00–9:15 A.M.	Greeting. Children independently read while the teacher completes tasks like attendance. This practice is best supported if students have browsing boxes of books or a personally selected book on their desk or table space.
9:15–10:45 A.M.	Literacy Block. Students independently read as others work with the teacher during guided reading time. Students might read leveled text tied to their core program and then other text that relates to the theme of study or freely chosen text.
10:45–11:00 A.M.	Recess
11:00–11:30 A.M.	Literacy Intervention. Typically during interventions for students there is direct instruction, often guided by a program. For children at grade level or above, the teacher has more freedom of the instructional content. For these children, reading aloud with an independent reading follow-up is appropriate.
11:30–12:00 P.M.	Writing Block. The teacher can often include a read-aloud for modeling a writing strategy or skill.
12:00–12:45 P.M.	Lunch and Recess
12:45–1:15 P.M.	Special Class
1:15–2:15 P.M.	Math. Periodically, the teacher includes a read-aloud tied to a math concept.
2:15–2:30 P.M.	Read-Aloud
2:30–3:00 P.M.	Social Studies or Science (taught on a rotating basis). As with the math block, the teacher includes a read-aloud tied to a specific content.

FIGURE 2.1. Sample daily schedule.

longer because students usually require a few moments to settle down before they can listen and observe.

In my experience, motivated teachers have found creative ways to build in a daily-read aloud. In one school, having found it impossible to fit in a daily read-aloud, teachers chose to extend their day a bit. Because the majority of children in their school qualified for the free and reduced breakfast programs, teachers took advantage of this time and read aloud while children ate breakfast in the cafeteria. A different teacher read daily, typically the teacher who was scheduled to supervise breakfast. For most teachers, this meant a twice-a-month commitment and did not lengthen their teachers' workday. In a variation, teachers at another school had children collect their breakfast and come back to their classrooms to eat while their teacher read to them. These smaller groups allowed for increased student discussion. In my visits, teachers were enthusiastic about the before-school reading; it was a nice transition to the schoolday and, because it took place before the traditional day began, they felt freer to just enjoy books with their students.

Another way to build bridges and strengthen more formal literacy instruction and the read-aloud is through connections to a theme shared in a core reading program. This primes students for the read-aloud because background knowledge has already begun to be developed during previous literacy instruction. For instance, if the core reading theme is friendship and the teacher organizes a read-aloud with books about friendship, the earlier instruction is enhanced. This strategy is certainly applicable to informational text as well where background has been developed in earlier reading events (Barone & Youngs, 2008a, 2008b). For example, one program has a theme of challenges, which is particularly appropriate as a foundation for exploration of biographies or informational books about weather or health.

WHY READING ALOUD IS IMPORTANT

Reading aloud has many advocates. Among the most passionate, vocal, and eloquent are Mem Fox, Jim Trelease, Ralph Peterson and Maryann Eeds:

Mem Fox

The fire of literacy is created by the emotional sparks between a child, a book, and the person reading. It isn't achieved by the book alone, nor by the adult who's reading aloud—it's the relationship winding between all three, bringing them together in easy harmony. (2008, p. 10)

Reading aloud and talking about what we're reading sharpens children's brains. It helps develop their ability to concentrate at length, to solve problems logically, and to express themselves more easily and clearly. The stories they hear provide them with witty phrases, new sentences, and words of subtle meaning. (2008, pp. 15–16)

Jim Trelease

Whenever I visited a classroom, I'd save some time at the end to talk about reading. I'd begin by asking, "What have you read lately? Anybody read any good books lately?" To my dismay, I discovered they weren't reading much at all. I slowly began to notice one difference. There were isolated classrooms in which kids were reading—reading a ton. . . . In every one of the turned-on classrooms, the teacher read to the class on a regular basis. (2006, p. xxi)

We read aloud to children for all the same reasons we talk with children: to reassure, to entertain, to bond, to inform or explain, to arouse curiosity, to inspire. But in reading aloud, we also:

- Condition the child's brain to associate reading with pleasure;
- Create background knowledge;
- Build vocabulary; and
- Provide a reading role model. (2006, p. 4)

Ralph Peterson and Maryann Eeds

> Reading aloud is also meant to promote pleasure and enjoyment—to bring joy to life in school. (2007, p. 8)

> Reading aloud also gives children the opportunity to take up ways of thinking about a story that can deepen their understanding. Sometimes a comment by the teacher or another student following a selection read aloud can illuminate meaning for all. (2007, p. 10)

The words of these writers are important for encouragement and are worthwhile to return to for inspiration on days when finding time to read aloud just didn't happen.

Children reap vast rewards through read-alouds, concisely summarized as follows. Reading aloud:

1. Increases test scores (Anderson, Hiebert, Scott, & Wilkinson, 1985; Kersten, Apol, & Pagtaray-Ching, 2007; Serafini & Giorgis, 2003)
2. Promotes positive emotional connections between books and readers (Butler, 1975; Cochran-Smith, 1984; Esquith, 2007; Fox, 2008; Peterson & Eeds, 2007; Trelease, 2006)
3. Extends a child's attention span (Fox, 2008; Trelease, 2006)
4. Expands vocabulary knowledge (Fox, 2008; Hancock, 2000; Trelease, 2006)
5. Provides rich, language models (Barone & Xu, 2008; Gunning, 2010; Trelease, 2006)
6. Expands literal, inferential, and critical comprehension (Gunning, 2010; Keene & Zimmermann, 2007; Peterson & Eeds, 2007; Sumara, 2002; Tompkins, 2010; Wolf, 2004)
7. Builds connections to other books, life, and world events (Peterson & Eeds, 2007; White, 1956; Wolf, 2004; Wolf & Heath, 1992)
8. Widens children's imagination (Cooper, 2009; Wolf, 2004; Wolf & Heath, 1992)
9. Creates lifelong readers (Butler, 1975; Peterson & Eeds, 2007; Trelease, 2006)
10. Develops and creates background knowledge (Fox, 2008; Trelease, 2006)
11. Builds a community of learners (Esquith, 2007; Gambrell, 1996; Guthrie, 2004; Johnson & Giorgis, 2007; Peterson & Eeds, 2007; Serafini & Giorgis, 2003; Wolf, 2004)
12. Develops students' reading engagement (Hancock, 2000; Peterson & Eeds, 2007; Tunnell & Jacobs, 2008; Wilhelm, 2008)
13. Supports developing knowledge of authors, illustrators, titles, literary genres, and text structures (Barone & Youngs, 2008a, 2008b; Serafini & Giorgis, 2003; Wolf, 2004)
14. Promotes research skills (Cochran-Smith, 1984; Gunning, 2010; Hancock, 2000; Serafini & Giorgis, 2003)
15. Models that books are valued possessions (Cochran-Smith, 1984)

16. Affords opportunities for conversation centered on text and illustration (Barone & Youngs, 2008a, 2008b; Peterson & Eeds, 2007; Serafini & Giorgis, 2003; Wilhelm, 2008)
17. Increases students' interest in independent reading (Esquith, 2007; Serafini & Giorgis, 2003)
18. Offers models for writing (Hancock, 2000; Serafini & Giorgis, 2003; Tompkins, 2010)
19. Builds fluency through listening to fluent models (Bandré, Colabucci, Parsons, & Son, 2007; Serafini & Giorgis, 2003)
20. Refines self-identity (Sumara, 2002)

These benefits are realized through the process of reading aloud enriched with student discussion or other forms of response. They should help teachers relax a bit, because they validate that reading to students honors the literacy expectations that are part of their curriculum.

Reading Fiction Aloud

Most adults remember those moments when their teacher read aloud to them. For many, it was the best part of the schoolday where they could escape to some exotic location, share in funny events, or wonder why a character did what he or she did (Bandré et al., 2007). Students were often unaware that when their teacher read aloud, they were learning. In these circumstances teachers introduced a book, most often fiction, and then read it from the beginning to the end on successive days. Sometimes students were encouraged to chat about the book as it was read, and other times they were to remain quiet until the end of the reading event.

Typically, the fiction read-aloud is guided through the selection of a good book that might be related to a theme that is being explored or just one that the teacher feels will be valuable or enjoyable for students to hear. The teacher might share his or her thinking as the book is read; for example, "I am confused. What is happening here?" She or he might then reread and engage in a discussion to clarify the plot. The teacher may stop reading at other times to allow room for students to make connections or to pose questions (Manning, 2005). In some classrooms, students return to follow-up the read-aloud by writing or drawing in a read-aloud journal. Through this process, students have a record of their feelings or ideas as they worked through a book or poem (Manning, 2005).

Gunning (2010) offers teachers a few suggestions to prepare for a read-aloud. Of primary importance is designating a location in the classroom for read-alouds. It may be that students join the teacher on the carpet in an area near the classroom library or remain at their desks or tables. Typically, teachers of younger children have them move to the carpet, where they can sit together. This practice is less common in intermediate classrooms. Teale's (2008) research showed that students sitting closest to the teacher reaped the most benefit during a read-aloud, so it is important to periodically change seating places, so that all children have equal opportunities to sit close to the teacher. Placement is also important to consider when students remain at their desks or tables during read-aloud. The teacher could vary his or her location during reading to accommodate all students.

Prior to the read-aloud, it is important for the teacher to read the book selected. By previewing, a teacher can determine whether the book is appropriate for the class and can anticipate where reading can stop in order to engage students in discussion. Also, by knowing the story in advance, the teacher can evoke emotion in his or her voice to correspond with the action (i.e., reading with excitement or reading quietly and calmly).

When the read-aloud begins, the teacher starts by sharing the cover (front and back), peritextual elements like the front and back pages, dedication, and information about the author/illustrator. Some of these elements may be missing if the teacher is using a paperback copy of a picturebook. When reading a picturebook, it is important that students see the pages as the text is read. This showing of text and illustration is less important in novels, unless they qualify as graphic novels where illustrations are equally important. If the illustrations are very complex, the teacher may want to place the book on a projector so that students can see the details as the book is read. It is vital that books that are read be available for students' independent reading so that they can spend more time on their own with text or illustrations. Teachers may even choose to reread texts as students gain deeper comprehension on each subsequent reading, as discussed in Chapter 1.

A teacher may ask students to predict, based on the book cover, what might happen and then again at stopping points along the way; however, he or she may want to break from this routine and pause in reading to allow more open student response. On the basis of my classroom observations, I find that student engagement is high when the teacher allows them to share with partners or small groups in this more open-ended way. Serafini and Ladd (2008) call this an interpretive space where students have opportunities to become "active constructors of meaning and forced to deal with the openness and indeterminacies of the written and visual representations included in picturebooks" (p. 6). Often when the conversation comes to a close, the teacher just shares a few comments he or she heard rather than calling on individual students to share. Once the reading is complete, the teacher does not want to just close the book and move to the next instructional event. This is a time when children can reflect on what they heard or saw. They may ask the teacher to turn to a specific page so that they can once again consider it. They may chat about a character and what the result of an action was. They may want to reconsider all of the illustrations to better understand the artist's craft. If there is time, students might write or draw their ideas in a read-aloud journal and then they can discuss their ideas with other students.

For variety in read-alouds, the teacher may ask the librarian or principal to read a favorite book to students or, as a variation, use a read-aloud from an online source. The Storyline Online website (*www.storylineonline.net*) has read-alouds by actors and authors, such as Pamela Reed reading *Stellaluna* (Cannon, 1997) or Sean Astin reading *A Bad Case of Stripes* (Shannon, 2004). Tumble Book Library (*www.tumblebooks.com*), a division of the New York Public Library, has an expert narrator who reads aloud many popular children's books that are perfect for students to listen to independently. Unfortunately, Reading Rainbow (*pbskids.org*) has been discontinued. At this site hundreds of children's books were read aloud. The read alouds are now available in a DVD set.

Reading Informational Text Aloud

Nonfiction read alouds, like those for fiction, require the teacher to establish a comfortable place to read, preread the selection, and offer opportunities for student conversation. Young (2009) makes several additional recommendations for reading aloud informational text:

- *Cover to cover.* These books are high quality and are appreciated as works of literature. They may tie to a unit of study and their content extends understanding, or they may be a genre focus, like biography, and should be read cover to cover. *Theodore* (Keating, 2006), a picturebook biography, is a good example. The author has Theodore Roosevelt tell about his life by talking directly to the reader—for example: "My mother named me Theodore, but everyone remembers me as Teddy" (unpaged).
- *Chapter or excerpt.* This sharing is noted as "bits and pieces" (Moss, 2003, p. 61) where the teacher shares specific parts of text that is targeted to student learning. For instance, the teacher may read just a short section from a Lincoln biography clarifying his childhood. Another reason for sharing just a small piece of text is to motivate students to read the rest of the book or to prepare them for a different text on the same topic. An example of a book that would best be read in pieces is *Something Out of Nothing: Marie Curie and Radium* (McClafferty, 2006). The book begins by exploring the early life of Marie Curie with photos of her and her siblings. This bit of reading provides enough interest for students to pursue this book on their own.
- *Participatory.* Students may read part of the text. This works especially well with diaries or dialogue. The *My America* series offers the opportunity for students to read journal entries from children. For example, using *A Perfect Place: Joshua's Oregon Trail Diary* (Hermes, 2002), a student might read just one or two of Joshua's journal entries describing his experience, with the teacher continuing the reading thereafter.
- *Captions.* The teacher skims through the book highlighting illustrations, photos, maps, and captions. This kind of reading gives students a preview of the content of the text. *Komodo Dragons* (Reeder, 2005) is a perfect vehicle to share illustrations and captions because they are found on every page.
- *Reference material.* The teacher highlights the table of contents, index, or glossary of a book. For example, the teacher might have children select a term from the glossary and then move to where it is explained in text, thus modeling how a glossary supports meaning. *Komodo Dragons* (Reeder, 2005) is a good example because it allows teachers to share the table of contents, glossary, and index.

• *Modeling informational text features.* A teacher may just read the sidebars, headings, or captions or identify different type fonts to model how they contribute to nonfiction. Morley's (1995) *How Would You Survive as an Ancient Egyptian?* serves as an example of a book where teachers can share sidebars and headings, and point out a wide variety of font formats. Each page contains multiple sidebars and captions.

Combining Genres in Read-Alouds

Teachers might consider a themed approach to read-aloud events (Gunning, 2010). For instance, on one day the teacher might read an informational book about dragons like *Komodo Dragons.* On other days, the teacher may select from the following genres that target real or imaginary dragons (see Figure 2.2). By grouping texts in this way, students come to understand the differences between fiction and informational text and the genres related to each.

In this set, students study Komodo dragons and other animals and compare them with fictional dragons. They also explore fictional tales of dragons, an immigration story in *The Dragon's Child: A Story of Angel Island*, stories about Chinese New Year, and poetry in *The Dragons are Singing Tonight*. The books range in complexity from simple (*Komodo Dragons* and *The Knight and the Dragon*) to complex (*The Dragon's Eye* and *The Dragon's Child: A Story of Angel Island*).

Name of Book	Author (year)
Informational Text	
Komodo Dragons	Tracey Reeder (2005)
Behold . . . the Dragons	Gail Gibbons (1999)
Your Safari Dragons: In Search of the Real Komodo Dragon	Daniel White (2005)
Real-Life Dragons	Matt Doeden (2008)
Reign of the Sea Dragons	Sneed Collard (2008)
Fiction	
A Dragon's Birth	Terry Reschke (2005)
The Dragon New Year: A Chinese Legend	David Buchard (1999)
The Knight and the Dragon	Tomie dePaola (1998)
The Dragon's Eye	Dugald Steer (2006)
Day of the Dragon King	Mary Pope Osborne (1999)
The Book of Dragons	Michael Hague (2005)
The Dragon's Child: A Story of Angel Island	Laurence Yep (2008)
The Dragons are Singing Tonight	Jack Prelutsky (1993)

FIGURE 2.2. Dragon text set.

Teachers might also decide to partner two books together: fiction and information, poetry and information, and so on. For instance, *Flotsam* (Wiesner, 2006), a fiction book, centered on a camera that floats to the beach and *Tracking Trash: Flotsam, Jetsam, and the Science of Ocean Movement* (Burns, 2007), an informational book about trash and ocean movement, partner nicely. Another pairing is MacLachlan and Charest's (2006) book of dog poems, *Once I Ate a Pie*, showcasing dog behavior from a dog's point of view and *Good Dog! Kids Teach Kids about Dog Behavior and Training* (Pang & Louie, 2008). These genre pairings help students learn about genres and how they complement one another; and are easier for teachers to compile than a whole text set.

Finally, Hartman and Hartman (1993) offer teachers a variety of ways to compile text sets, summarized as follows:

- *Companion texts.* A collection of books to supplement a set of texts (e.g., the *Shiloh* series by Naylor).
- *Complementary texts.* Books centered on a single topic, like the dragon text set listed in Figure 2.2.
- *Synoptic texts.* Books that focus on a single idea, story, or event (e.g., books about President Lincoln).
- *Disruptive texts.* A collection of books that share conflicting or alternative views about a topic, idea, or story (e.g., books about the Civil War).
- *Rereading texts.* A collection of books students reread to gain deeper meaning.

HOW TO CHOOSE BOOKS

Choosing fiction and informational text to read aloud involves many decisions for teachers. First, the books need to be ones that students will enjoy and understand. It is also beneficial to select books tied to a current curricular theme so that each book builds upon the other and connects to important content expectations. Moreover, teachers want to select from various genres within fiction, such as mystery, folktales, or poetry, and within informational texts, such as biography, photo essays, or memoirs.

Choosing informational books to read aloud requires additional guidelines to the general ones recommended for fiction. As Moss (2003) indicates, in most circumstances, teachers choose informational text that matches curriculum topics or provides support for student reports. She suggests that teachers extend this thinking because many students, like adults, see informational text as pleasure reading. With this added reason for informational text, it then regularly appears in the classroom library or is displayed in the room for student selection, and not necessarily only selected based on current curriculum topics.

Additionally, teachers' selection of informational text books should be based on several criteria (Moss, 2003). First, teachers should consider the *authority* of the author. Is the author an expert or has the author worked with experts on a topic? Second, is the information *accurate and up to date?* In most current nonfiction, authors list experts, books, or websites to support the accuracy of their information. A vivid example of information being up to date comes from the recent astronomy discoveries regarding Pluto. Older books do not present this new information and can thus be misleading to students. Third, the *appropriateness* of the book for the student audience must be considered. Books that talk down to students are never appropriate. They should also include information that is interesting to novice learners. Fourth, the book must be *artistic*. Readers should experience quality in text and illustration. Fifth, the *author's voice* should be clear and demonstrate a passion about the text.

Teachers may be gasping right now if they believe this process of selecting informational text is laborious and difficult. Most of the selection process requires skimming and is not time intensive. More careful reading might be required to ensure accuracy of information, especially if the text is long. In the following, I describe my book selection process for informational text using the book *Tracking Trash: Flotsam, Jetsam, and the Science of Ocean Movement* (Burns, 2007) as a model.

In this process, I first checked the authority of the author. Loree Burns has her PhD in medicine from the University of Massachusetts Medical School. I am thinking that she has a doctorate but not in oceanography, so is she an expert on this topic? In the author information provided, I discover that Burns made several research trips to the Pacific Coast for this book and worked closely with renown American oceanographer Dr. Curtis Ebbesmeyer, chronicling the development of his research program. I then check the book's references. Burns suggests books that students might enjoy and websites to explore and provides her reference materials and names of experts who helped her. *Tracking Trash* has also won the Boston Globe–Horn Book Award for nonfiction. On the basis of all this information, I conclude that Burns has author authority. With a publication date of 2007 I feel confident that the book is up to date and accurate. Also, the book's topic, ocean movement, is a fairly stable, constant branch of science. Burns assumes her reader is sophisticated and interested in wave movement and currents. She begins the book from a historical perspective, sharing Benjamin Franklin's interest in finding the fastest routes from Europe to the American colonies and his discussions with ship captains from whom he learned that traveling from West to East was faster than the reverse. Burns uses Franklin, a figure familiar to students, and his real-life question as an entry to the book, thus appealing to students. Her chapters also build upon each other, with the reader positioned as a scientific detective. *Tracking Trash* is appealing not only for its topic but for its numerous visuals: photographs showing trash (often toys or shoes) and where it washed up and of scientists working and newspaper clippings. The text lends itself perfectly to be read in bits and pieces so that students can absorb smaller portions of information rather than being overwhelmed.

Although this selection process may seem laborious, I accomplished it quickly by scanning the author information, reading a few snippets of text, and skimming the book to note visual support. Importantly, this book will not be read on just one day; it will be returned to on numerous occasions. Students will explore this book independently as well, so the time spent evaluating it was worthwhile. Moreover, once this process is complete for a book, it can be used in subsequent years without the selection process, unless, of course, scientific changes have occurred in the meantime, rendering the book outdated.

There are many sources to help teachers with book selection, and the good news is these sources are, for the most part, updated yearly. Some sources for book selection follow:

1. *School library or local library*. Most librarians are familiar with children's books and can make valuable recommendations for read-alouds.
2. *Classroom library*. Most teachers have created student libraries that serve as a source for read-alouds. They can also borrow books from neighboring teachers.
3. *Local bookstores*. Although the number of independent children's bookstores are dwindling, the owners of these stores are often very knowledgeable and can recommend the perfect books for read-alouds, helping teachers tailor their book selection. Larger bookstore chains are also familiar with read-aloud choices, although much of their inventory targets consumers, so caution is urged.
4. *The Read-Aloud Handbook* by Jim Trelease. This book, now in its sixth edition, offers support for reading aloud and recommendations for more than 1,000 books.
5. *The Best Children's Books of the Year (2009 edition)*. This book, published yearly by the Children's Book Committee from Bank Street College of Education, is a reliable source that groups books by age and topic (e.g., Life in a New Land).
6. *National Council of Teachers of English* (NCTE; *www.ncte.org*). In its bimonthly journal *Language Arts*, NCTE highlights quality children's books along with book reviews.
7. *International Reading Association* (IRA; *www.reading.org*). IRA publishes yearly lists of children's, teachers', and parents' book choices. Each issue of its journal *The Reading Teacher* features quality children's books with reviews.
8. *Book Links (www.ala.org)*. *Book Links* is a quarterly supplement to the American Library Association's *Booklist* subscription magazine. Each issue is filled with wonderful literature, text sets, and creative ideas for bringing literature into the classroom.
9. *The Horn Book Magazine (www.hbook.com)*. This journal is focused on children's and young adult literature with articles and reviews.
10. *Children's Book Council (www.cbcbooks.org)*. This website maintains a database of children's choice book award winners grouped by grade level as well as award-winning authors and illustrators. Reading lists for science and social studies are also available.

11. *www.carolhurst.com*. This children's literature site publishes free newsletters about children's books and is a source for book collections organized by theme or curricular area.

Teachers might also consider awards given for children's books as a basis for selection. Some of the more prominent awards are as follows:

- Jane Addams Book Award (*home.igc.org/~japa/jacba/index_jacba.html*): honors books that promote peace and social justice.
- Hans Christian Andersen Award (*www.ibby.org/index.php?id=273*): recognizes authors and illustrators who have made a lasting contribution to children's literature.
- Mildred Batchelder Award (*www.ala.org*): recognizes books that were first published in a foreign country and then in the United States.
- Boston Globe–Horn Book Award (*www.hbook.org*): recognizes one book in each of the following categories: fiction, nonfiction, and illustration.
- Randolph Caldecott Medal (*www.ala.org*): recognizes the work of illustrators.
- International Reading Association Children's Book Award (*www.reading.org*): recognizes excellence in three categories: young children's books; older children's books; and nonfiction.
- Ezra Jack Keats New Writers Award (*www.ezra-jack-keats.org/bookawards/index.html*): honors a new writer or illustrator, one who has six or fewer published children's books.
- Coretta Scott King Award (*aalbc.com/books/related.htm*): honors excellence among African American authors and illustrators.
- National Council of Teachers of English Award for Excellence in Poetry for Children (*www.ncte.org*): awarded every 3 years to an American poet for his or her entire body of work.
- John Newbery Medal (*www.ala.org*): awarded yearly to an author of children's books.
- Orbis Pictus Award for Outstanding Nonfiction for Children (*www.ncte.org*): awarded yearly for outstanding nonfiction for children.
- Scott O'Dell Historical Fiction Award (*www.scottodell.com/odellaward.html*): recognizes outstanding books of historical fiction written by a U.S. citizen.
- Tomás Rivera Mexican American Children's Book Award (*www.education.txstate.edu/departments/Tomas-Rivera-Book-Award-Project-Link.html*): granted to a book, fiction or nonfiction, that depicts the Mexican American experience.
- Robert Sibert Informational Book Award (*www.ala.org*): honors the author and illustrator of an outstanding informational book.
- Laura Ingalls Wilder Award (*www.ala.org*): awarded every 2 years to an author or illustrator for his or her contribution to children's literature over numerous years.

Although all of the previous suggestions for choosing books can be valuable, perhaps the best way is for teachers to be avid readers of children's books themselves (Miller, 2009). For some teachers, reading children's books may be a way to reignite their own thirst for reading. Surprising as it may be, Applegate and Applegate's (2004) research discovered that 54% of preservice teachers were unenthusiastic readers, not a very positive sign if teachers are to inspire students themselves. Whether you qualify as an enthusiastic or unenthusiastic reader, the best way to learn about children's books is to commit to reading at least 15 minutes everyday; read books recommended by students; read children's books that are recommended by others, like the International Reading Association; record what you read in a notebook; and reflect on the book, including your likes and dislikes.

There are multiple supports to help teachers locate books for read-aloud and other instructional classroom events. Rather than building a collection of read-alouds independently, teachers may want to collaborate. Rather than engaging in this process alone, it would be much more meaningful to visit the library or bookstore with colleagues, discussing books and make choices together.

INDEPENDENT READING

Independent reading allows students to choose their own books and read at their own pace. Miller (2009) writes, "Reading is not an add-on to the class. It is the cornerstone. The books we are reading and what we notice and wonder about our books feeds all of the instruction and learning in the class" (p. 50). Her words highlight the centrality of independent reading to foster reading development. Opportunities to read independently support students in multiple ways:

- Students gain practice in using the skills and strategies taught by their teachers and become better readers (Allington & McGill-Franzen, 2003).
- Independent reading provide authentic literacy experiences where students can select their own books.
- Students learn to select texts (Kelley & Clausen-Grace, 2009).
- Independent reading enhances motivation for readers (Gambrell, 2009).
- Students become lifelong readers (Tompkins, 2010).

Even with these strengths of independent reading, some teachers may still view it as a supplement to reading instruction. Gunning (2008) argues that there is no core reading program that provides sufficient fiction and informational material for students to fully develop literacy. Although the research on independent reading is robust in its support of literacy gains, it also indicates that students are spending less time reading in their classrooms and at home (U.S. Department of Education, 2005). Gambrell (1984) observed that first graders actually read for about 3 minutes per day and second and third graders about 5 minutes per day. More recently, Brenner, Hiebert, and Tompkins

(2009) noted that third graders spend about 18 minutes per day really reading. Important to this research is that the amount of time reading on the Internet and composing e-mail or text messages was not included, so the time reported may not accurately reflect reading opportunities. This amount of time spent reading begs the question as to whether it is sufficient practice for novice readers to develop proficiency.

If, as a teacher, you believe as I do that these reported times for independent reading are not sufficient to develop engaged readers, the next question is, what can teachers do to increase these times? Teachers might first consider the value of choice in independent reading, a critical element in developing motivation to read. Choice is the central theme in the book *Moxy Maxwell Does Not Love Stuart Little* (Gifford, 2008) and makes for a great read-aloud. In this story, Moxy has been assigned to read *Stuart Little* over the summer and knows there will be a quiz on it the first day of school. The whole book is about avoiding reading *Stuart Little.* Using humor, it emphasizes the importance of readers' choice and that students like to make book choice decisions, at least sometimes. *Moxy Maxwell* could serve as a discussion starter about choice and the importance of independent reading. Students will also have much to say about quizzes after reading and their influence on how a reader reads. Get ready for lots of feedback from students!

Rather than allowing students free choice, some teachers preselect a group of books from which students can choose, narrowing options but allowing students to read books that are somewhat related. This preselection might push students to choose a genre or an author they have not previously read. When I was in Mr. Bussoni's fifth-grade classroom (Barone, 2006), I observed this process in action. He preselected five books for independent reading: *Saving Shiloh* (Naylor, 1999), *Skitterbrain* (Brown, 1992), *Cousins* (Hamilton, 1992), *The Black Pearl* (O'Dell, 1996), and *Jeremy Thatcher, Dragon Hatcher* (Covill, 1991). Mr. Bussoni gave a short talk on each book, where he shared the author, other books by the author, an approximate reading level, and the book's genre. Once the book talks were concluded, students previewed each book during the day and signed up for their first and second choices. The next day students entered their classroom to find a copy of their first or second choice at their desks for independent reading and a contract for reading their choice book with other students. The contract suggested the chapters they should read and an approximate time to complete them. Students were encouraged to talk daily with other students reading the same book and to record ideas in a notebook. Students, even those who were reluctant readers, were excited to begin reading and checked out what all of their friends were reading before they opened their books.

In other classrooms, teachers may require students to read from specific genres during the year. They may have all students select from one genre and read a selection during a specified period of time. Or they may just share a list of genres and allow students to self-select throughout the year. Another way to organize independent reading is to have students select a book that represents a theme for instruction. In this case, all students would read books about self-identity or the wilderness, for example. Both of these structures allow for student discussion across books as students; they could discuss a genre or how each character understood him- or herself. Teachers might have students explore numerous books by one author or illustrator to learn more deeply about the individual who has crafted them. As is easily seen, there is a multitude of ways to organize book selection while still offering students choice.

After books are selected, teachers need to find time for independent reading. Again, this does not need to be separate time, although that would be ideal. Rather, students can read independently when they are not working in small, guided reading groups with the teacher. It needs to be made clear to students that they are expected to read when the teacher is working with others. Teachers must also be careful that the books for independent reading are within the reading capabilities of independent readers so that students can successfully read them. Suggestions for meeting the reading abilities of students are shared later in this chapter.

A well-stocked library supports student independent reading. Teachers can borrow books and magazines from the school or community library for student reading as they develop their own classroom libraries. Teachers will also want a display area where they place books related to a theme of study. If teachers choose to read aloud the books shared about dragons, for instance, they would also display other dragon books and those read aloud for student independent reading. Students love to reread the book the teacher just read aloud to the class because they can understand the story or information and can read successfully. Displaying books, especially for younger readers, makes them appealing to choose from. In addition to print media, teachers will want to make online reading accessible to students by having sites or specific books bookmarked for easy access.

Teachers sometimes worry about management issues related to independent reading: Did the students really read? Although teachers have numerous ways to guarantee this, I have observed that teachers who ask students to record the books they read independently and write entries into a journal have the most success. Later in the year, students can return to these notebooks to determine the genre or the author/illustrator they prefer. The teacher might nudge them to experience other genres or authors/illustrators to build their reading repertoire. Students can also reflect on the comments they write or draw about books and learn about themselves as readers. For example, do they always write about the plot, or are they interested in how the book makes them feel?

Another way to ensure that students are actually reading is to have one-on-one conversations (Reutzel, Jones, Fawson, & Smith, 2008). Teachers might find time to chat with a student between guided reading groups. Although these conversations may seem arbitrary, they are carefully documented so that teachers know they have met with each student in the room. If teachers find that this transitional time for conversations is not very satisfactory for more in-depth discussion, they might decide to schedule one fewer guided reading group each day. During the time that was previously set aside for guided reading, they can chat with multiple students individually about their reading. These conversations allow teachers to notice what is most important to a student as he or she reads, whether the student is using previously taught comprehension strategies, what the student notices about an author or illustrator, and whether the student is personally enjoying the reading.

These conversations around reading, although they may appear to be easy, take practice. In order to foster students' critical thinking, teachers need to move away from the standard question-and-answer format—Who are the characters? What was the most exciting part? What facts did you learn?—and focus on questions that encourage conversation: What did you notice while you read? How do you think the character felt? Students take leadership in these conversations by sharing ideas or emotions that evolved from their reading. Through this type of conversation, teachers demonstrate that they are interested in their students' comments by responding to their ideas and serving as builders of meaning (Hassett & Curwood, 2009). For example, a student shares from his reading of *A Dog's Life* (Martin, 2005): "I hated the way people treated Squirrel. You would think that if they took him to be their pet they would at least feed him." The teacher responds: "I wondered if he would ever find a family that was nice to him. Some even started off nice, and then they just left him. I think I felt as lonely as he did when he lived in the woods." From these initial comments, the conversation continued and both teacher and student shared their feelings and thoughts.

A second issue with independent reading is the need for books that students can successfully independently read. Children in classrooms with no books matched for their reading level will engage in pretend reading or will select books but never open them. Teachers need a variety of books that range from easy to difficult for student choice. They can also include magazines and Internet sites to expand the traditional resources available. Teachers can also make books on CD available; students can listen to these until they develop sufficient skills to read independently. In intermediate classrooms, picturebooks must be valued as much as longer, more difficult text, so that struggling students are not embarrassed by their book choices. The result of these careful choices by teachers is that there is always a wide range of reading materials for students to select from.

RESPONDING TO LITERATURE

Reader response happens as a person is read to or reads independently. Response is grounded in the belief that reading is an active process, with meaning being constructed continuously through intellectual and emotional connections. Three components influence response: the reader, the literature, and the context for response (Galda, 1988; Hancock, 2000). For example, the reader may be a student, who listens to a book read by the teacher, and is asked to respond freely in a journal. The reader brings to the text all previous experiences with reading, academic learning, personal experience, and so on. For instance, in order for a reader to understand a fractured version of a fairytale, he or she must understand the original version. If not, a child interprets a fractured version as though it has no literary tradition. A child who never heard about Little Red Riding Hood will not appreciate the variant *Into the Forest* (Browne, 2004). The child most likely will not recognize that a boy is going into the forest and he has a red jacket, similar but different from the original, and any of the other subtle visual connections to other fairytales within the text.

The second part of this response triad is the literature. If children have only listened to or read fiction, then an informational reading event might prove difficult for them to understand. Genre, text structure, literary elements such as a writer's style, and the content of text all influence the reader.

The last component of the triad is the context. Teachers may expect students to respond in a certain way, for instance, providing a summary of what they read. If this is the regular expectation, children in this classroom will find it difficult to respond in other ways, because they have not been officially sanctioned as appropriate in the classroom. In classrooms where diversity of response is routine, students will be free to respond in ways they find appropriate to the text. A second aspect of context to consider is students' family backgrounds. For instance, religious beliefs might influence the way a child responds. For example, Jacob, whose family was very spiritual, wrote about the use of the word *underwear* in a book: "I don't think the author should use that word. It seemed wrong to read it in a book." Jacob abandoned this book because he was uncomfortable reading it and reconciling his personal religious beliefs.

Most teachers have become familiar with responding to literature through the work of Rosenblatt (1938, 2005). Rosenblatt identified two primary ways of responding to text: efferent and aesthetic. Efferent responding is more focused on understanding ideas or facts. Aesthetic responding is more concerned with emotional or artistic response. Important to this division of response is that most readers engage in both while reading. Readers engaged with informational text may appreciate the writer's style while acquiring information, or those engaged with fiction may wonder about details of the setting as they are appreciating the plot. Previous reading experiences and personal experience influence the way readers respond to a book. An addition to the ways of responding to text described by Rosenblatt includes critical response (Pearson, 2008). Critical response allows readers to challenge a text by considering the representation of a character, an event or issue, or the author's purpose.

A second influential voice on the topic of response is that of Iser (1978). His work focused on the gaps in literature and how the reader fills them. The first gaps are easily completed by the reader because they are based on real life. For example, the reader assumes that a character has two eyes, a nose, and so on. The reader also assumes that the author will share any unusual characteristics, such as a monster with one eye. The second gap is purposely left by the writer to stimulate reader participation. This gap may be difficult for some readers to complete because they lack sufficient background knowledge. For instance, in *Bud, Not Buddy* (Curtis, 1999), the reader has to know about segregation in the 1930s in a northern state. Without this knowledge, the reader will struggle with creating meaning. The third gap stimulates a reader's imagination. In *Holes*, Sachar (1998) tells readers directly that he has left gaps for them to complete—"You will have to fill in the holes yourself" (p. 231)—such as what happened to Stanley after he returned home with jewels and papers that were redeemed for a sizable sum of money. This gap is easier to complete because the readers are free to use their imagination to complete it.

Iser's work (1978) helps teachers recognize how the reader completes the text and how the text needs the reader to make meaning. In some cases the gaps are filled by common experience or the imagination. However, for gaps that require background knowledge, such as knowledge of a historical event, the teacher is critical in helping a student fill in these gaps when this knowledge is not internally held.

Physical

Physical response to books just happens. When children are scared, they may cover their eyes or gasp. When a book has a pleasant ending, they smile; with a sad ending, they cry. When I was reading *The Witches* (Dahl, 1983b) to a group of young children, they backed away *quickly*, after I read the following text from the introduction. I think students were surprised when I laughed as they moved away from me.

> In fairy-tales, witches always wear silly black hats and black cloaks, and they ride on broomsticks.
>
> But this is not a fairy-tale. This is about REAL WITCHES. . . .
>
> For all you know, a witch might be living next door to you right now.
>
> Or she might be the woman with the bright eye who sat opposite you on the bus this morning.
>
> She might be the lady with the dazzling smile who offered you a sweet from a white paper bag in the street before lunch.
>
> She might even—and this will make you jump—she might even be your lovely school-teacher who is reading these words to you at this very moment. Look carefully at that teacher. Perhaps she is smiling at the absurdity of such a suggestion. Don't let that put you off. It could be part of her cleverness. (Dahl, 1983b, pp. 7–10)

As a teacher, I knew they were hooked in the first few pages of this book just by their movement. Although teachers don't have to require physical response, watching children while reading aloud reveals their emotional response to the text.

Oral

Conversation surrounding reading allows students to share what they think or feel about a text and to extend meaning as they learn from the comments of others. Peterson and

Eeds (2007) called these "grand conversations." These conversations often move from commenting about a character or event to sharing puzzles about the text: "Why did the illustrator use dark colors?" or "When Alex did that, it reminded me of when my big brother . . . ." Nystrand (1997) observed that teachers' questions and discussion technique influence how students respond to books. He noted that asking open-ended questions or just providing discussion space allows students the freedom to negotiate meaning with other students, resulting in more sophisticated understanding. Some sample questions or stems to encourage discussion might include:

I think . . .
I notice . . .
I wonder . . .
My opinion is . . .
How is this story or informational text similar to others we have read?
How is this character, setting, or plot making you feel? (Just ask about one of these.)
What are you learning?

What is tricky about conversation is for teachers to just participate instead of asking a series of questions, even if they are open ended. Moving from the role of question giver to participant can take practice. Teachers can shift to the role of participant by allowing students to talk to partners or in a small group and then visiting or listening to each pair or group. Just making this small change helps teachers shift away from being the presenter of questions to inquisitive readers.

The following is a conversation from Mr. Bussoni's class as he was reading aloud *Sounder* (Armstrong, 1969). It is clear that Mr. Bussoni has mastered the art of listening to students rather than asking them to respond to a series of questions. There is not one question posed by the teacher in this short exchange; he just allowed space for student response.

STUDENT 1: He is reading about a school he wants to go to.

STUDENT 2: He crosses the street because he is afraid of people, White people.

STUDENT 3: It is a school for Whites.

STUDENT 4: African Americans can't go there.

STUDENT 5: He lives in the South. I think they had schools for White kids and for Black kids.

Students continued the discussion about schools being segregated, and then Mr. Bussoni began reading, pausing along the way to allow for additional student comments. At the end of the read-aloud, he asked students to think about what was important. He let students think for a bit, and then they shared with partners before being transitioned to the next learning event.

Not all conversations happen during a whole-class read-aloud. When students are organized into small groups by book choice, there are opportunities for conversations as well. I listened in as a group of fifth graders talked about the book *Oh, Brother* (Wilson, 1989). These students sat near each other as they read silently, and every so often a student offered a question or comment that spurred conversation.

STUDENT 1: This is the same as my family. My brothers treat me like he does.

STUDENT 2: They talk back to their parents.

STUDENT 3: My sister took money out of my dad's wallet and she got into big trouble.

STUDENT 4: Andrew might steal from Alex.

STUDENT 5: When the mom talks to them they kind of listen, but when the dad talks they stop.

STUDENT 6: I think the dad hollers at them.

STUDENT 7: I think they worry about their mom. Maybe they are scared of her.

The students returned to reading, but frequently interrupted themselves for these brief but valuable conversations.

Students deepen their comprehension and appreciation of a book by chatting about it. Conversation about books can center on text, illustrations, or their interaction. Students reading informational text might chat about interesting ideas or facts they have just discovered.

Written

Written response involves students writing in a journal before, during, or after reading. Harvey and Goudvis (2000) offer a simple way to support written response: Encourage readers to "leave tracks of their thinking" (p. 19). Adult readers do this when they write down ideas to remember, questions, or connections to text in the margins of their books. Often children are not able to write in their books, but sticky notes can work well. These notes serve as a vehicle for discussion or just as a way for students to learn about themselves as readers.

Written response, can also include writing in a literature response journal, a simple notebook. A structure for a journal could be a page where a student lists the books he or she read, a page for books the student wants to read, and pages for response. Teachers may just expect students to write an entry each day in their journal after they complete reading (Barone, 1990; Hancock, 2000). If teachers respond to a student's ideas in writing, the journal becomes a dialogue journal, where the teacher and student converse about a book. They might chat about the plot and what they think will happen, or they might write about a character and why they like or dislike him or her. Students can also engage in this dialogic writing with another student, where they respond to each other's entries. The following is an example of an entry in Mary's literature response journal about *What's the Big Idea, Ben Franklin?* (Fritz, 1976).

> Mary: Ben didn't know what to do for a living so he tried different things. He was really smart. His dad wanted him to work with his brother publishing, but Ben didn't like the job.
>
> Teacher: Ben really tried lots of jobs before he found the perfect one. I wonder what his dad is thinking about him now that he didn't want to be in publishing.

The entry serves as a vehicle for the student to write about what was most important in reading and for the teacher to respond to the student and nudge her to deeper understanding.

A variation on the form of an entry in a literature response journal is the double-entry draft (Barone, 1990). For this entry, a student copies an important piece of text on the left side of a paper, selecting a snippet that is meaningful to him or her. On the right side, the student explains why this text snippet was chosen. In the following example, Michael responds with a double-entry draft to *What's the Big Idea, Ben Franklin?*

	D. E. D.
Michael: Some people are blacksmiths	That reminds me of my dad. He used to be a blacksmith but now he does television. He likes television more than being a blacksmith.

> Teacher: I didn't know that your dad was a blacksmith like Ben Franklin. What did your dad like and not like about being a blacksmith?

The double-draft entry typically moves a student beyond literal comprehension to inferential and, in particular, to personal connections to the text, as is seen in Michael's response.

The previous examples have centered on traditional writing on paper. With technology, students can share their ideas or emotions about reading through book blogs, where they comment and other students respond and extend the conversation (Barone & Wright, 2008). Any of the ways that teachers engage students to write about their reading can certainly be accomplished with technology.

Artistic

Artistic responses for reading aloud and independent reading most often take the form of sketches. Students might draw a character or an event from the plot. Visual response might be a representation of an emotional response or a chart with important information (Hancock, 2000). Figure 2.3 shares an example of an artistic response from Elder, a

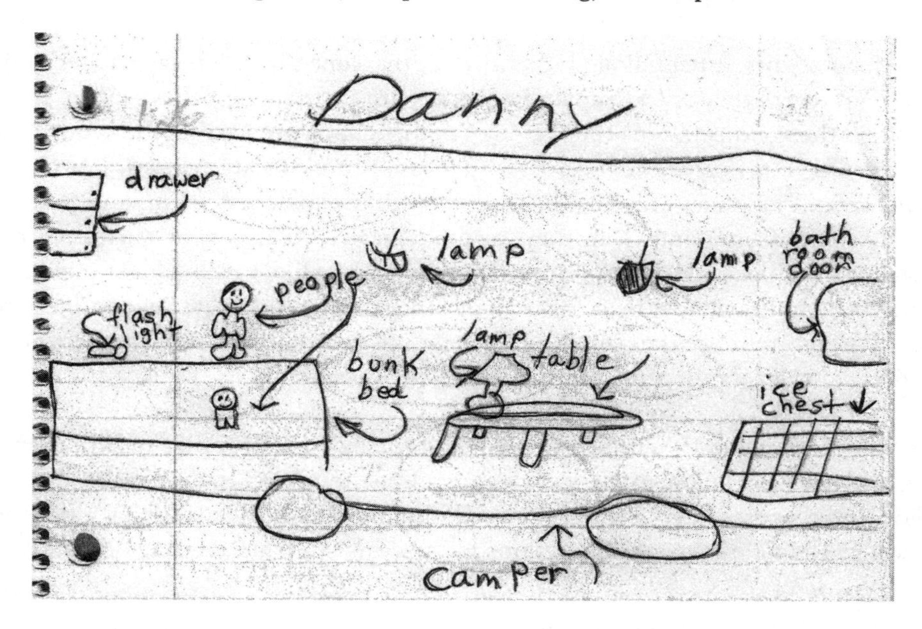

FIGURE 2.3. Elder's artistic response.

third grader, who was reading *Danny the Champion of the World* (Dahl, 1975). Elder was confused when he learned that Danny lived in a caravan, so he drew a sketch of what he thought Danny's caravan might look like to help with meaning.

In response to picturebooks, students may also want to draw using the media of an illustrator. Through this process, they gain a better understanding of how a particular medium contributes to the meaning of a text. They may also explore other visual elements like line, color, shape, and so on to experience the effects of each (Serafini & Giorgis, 2003).

All of the ways of responding in this chapter allow students to make decisions about their topics of conversation, writing, or visual response. They do not involve points or grades; rather, the focus is on engagement with books and reading. If teachers allow students these choices, they can learn about what their students find important or frustrating in text, what their students make connections to, and how emotionally connected students are to text. Additionally, through responding, students deepen their understanding of text and are more engaged with it.

ENGAGING STUDENTS

In the Responding to Literature section, I suggested ways that students can physically, orally, artistically, and in writing respond to reading. However, these suggestions did not touch on the practical concerns surrounding students reading independently. Perhaps fundamental to any discussion of independent work is that teachers have routines in place for students. A read-aloud is planned for the same time each day so that students are aware of where they need to sit and how they are expected to behave. Once students understand these expectations they can more quickly prepare for the read-aloud and are more engaged. For independent reading additional routines are needed. For instance, students must know how to select books, when they can access them, and how many they may select at one time. Can they keep books at their desks, or must they return them to a central location? They need to have materials, like notebooks or paper, available and need to know how to access and put these materials away. Beyond these pragmatic concerns are those that center on the reading development of students, which are critical to consider if independent reading is to be successful.

1. *Varying reading levels.* Within a classroom students typically range in skill from novice readers, with below-grade-level expectations, to above-grade-level readers. This wide range necessitates a variety of reading materials be available for independent reading. The following are suggestions for meeting students' reading needs:
   a. Select books that are grouped thematically. If books are selected to meet an expectation of theme, simple to more complicated books can be offered to students. Struggling readers can participate as successfully as proficient readers because they can find a book they can read, talk about, and write about.
   b. When conducting author studies, select authors of picturebooks and novels so that all students can assess his or her books. Each book will contribute to learning about an author's craft.
   c. Read aloud books that may be difficult for some students to read independently. Once struggling readers have heard a book, they can more easily read it independently.
   d. With a specific topic selected (e.g., bugs, the Westward expansion), provide books at a variety of reading levels. As students read simple books, they build background knowledge so they can successfully engage with more complex ones.
   e. Add to the media for independent reading by including Internet text or appropriate websites and magazines. These more visual materials often appeal to struggling readers.
   f. Create a podcast or a CD of a book. Students who want to access more difficult text can have oral support. More proficient readers, parents, or teacher aides can create these recordings.
2. *Management issues for independent reading.* Teachers can have a simple chart to note when they have conferred with students. Figure 2.4 is an example. Each block has a student's name and a place to record the date and the book title. Based on this information, teachers can know when a student completes a book, continually chooses new books but never finishing one, or chooses books that are too difficult to read. These observations can be used to facilitate book selection for students so they can experience success with their reading.

John **Date** **Book**	Emily **Date** **Book**	Michael **Date** **Book**	Vanessa **Date** **Book**	Jared **Date** **Book**	Kendra **Date** **Book**

FIGURE 2.4. Conference chart.

Students can also be tasked with creating a record of their independent reading. A sample form appears in Figure 2.5.

This record of independent reading lets students note how long they are involved with a book and shows them the importance the teacher places on independent reading. Later they can refer to this list to note genres or authors or illustrators they prefer. Their notes are a record of their first thoughts about a book and can help them identify what they find most important in books or how they emotionally connect to text.

At the end of this chapter, it is time to take a few moments to reflect:

1. Think about your experiences either being read aloud to or when you are reading aloud. What do you see as the strengths of these experiences? What are the challenges?
2. How do you choose books to read aloud? What genres do you prefer?
3. Visit the website for the American Library Association (*www.ala.org*), and go to either the Caldecott Medal or the Newbery Medal award page. Choose one of the recent winners and a winner from the past. Go to the library and read each. What did you notice?

Name ______________________________

Date	**Book Read**	**Thoughts**

FIGURE 2.5. Record of independent reading.

4. What books do your students elect to read during independent reading? What genres or authors do they prefer? Are these books available to them?
5. How do your students respond to reading? Do they write and draw about their books? What do you notice about their responses?

RECOMMENDED READING

For readers who would like to know about some of the topics in this chapter, the following books and article provide additional information.

Reutzel, D. R., Jones, C., Fawson, P., & Smith, J. (2008). Scaffolded silent reading: A complement to guided repeated oral reading that works! *The Reading Teacher, 62*, 194–207.

This article shares strategies to make independent reading more effective for students.

Miller, D. (2009). *The book whisperer: Awakening the inner reading in every child.* San Francisco: Jossey-Bass.

This book is written by a teacher and demonstrates how read-aloud and independent reading can be supported in a classroom. She offers practical suggestions to help teachers and provides numerous book suggestions.

Stead, T. (2009). *Good choice! Supporting independent reading and response K–6.* Portland, ME: Stenhouse.

This book offers many practical suggestions to help teachers with independent reading and response activities. Stead provides numerous forms to help teachers.

Student Voices

Island of the Blue Dolphins (O'Dell, 1971)

"*Island of the Blue Dolphins* is a good book because of the adventure. Karana is all alone, and she finds food and shelter. She is brave, strong, and creative. She made a house all by herself. I wouldn't be able to do what she did because I am not used to doing things all by myself or being alone. I would be too afraid."—Gabrielle, a fourth grader

CHAPTER 3

Exploring Narrative Genres

> When you visit the zoo now, you surely won't mind
> If the animals seem just a bit hard to find . . .
> They are snug in their niches, their nests, and their nooks,
> Going wild, simply wild, about wonderful books.
> —JUDY SIERRA, *Wild About Books* (2004, unpaged)

In the book *Wild About Books*, a librarian happens to take her bookmobile into the zoo. The animals are excited about reading, especially their favorites (it's always interesting to me how easy it is for animals to read). In rhyme, the author writes about otters liking *Harry Potter*, llamas enjoying drama, and the kangaroos preferring *Nancy Drew*. What is fun about this book is that it provides a brief, enjoyable introduction to genre (literature sharing common characteristics) and certainly could serve as a stimulus for students to talk about their favorite genres.

The first genre distinction made for children's literature is that children's literature, itself, is a genre (Nodelman & Reimer, 2003), a subset of literature in general. Thinking back to the discussion in Chapter 1 about the definition of children's literature, it is obvious that a blurry boundary exists between children's literature and adult literature. The next blurry boundary is centered on genre distinctions within children's literature, because they are complicated even when just considering the dichotomy of fiction and nonfiction or informational text (Lukens, 2007). For example, fiction is usually thought of as encompassing books that contain stories or poems and informational text as carrying only factual information. However, some books combine these two genres. For example, *The Magic Tree House* series (Osborne) are fictional stories centered on two time-traveling characters, Jack and Annie, who bring what they learn to their readers. For instance, in *Buffalo Before Breakfast* (Osborne, 1999), the children travel back 200 years, befriend the Lakota, and learn about bison and the life of this Native American tribe.

Another similar collection written for young children is *The Magic School Bus* series (various authors). The main character, Ms. Frizzle, is a teacher who loves science and takes her class on numerous field trips where they learn about, for example, space, bats, the food chain, and germs.

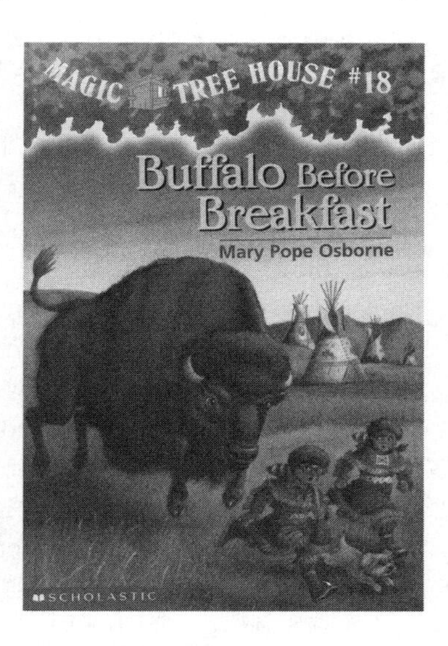

Considering just these two popular series, it is easy to see how authors combine fiction and information. Although the fiction and informational aspects of these texts are clear—in *Buffalo Before Breakfast* information about bison is identified using a separate font—both are contained within a single book, thus making the categorizing of books as fiction or information problematic.

Although these broad divisions between information and fiction seem apparent to adults, they are not so clear-cut for students. For example, when I chatted with first graders about the *Magic Tree House* books, many assumed that everything in them was real. They believed that the children actually talked to the Lakota. A few others decided that the covers of the *Magic Tree House* books make them stories because the images were drawings, not photos. An activity to help students with these grand divisions would be for teachers to provide a sample of fiction and informational books to small groups of students. For younger students teachers may select books that clearly sort into each category. For more experienced readers, teachers may choose poetry books that include poems about animals or books that include information and narrative so that students experience conflict in sorting and have to carefully reason through their decisions. Once books are selected, students would then be expected to sort them into binary stacks of fiction and information, noting the reasons for these categorizations. Teachers will become aware of how students make these decisions through their comments. They might even create charts noting the important parts of narrative or informational text. It will be interesting to discover whether they form these decisions from the cover art, from previous experience, or from a careful review of the contents of the book.

With the acknowledgment of the arbitrariness of genre sorting, identifying common elements of books and placing them into categories does help students develop background knowledge, or a road map for the structure of a text, that supports comprehension (Youngs & Barone, 2007). For instance, when reading a fairytale, students know that there are fanciful elements like talking animals, magic coaches, and so on; they know that there are good characters and evil characters; and they know the story ends with a happy resolution. In order for students to truly understand a genre, they must read widely within it as they determine its characteristics. Teachers can support students in genre learning by collaboratively creating genre charts with students where they add additional characteristics with each exploration of a genre.

These charts might begin in a similar fashion to a KWL (Ogle, 1986), where students offer what they already know about a genre. It is easiest for teachers, especially those in the primary grades, to begin with one genre at a time. Teachers of intermediate students may have several genre charts available for students to add to, thus refining their knowledge of genres. As the teachers read more books in a genre and as students independently read a genre, students can add to the charts. This explicit focus on genre allows students to recognize books by genre and bring these expectations to text. This background knowledge supports students in focusing on the unique ideas within a book rather than spending time negotiating the key aspects to a genre.

Elementary teachers often organize class libraries to help students identify books within genres. Figure 3.1 shows the genre organization of books in Diane Frank's fourth-grade classroom. She organized books in this way so that students become familiar with the different characteristics of each genre and have opportunities to read in each category. Primary teachers in their genre organization schemes might further divide traditional literature and include categories like alphabet or number books.

Teacher readers may be thinking, "I already know about genre. Why is this chapter included?" Although this knowledge is certainly familiar to teachers, I present it so that teachers are aware of the importance of sharing this knowledge in routine ways with students. Teachers may want to use their knowledge of genres to self-check the books they read aloud to students. Often teachers have a personal preference for a specific genre and forget to share other kinds of books. Or they share a genre that is nestled within a larger genre but never share this organization with students. For example, I often see teachers share a fairytale unit with students. Children love hearing and reading these stories. They become familiar with these tales and the characters that inhabit them. However, I wonder if they know that they are part of the traditional literature that is shared in

FIGURE 3.1. Diane Frank's classroom library.

the United States? This understanding can happen only when teachers broaden a unit centered on fairytales to other genres within traditional literature. Through an exploration of traditional literature, students learn about the nuanced differences between legends and myths, for example. I ask teachers to reconsider genre and to think of it as more than categories for narratives. For instance, wouldn't students love to be given the challenge of determining when a book is classified as fantasy or science fiction? Rather than telling students about the differences, wouldn't they enjoy discovering these differences from reading? Once students have clear understandings of each narrative genre, they can appreciate when authors and illustrators borrow from other genres or combine genres within their books.

In this chapter, I have organized the fiction genres by category. I have separated books for the very young from these categorization schemes because many are informational as well as fiction. To avoid redundancy and focusing on these books in both this chapter and the next, I share them here only. Books for the earliest readers are important to include as children develop as readers at home and in preschool, and these books influence in-school reading.

The fiction category includes traditional literature, fantasy, poetry, historical fiction, realistic fiction, multicultural literature, international literature, graphic books, and postmodern picturebooks. Some of these categories, like international or multicultural literature, might also encompass fiction, but they just have an additional designation. Within each category, I share some familiar book examples so that teachers can feel satisfied with their knowledge of these books and can remember successfully sharing them with students. I also include newer books that may not be as well known but are worth exploring with students. I end the chapter with school-based genres. Only in schools are the genres of decodable, predictable, and leveled text used with regularity and commonly understood as categories of literature. Like books for young children, these school-based genres include narrative and informational text. To avoid redundancy, I included them in this chapter.

BOOKS FOR THE VERY YOUNG

Parents begin the process of sharing literature with their infants and young children. Often a baby's first book is one that can be explored using the senses. In *Pat the Bunny* (Kunhardt, 1940), for example, a baby can interact with the book, feeling the bunny's fur or looking in a mirror, as his or her parents reads. Some first books focus on naming things, include nursery rhymes. On your next visit to a bookstore, investigate how many books are available for infants and young children. The extensive line of board books, books made of cardboard pages, is evidence of their increasing popularity among parents. On one recent visit, I noticed a full wall dedicated to board books alone.

Early exposure to books, the physical comfort that surrounds a book-reading activity, and the conversations centered on a book provide children with enjoyment and the understanding that reading is a pleasant experience. Along with experiencing the emotional qualities of being read to, children are also learning, among other things, the structure of stories, the appreciation of a character, and the alphabet. Children who have been read to at home and/or in preschool are acquainted with narratives, the alphabet, and how books work. And they have preferences in what they want read to them. This knowledge and experience accompany them into elementary classrooms.

Alphabet Books

Although alphabet books are intended for the very young, they appeal to students in later grades as well. Some alphabet books are straightforward, with one letter and an object on each page. Others are quite complex and the connections are not so obvious, or the alphabet format serves to share information. Figure 3.2 presents a list of alphabet books ranging in content, from simple to complex.

Primary students love alphabet books because they are familiar with the structure. They enjoy seeing what an author/illustrator chooses for *X* and *Q*, because they know these are difficult letters to represent. Teachers can easily use this format to create class books. However, rather than just deciding on what should be used for a letter's illustration, students can be encouraged to reproduce the style of the original book shared by the teacher. Youngest students might recreate the style used in *I Spy Little Letters* (Marzolla, 2000), for instance. Each student would be given a letter or a page with a large, drawn letter that is outlined so it has space within. (It is best perhaps if the letters are precut for young students using a die cut machine.) On the letter students draw items that begin with the letter. The style includes bright colors and simple designs. Once each page is complete, it becomes part of a class book for students to read. Another project idea is for teachers to use a digital camera to photograph images that represent letters. Students have a "field trip" within their classroom and school, and teachers photograph images for each letter that students identify: for example, *P* for principal, *C* for cafeteria. These images can become part of the alphabet wall display making it much more meaningful to the students, because they created it.

Older students always feel that an alphabet book is beneath their sophisticated status. I have had fourth graders say to me, "I already know the alphabet. Why would you bring those books here?" The answer is that these are more complicated and are geared to older students. Books like *Tomorrow's Alphabet* or *Q is for Duck*, for example, require students to think more abstractly about a letter. Coming up with an appropriate illustration that suggests something related to the primary item is often difficult: for example, a picture of a tire for the letter *C* because cars have tires. Other alphabet books are complex in their visual structure (e.g., a letter turns into the next, like an *m* becoming an *n*). These visual representations provide intellectual and artistic challenges for students.

Name of Book	Author/Illustrator (year)	Brief Description
Chicka, Chicka, Boom, Boom	Bill Martin, Jr. & John Archambault; IL Lois Ehlert (1989)	This book shares the names of alphabet letters to a catchy rhythm.
ABC3D	Marion Bataille (2008)	On each page of this book a letter pops up to a 3-D view, and some are transformed from one letter to another (e.g., *C* turns into *D*).
My Big Alphabet Book	DK Publishing (1999)	Each letter is represented by several objects that begin with the letter.
City Seen from A to Z	Rachel Isadora (1983)	Each page shares something you would see in the city with the first letter capitalized (e.g., Ice cream).
An Edward Lear Alphabet	Edward Lear; IL Vladimir Radunsky (1983)	Edward Lear's tongue-twisting verse accompanies each letter.
Tomorrow's Alphabet	George Shannon; IL Donald Crews (1999)	This alphabet book does not represent letters with objects that begin with them. For instance, *A* is for seed because the seed results in an apple.
Q is for Duck: An Alphabet Guessing Game	Mary Elting & Michael Folsom; IL Jack Kent (2005)	This alphabet book asks students questions about letters (e.g., *A* is for zoo. Why? Because animals live in the zoo).
The Graphic Alphabet	David Pelletier (1996)	This alphabet book is more complex because each letter influences the next; for example, the *A* crumbles as the result of an avalanche and the *B* bounces with electrified energy.
I Spy: An Alphabet in Art	Lucy Micklethwait (1996)	The book asks readers to spy something that begins with a letter in a work of art (e.g., the *a* is the apple in Magritte's Son of Man).
Anno's Alphabet	Mitsumasa Anno (1974)	The letters are created in woodcuts with an illustration and intricate border on the partnering page. Anno helps students recognize some of the items with a list at the back of the book.

(cont.)

FIGURE 3.2. Alphabet books.

Name of Book	Author/Illustrator (year)	Brief Description
Aardvarks, Disembark!	Ann Jonas (1990)	After the great flood, Noah orders animals off the ark in alphabetical order. He realizes, however, that many animals did not listen so he repeats his list starting with *z*. The book includes many animals that are unfamiliar to students, but there is a glossary to help.
The Z Was Zapped	Chris Van Allsburg (1987)	This is a drama with the alphabet featured.
S is for Shamrock: An Ireland Alphabet	Eve Bunting; IL Matt Faulkner (2007)	Each page shares interesting information about Ireland. There are alphabet books for other countries and states as well written by a variety of authors.
Jazz A • B • Z	Wynton Marsalis; IL Paul Rogers (2005)	Each letter offers the opportunity to share information about a jazz musician.
The Ultimate Alphabet	Mike Wilks (1986)	The author/illustrator begins by sharing how the book was crafted. On each page he tells the reader how many items begin with a letter–360 for *A* alone.
The Dangerous Alphabet	Neil Gaiman; IL Cris Grimly (2008a)	This alphabet book shares a full story about a journey using the alphabet as a structure.
Alphabeasties and other Amazing Types	Sharon Werner & Sarah Forss (2009)	This book uses type/font in unusual ways to create animals/objects that represent letters.

FIGURE 3.2. *(cont.)*

Moving from the visual, older students may also be up to the challenge of creating a story similar to *The Dangerous Alphabet*. This type of writing requires several visits to the original text to see how the author—in this case Gaiman—constructed it exactly. Teachers would encourage students to rough out the key events of the story and then place the characters within. Rather than creating the rhyming patterns used by Gaiman, students could just create a narrative that cleverly includes the alphabet, either in the form of characters' names or places. This complex writing would take several days to complete in a writing workshop.

Counting Books

Similar to alphabet books, counting books can be simple or complicated. Early counting books support one-to-one correspondence. See, for example, Molly Bang's *Ten, Nine, Eight* (1991) and Eric Carle's *1, 2, 3, to the Zoo* (1968).

Books that target counting at a slightly more complicated level include *Fire Truck* by Peter Sis (1998), *Anno's Counting Book* (Anno, 1986), Rose's *One Nighttime Sea* (2003), and Pallotta's *Ocean Counting Odd Numbers* (2005). Sis's *Fire Truck* is a story of a young boy who loves fire trucks; he sleeps in a fire truck bed, reads about them, and plays with them. One day he wakes to find that he is a fire truck and counts the items on the fire truck. I wonder what students will think about a child who turns into his favorite thing. What complications might this bring? How can a child go to school if he is a fire truck? *Anno's Counting Book* is complex in that the things that are counted are embedded in full illustration. For instance, for the numeral 1, there is one unifix cube, one snowman with a flag with "1" on it, one bird, one dog, one skier, one bridge, one sun, one chimney with smoke (although there were two chimneys), one boy, and one shovel. Like Anno's other books, what appears to be simple and calm in illustration is quite complex. After children have counted everything they can on the pages, they may step back, with a teacher's support, and consider the calmness of the illustrations. Anno's books, no matter the topic, are always satisfying to readers/viewers in their composition and color palette.

Several recent counting books are just too good to overlook. In Cave's (2003) *One Child, One Seed*, a young South African child plants a seed, watching over it and nourishing it until it grows into a pumpkin. Each page not only represents a numeral but reflects the growth of the vegetable, until it is finally eaten. Jay's (2007) *1-2-3: A Child's First Counting Book* is a counting fairytale. The book resembles an older book in the tone and construction of its illustrations because they are balanced and often framed. Young children will enjoy the fairytales that are woven into each illustration, although they will have to look closely, and may even need adult support, to discover them. Finally, *Counting with Wayne Thiebaud* (Rubin, 2007) includes the contemporary paintings of Thiebaud as the focus for counting. Young children just enjoy the paintings, not recognizing they are works of art. They might describe how familiar things like ice cream cones can represent numerals. Older students can step back from the form of counting book and explore the artwork. It is exciting for them to see how cleverly the contemporary paintings are used to reinforce counting lessons. Because Thiebaud's artwork is so accessible to students in that he uses familiar objects, teachers can have students create books, perhaps a number book, in his style. Students can view his paintings at *www.artnet.com/artist/16543/wayne-thiebaud.html* to learn about his work in support of their own creations. Teachers might also use this book as a springboard to exploring other artists and how their work might be repositioned to create a number book.

Engineered Books

Engineered books are those that are interactive in some way. Most times, they have flaps, cut-outs, or 3-D effects, like the *ABC3D* alphabet book (Bataille, 2008), a very visually complex book. Simpler books include *Pat the Bunny* (Kunhardt, 1940), where children can touch fur or view themselves in a mirror. Scratch-and-sniff books, where children scratch a sticker to release a smell such as chocolate or blueberry, have waned in popularity, unlike flap books. One of the most popular flap book series, features

Spot, a spotted puppy whose adventures require readers, to lift a flap to gain necessary information to support the plot. In *Spot's First Walk* (Hill, 1981), Spot's mother tells him not to get lost as Spot embarks on his first solo walk. As children lift flaps, they see that Spot encounters a snail, a cat, a chicken, a woodpecker, and so on. Although there is little text, the illustrations behind the flaps extend the story, and young children love exploring what happens.

More complicated engineered books include *The Snowmen* (Buehner, 2002), where the pop-up provides action. For instance, on the first page, the boy moves to attach a carrot to the snowman for his nose. Whereas in *Spot* the flaps let the readers view another illustration, in *The Snowmen* the pop-ups are three-dimensional, enhancing the illustrations. In addition to the pop-ups, there are tabs that allow the readers to move a snowman (e.g., letting it tube down a snowy hill). Other pop-ups that stir imagination and wonder are *600 Black Spots* (Carter, 2007) and *Trail* (Pelham, 2007). In *600 Black Spots* there are 600 dots to be counted that are shared in amazing structures like roller coasters and pagodas. *Trail* is considered to be paper poetry where all the pages are white with verse to accompany them. This is a book that, once opened, is hard to put down because each page is incredibly intricate and the reader craves observing each detail (see image to the right).

Although students may find it difficult to create whole books in the style of *Trail*, they may enjoy creating a single illustration. Teachers should be forewarned, however, that this kind of creative project can be frustrating to some students, ending in tears or even anger. If you have ever asked students to create torn-paper art, you can resonate with how they might feel creating a cut-paper pop-up. I envision this creative illustration coupled with a poem that students have already written or one that they have chosen from a poet. Once the poems are complete, they can pair them with a pop-up cutout like those in *Trail*. They will start with a single focus, like the unicorn in the image presented above. For this initial piece, they can draw on a piece of paper and then cut it out, leaving flaps at the bottom so it can be glued to another paper. Once satisfied with this image, students can add additional details following the same format. In *Trail* all the images are white, so teachers may ask students to limit their color choice to a single color. As students create these images, they will discover how the art in *Trail* contributes to the poetry and how complex this style of illustration is. They will also enjoy their poetry and artistic rendering.

Wordless Books

Wordless books are just that: books with few or no words—the story is relayed through the illustrations. Similar to alphabet and counting books, they range from straightforward to challenging. Some of the first wordless books were created by Mercer Mayer, who frequently used the theme of friendship but with a humorous twist. In *Hiccup* (1976) two hippopotami are in a rowboat when the girl hippopotamus gets the hiccups. The boy hippopotamus attempts to get rid of them by scaring and hitting her. The book ends with the boy hippopotamus getting the hiccups. The book is illustrated with simple line drawings and is quite funny, especially if you are 5. Tomie dePaola, in *Pancakes for Breakfast* (1978), shares a silly story about creating pancakes, although he uses full-color illustrations that frequently resemble comic strips, with four separate, but connected, illustrations on a two-page spread. This story, like *Hiccup*, is comical and results in lots of giggling.

Alexandra Day created a whole wordless book series around a Rottweiler named Carl, who takes care of a young baby. The illustrations show humorous situations when Carl is babysitting with a happy resolution when the mother reappears. *Will's Mammoth* (Martin, 1989) is similar in story to *Where the Wild Things Are* (Sendak, 1963/1988). Will is in his bedroom drawing mammoths and his parents keep telling him they don't exist. Will is convinced they do and the majority of the book shows him riding a mammoth. The book ends with his return home, just in time for supper. *Deep in the Forest* (Turkle, 1976), another wordless book, is a variant of *The Three Bears*, only this time the littlest bear goes into Goldilocks's home. Children who are familiar with the traditional story of *The Three Bears* will giggle as they see the bear tasting porridge, breaking a chair, and sleeping in Goldilocks's bed.

More complicated wordless books include several by David Wiesner: *Tuesday* (1997), *Free Fall* (1998/2008), *Sector 7* (1999), and *Flotsam* (2006). *Tuesday* received the Caldecott Medal and features frogs flying. However, there are messages within, such as an adult robotically watching television and the frog taking control of the remote control. Although there is much to talk about in *Tuesday*, students can be nudged to consider what Wiesner thinks about television by interpreting the illustration of the frog taking the remote. In *Free Fall*, a boy falls asleep as he reads an atlas and then floats above earth; however, his adventure is not logical but rather very confusing. In *Sector 7*, another child has an adventure in the clouds when he leaves his field trip to the Empire State Building. Finally, in *Flotsam*, a young child finds a camera that has washed up on a beach. These wordless books contain complicated stories that are enriched with each viewing and cause students to ponder each illustration, moving ahead and then back to make sense of the story. Typically, students do not agree on what is happening within Wiesner's books, resulting in enthusiastic discussions as they explain their interpretations. I have observed teachers partnering students with Wiesner's books so that they have time to carefully study each illustration and create meaning with a partner. The conversations are energized, with each student wanting to convince the partner of his or her own interpretation.

Perhaps the most complicated wordless book I have used is *The Grey Lady and the Strawberry Snatcher* (Bang, 1980). This book is complex because the background often becomes the foreground, and it is hard to decipher which is which. The grey lady carries her strawberries as a goblin-type creature tries to snatch them in a very convoluted chase. Bang writes about her book and the difficulties she had getting it published (*www.*

mollybang.com). She also provides insight for viewers as they try to make sense of this tale. Most teachers and students will welcome her words to help to understand the book; even after revisiting this book multiple times, I am still puzzled by many of its illustrations. However, I never tire of trying to decipher more of the plot with each visit.

TRADITIONAL LITERATURE

Traditional literature encompasses books rendered from oral tradition—stories that have been passed down for ages (Kiefer, 2007)—and as a result are commonly shared throughout the world. This literature includes folktales, myths, fables, and legends. These stories are short and often plot driven, with characters that are either good or evil.

Folktales

Folktales appear to be set in the past, although the past and exact setting are difficult to determine. They most often tell a story about a person or an animal who appears almost human. Common characteristics are:

- Plot filled with action involving a conflict.
- Characters not fully developed and often having a limited range of emotion.
- Setting in a time in the past and indicated by "Once upon a time" or "A long time ago."
- Themes centered on good prevailing over evil, intelligence being stronger than brawn, and the rewards gained by working hard.
- Style that is straightforward where the plot is clear and characters are easily identified.
- Motifs including magical transformations, hero acquiring a magical object, supernatural adversaries or helpers, and magical powers (Norton, 1995).

Familiar folktales include *tall tales* like Kellogg's *Johnny Appleseed* (1988) and *Pecos Bill* (1986). Kellogg has rewritten many tall tales with illustrations that beg readers to take in each detail. In *John Henry* (1994), Lester takes a more realistic view of American folk hero John Henry and whether he was a real person. The beginning of his book shares his research into John Henry and the building of the Chesapeake and Ohio Railroad. It shares a view of John Henry as a real person, someone who could have worked as hard as tales say he did. I believe that when children hear or read this book, they will be curious about other heroes in tall tales and will want to research them to find out the true story. Using a traditional literature genre like tall tales easily leads to informational research on each hero. I did a quick search of Johnny Appleseed and found information about him as a person. I also discovered Jacque Pratt's investigations of Johnny Appleseed published on the Internet (*www.hipark.austin.isd.tenet.edu/projects/second/ja/ja.html*). Each of her second-grade students created an illustration and wrote facts about

Johnny Appleseed. This site serves as a model for young children's research and Internet publication.

Cumulative tales are stories that begin with a simple idea that is repeated throughout. Examples include *Chicken Little* (Kellogg, 1985), *The Little Red Hen* (Galdone, 1973), and *The Mitten* (Brett, 1989). In each of these books, text repeats: for example, "Not I" in *The Little Red Hen* and "The sky is falling" in *Chicken Little*. These stories are perfect for young children to perform as Readers' Theatre. They quickly learn the repetitive pattern and enjoy showing off in front of their peers. It is best if children have a script, but the script can just include the part of text that is repeated. The teacher can read any of the narrator parts. The other advantage of Readers' Theatre is that practice is short, and no costumes are required.

Although these stories are familiar to most, authors and illustrators enjoy creating variants. For instance, Barry Downard (2004) illustrated *The Little Red Hen* with photographs of farm animals that are enhanced so the hen wears glasses and the cat is using earphones. The hen also rides a bike and the animals play pool. I love this version as a model for students to reillustrate other cumulative tales. Tales like *Chicken Little* are perfect for this process. Some students may have Chicken Little visit other animals, not those in the story, whereas others may change who Chicken Little visits totally. For example, Chicken Little could be living in the city and visit animals or people who live there.

Fairytales are a third category of folktales. Some of the most familiar are *Cinderella, Sleeping Beauty*, and *Little Red Riding Hood*. Authors and illustrators love to retell these stories, often with unique illustrations or twists. For example, *Little Red Riding Hood* has been a favorite choice of current writers and illustrators. Hyman (1983) created a version with framed illustrations and intricate borders on each page. This book received criticism, however, because Little Red Riding Hood carried wine to her grandmother. This version also has a happy ending, where the huntsman saved the grandmother and Little Red Riding Hood. *Lon Po Po* (Young, 1989) is a Chinese version of this story. Young's illustrations are muted and several pages have two to four separate panels. In this version Lon Po Po, the wolf, is visiting three girls while their mother is out. When I read it I was amazed at how the wolf, through Young's positioning of his face and highlighting of his eye, is the scariest wolf I have ever seen in a fairytale illustration. Browne's version of this story, *Into the Forest* (2004), moves furthest from the traditional story: A boy goes into the forest to visit his grandmother, who lives in a house that appears contemporary. As he walks through the forest, he meets Jack from *Jack and the Beanstalk*, Little Red Riding Hood, and Hansel and Gretel. The images are, for the most part, black and white, with the boy in color. Like other Anthony Browne books, this one is complicated in illustrations, and children will want the opportunity to talk about what they mean to the story.

Goldilocks and the Three Bears is another fairytale that is represented in numerous variations. Lauren Child's *Goldilocks and the Three Bears* (2009a) is a play, with dolls and stuffed animals representing the critical characters. Goldilocks has red shoes, which her mother expects her to protect as she walks in the woods. Unlike other versions, the reader learns that Goldilocks was sent to the woods because "her curiosity got the better

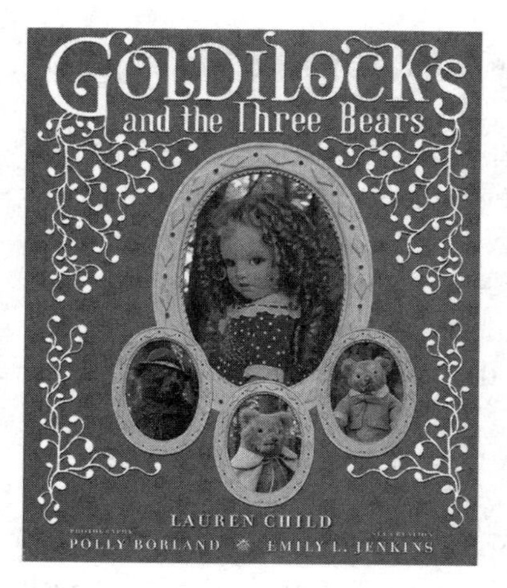

of her" (unpaged). Child writes that a little curiosity is okay but if you have too much, then expect trouble. The images of a doll wandering into real woods, a photograph, makes the viewer appreciate this story and see it as new. Readers, especially sophisticated ones, will appreciate the subtle humor throughout the book.

Cinderella is another book that authors enjoy tinkering with. *Glass Slipper Gold Sandal* (Fleischman, 2007) is a single version of this story with worldwide representation. For instance, the first page begins with "Once upon a time . . . " features a mother reading to her daughter, with a globe next to them. Each subsequent page is a version from another country: Mexican, Korean, Indian, and so on. The illustrations share traditional motifs from each country, like birds or flowers, and the country's name is written on the page. Rather than writing numerous versions, this one is a collection of multiple versions that complete a single rendition. Haddix (1999) wrote a variation of the traditional *Cinderella* story by creating a whole novel about Cinderella, *Just Ella*. Ella has a stepmother and Prince Charming in her life, but there is no magic like magic coaches or a fairy godmother. The author plays with the idea of what happens when the princess moves into the palace after the ball, and it isn't a happily ever after story.

Ferris has expanded the idea of fairytale in her book *Once Upon a Marigold* (2002) through the inclusion of humor. Princess Marigold is experiencing the usual dilemma for a princess: Her family wants her to be married, but she finds fault with each of her suitors. In a parallel circumstance, a troll, Ed, has been raising a run-away boy, Christian, since he found him wandering in the woods. Although Christian and Marigold find each other and want to be married, they are confronted with the issue of Christian being a commoner. As this plot is resolved, readers enjoy Ferris's humor in this modern fairytale of prince finding princess. Even boys might enjoy this fairytale because Christian is as central a character as Princess Marigold.

Books that make fun of numerous fairytales include *Revolting Rhymes* (Dahl, 1983a); *The Stinky Cheese Man and Other Fairly Stupid Tales* (Scieszka & Smith, 1992); and *Once Upon A Time, The End* (Kloske & Blitt, 2005). Dahl used rhyme to retell each story with humor, humor that makes even an adult laugh out loud. For example, Cinderella leaves the ball in her underwear, Snow White leads gambling dwarfs, and Little Red Riding Hood collects wolf skins. Scieszka and Smith start their humorous collection right on the cover, writing, "What is this doing here? This is ugly! Who is this ISBN guy?" It doesn't stop there as the front-page flap reads like an ad: "Only $17.99 USA—56 action-packed pages. 75% more than those old 32-page 'Brand X' books." Then the fractured versions of each tale begin with modified text, sometimes at an angle or upside down, and surrealistic illustrations. The final example is *Once Upon a Time, The End*, where each story consumes no more than one page so that parents can read to children but get them to bed in less than 60 seconds.

I have provided just a brief sampling of the fairytales and variants available to children. Carol Hurst (*www.carolhurst.com*) offers lists of fairytale variants. Another site that focuses on fairytales is Heidi Heiner's Sur La Lune (*www.surlalunefairytalkes.com*) where she provides information about fairytales and links to additional information about each.

Teachers are familiar with grouping fairytales from around the world for student exploration. Students might read and compare a variety of *Cinderella* stories, for instance. Another way to consider fairytales is to share traditional ones with students and encourage them to make notes about what they observe. Then teachers could move to variants of fairytales and students could share how the story changes. Does the author change the plot: The illustrations? Both? Once students are comfortable with these changes, they can select a favorite fairytale, sketch out the plot, and note the setting and characters. Just as contemporary authors have retooled traditional fairytales, students get to decide on one thing they might change as they write their own version. For instance: How would the story change if Little Red Riding Hood lives in a city? What if Cinderella had two stepbrothers instead of stepsisters? Students learn that just one simple change results in an entirely different version of the traditional fairytale.

Myths

Myths attempt to explain aspects of our world, such as how the world or animals came to exist. They often begin with phrases such as "Before Time Began." Gerald McDermott has explored numerous myths called *trickster tales*. He has written *Raven* (2001), *Arrow to the Sun* (1977), and *Creation* (2003), all beautiful books showing the creation of the world or creatures.

Other myths come from Greek, Roman, and Norse mythology and explain gods. Books like *D'Aulaires' Book of Greek Myths* (1962/1992) share information about Greek gods and goddesses like Zeus and Athena. Additional information about myths is available at the following websites: *www.ipl.org/div/kidspace* (worldwide myths), *www.windows.ucar.edu* (myths from around the world), and *www.acs.ucalgary.ca/~dkbrown/storfolk.html* (information about myths).

Riordan has written a narrative series centered on the ancient gods. The main character is Percy Jackson, who, until he was 12, thought he was an ordinary kid. In *The Lightning Thief* (2005), Percy discovers his relationship to an ancient god. Throughout the narrative series readers become familiar with the myths centered on the ancient gods. Unlike other myth books, this series incorporates this information into its plots and they are addictive to read. The gods become real persons who are jealous, mean, or helpful.

Fables

Fables are most often connected to Aesop. These stories always share a moral or a lesson to be learned, and the characters are most often animals. David Pinkney and

Arnold Lobel have written notable collections of Aesop's fables. Pinkney's lengthy version (2000) contains a mix of familiar and not-so-familiar 61 fables and beautiful illustrations. Children love hearing these fables, but this book can be overwhelming if read cover to cover. Rather, teachers might share a fable from this book with a version of the same fable in a different book. Children can share comparisons in how the fables were told.

Lobel's version (1983) is simpler for young children, although many have difficulty understanding the moral behind the fable (e.g., how slow and steady can be as good or better than fast). No doubt, young boys struggle with this concept. Similar to Pinkney's book, sharing parts of this book on repeated days would be a more effective way to read it to students. Cech's (2009) version, *Aesop's Fables*, contains numerous fables, and Marin Jarrie's artwork presents a contemporary spin. Similar to fairytales, students might select a favorite fable and illustrate it with a more contemporary style, as modeled in Cech's book.

Legends

Legends are similar to myths and tall tales. Many of the stories focus on King Arthur and his adventures, for example, Borgenicht and Pyle's (1996) *The Legend of King Arthur.* The Children's Literature Web Guide devotes a page to legends and contains additional valuable information: *www.acs.ucalgary.ca/~dkbrown/storfolk.html.* Students can also explore other legends about plants, dragons, and individuals. dePaola (2007) has compiled the legends of Bluebonnet, Indian Paintbrush, Poinsettia, and Bread in one volume: *Big Book of Favorite Legends.* This compilation helps children to see how simple things like a flower can have a legend written about it.

After students explore legends, teachers may have them write legends of themselves. Students select something they are very good at, brainstorm why this is important, and explain why this has made them a legend. For example, one student might share that she is masterful at jumping rope. She practices each day by jumping in front of her home. She explains how she trapped a thief with her jump rope right in front of her home. This event is written about in the newspaper, people congratulated her, and that is how she became a legend.

Each of the genres within traditional literature is perfect for Readers' Theatre. Don't worry! Teachers do not have to create the scripts. Whew! That would take far too much time. Aaron Shepard has created numerous Readers' Theatre scripts that are available for free at *www.aaronshep.com/rt/RTE.html.* There are many myths, fables, and legends to choose from. Students love to perform these scripts, and enjoy traditional literature even more with these dramatic complements.

Alternatively, teachers may decide to have students create "A Student's Guide to Traditional Literature" after they have explored traditional literature. Each page would list a genre of traditional literature, the important characteristics, and a book that fits the category. For technology-savvy teachers, this book could be displayed on a class website for others to learn from.

FANTASY

Fantasy takes readers to places that are beyond the scope of everyday experiences. "The imaginary element provides the bridge that separates fantasy from realism" (Hancock, 2000, p. 86). *Where the Wild Things Are* (Sendak, 1963/1988) provides a model of this shift from fantasy to reality as Max travels on his boat to the land of the wild things, a fantasy place, and then returns to the real world of his bedroom. Today fantasy is perhaps more popular than ever, as evidenced by the amazing sales of J. K. Rowling's *Harry Potter* series (Gamble & Yates, 2008).

Fantasy can be centered in stories about animals, unusual creatures, ghosts, or toys. They can be serious or humorous. There are distinctions within fantasy: High fantasy creates whole worlds, like Narnia in *The Chronicles of Narnia* series (Lewis), and low fantasy takes place in the real world, but with supernatural elements (Lukens, 2007). An example of low fantasy is *Charlie and the Chocolate Factory* (Dahl, 2001), where Charlie wins a ticket in the real world and visits the bizarre chocolate factory. Critical elements of quality fantasy include:

- A well-constructed plot.
- Convincing characters.
- A worthwhile theme.
- A story that makes the fantasy world or elements convincing (Kiefer, 2007).

Included within the fantasy category is science fiction. Temple et al. (2006) write that the primary difference between these two categories is that fantasy could never happen but science fiction has the possibility of happening.

Classic fantasy includes *Alice's Adventures in Wonderland* (Carroll, 1941), *The Tale of Peter Rabbit* (Potter, 1940), and *The Wonderful Wizard of Oz* (Baum, 1957), among many others. Moving from these classics, I share several more contemporary works. The first, *The Giver* (Lowry, 1993), allows readers to reflect on a utopian world that, at first glance, appears idyllic. As readers follow the experiences of Jonas, they discover that only one person holds memories and, as such, can experience pleasure or pain, color or dullness, and joy or despair. This book provokes strong discussion among students as they ponder freedom and control, among others issues. Teachers may want to pair this book with *The Hunger Games* (Collins, 2008) and its sequel *Catching Fire* (Collins, 2009). Teachers are forewarned that the content of these books is not for the fainthearted. In *The Hunger Games*, readers learn that the characters Katniss, Gale, and Peeta live in the ruins of North America. There are 12 districts away from the Capitol, with each district responsible for a necessary good, like coal or agriculture. The districts are kept separate from one another and in poverty circumstances, with little to no communication among them. They are kept obedient by the watchful eyes of Peacekeepers, who can punish them at will. Each year a boy and a girl from each district who have reached the age of 12 are chosen to participate in the Hunger Games. The Hunger Games involve surviving in a place created by the Gamemakers. The Gamemakers can choose the site for games—desert, mountains, and so on for the site of the games. Participants are led into the game site and must fight each other until only one is left. Each night those who die are highlighted against the sky. Similar to reality television, people in the districts are expected to watch the games on television. *The Hunger Games* focuses on the first time Katniss and Peeta are placed into this contest. The second book, *Catching Fire*, focuses on these characters as they endure a similar game the following year. The first book has readers on the edge of their seats as they consider the evil control of the Capitol and President Snow. Readers consider how characters are pawns and are expected to follow each command, even when it means the death of another. The second book shows how the characters move from obedience to revolution. This is a subtle change noted in the characters' feelings and inquiry. When I have listened in on discussions by sixth graders as they read *The Hunger Games*, I was amazed at how seriously they took the themes within the book. One group targeted obedience and disobedience. They considered the importance of following laws for the safety of others, and then they thought about what might happen if the rules were cruel. Another group focused on circumstances under which it was okay to kill another person. They knew it would be okay in a war or if they were threatened, but they wondered about President Snow and how he asked children to kill for entertainment. A third group pondered why children were selected for the games. Why wouldn't President Snow choose adults if he had to have the games? Serious conversations continued as students reflected on these issues.

Gaiman's (2008b) *The Graveyard Book* tells a story about a family that is killed with the exception of the youngest child, a boy named, Nobody, who finds his way to a graveyard and is raised by ghosts. As he is raised, he develops ghostly skills, like moving through walls and becoming invisible. These gifts serve him well when he is pursued by the killers. Within this fantasy is a mystery focused on Nobody's family murders and the current, real threats on his life. Students will find it surprising that a young child can survive in a graveyard through the kindness of ghosts. This book can be enriched by visiting *www.mousecircus.com*, and listening to Gaiman's read-alouds of each chapter. The book is broken down into chapters at the website, so it is easily adaptable for in-class read-aloud. Accompanying the chapter reading are short interviews where Gaiman has responded to readers' questions.

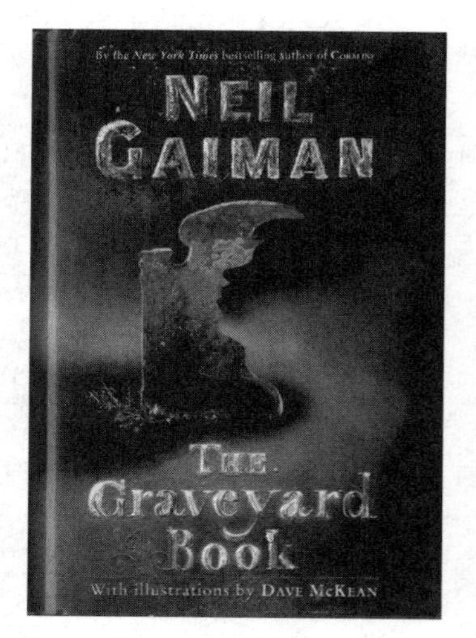

The third book, or rather books, are the *Poppy* series (Avi). Within this series, Avi has created a whole town, including Mousetown, and chronicles the numerous adventures of a mouse who leaves the safety of her home to explore the world. As she seeks out new places, she finds animal friends who share her adventures. This book provokes students to discuss the issue of taking risks or remaining safe.

Within each of these fantasies are dilemmas that center on risk, obedience, and survival. Necessary to each of these books is a well-detailed setting. An understanding of the risks that Poppy took to find a new home or that Katniss took to protect her family is embedded within a specific setting. To encourage students to consider the importance of setting within fantasies, they might choose one setting clearly described by the author. Then they can sketch the setting, including all details. From this sketch, they might refine the setting to include just one small point of interest. For instance, students might draw the barn that Poppy visits, a grave from the graveyard where Nobody lives, or one home in District 12 where Katniss lives.

POETRY

Poetry allows children to enjoy the sound of language and to appreciate the uniqueness of a word the poet chose. Poetry for the youngest children often begins with collections of *Mother Goose* rhymes. Children learn about Humpty Dumpty or Peter Piper in these simple rhymes. These poems are filled with rhyme and rhythm, two prominent characteristics of poetry, as well as imagery or word pictures, onomatopoeia or word sounds, repetition of words or stanzas, and compact, precise language (Mitchell, 2003).

Once children graduate from *Mother Goose*, parents often select Dr. Seuss books. They, like their young children, enjoy reading simple stories filled with rhyme. Random House, under the leadership of Bennet Cerf, created two Dr. Seuss lines for young children: Beginner Books and Bright and Early Books (Kudlinski, 2005). For the first Beginner Books, Dr. Seuss was challenged to use fewer than 25 words in a single book. *The Cat in the Hat* (1957c), *How the Grinch Stole Christmas* (1957b), and *Green Eggs and Ham* (1960) were among the first books in this series. For the Bright and Early Books, where he used even fewer words and often also signed his books as Theo. LeSieg, he wrote *The Foot Book* (1968) and *Mr. Brown Can Moo! Can You?* (1970).

Poetry shared in picturebooks is typically organized in either one of two formats: collections or a single poem throughout a book. One example of a collection is *The Dragons Are Singing Tonight* (Prelutsky, 1993). Peter Sis created the illustrations for this collection, and they complement the poems in a very satisfying way. For instance, for the poem *If You Don't Believe in Dragons*, there is a boy in full color contemplating a dragon that is in black and white and translucent. An example of the second collection is *Once I Ate a Pie* (MacLachlan & Charest, 2006), where each poem is written from the perspective of a dog. For example, in *Puppy*, the first line is "The world is big. Trees too tall. Sky too high" (unpaged). The poem shares what it must feel like to be a new puppy. Along with beautiful illustrations by Katy Schneider, the font changes in size and orientation, making the poems a delight to read aloud.

Two examples of books that share a single poem are *Life Doesn't Frighten Me* (Angelou, 1993) and *Jabberwocky* (Myers, 2007). Matched with Angelou's poem are paintings by Jean-Michel Basquiat. Angelou's poem is described as "defiant" and "celebrating courage" on the book cover, and the artwork complements and extends these emotions, although not in a comfortable way. Each page requires readers to stop and move from illustration to words and repeat this process numerous times before being satisfied to move on. In *Jabberwocky*, Myers used the poem written by Lewis Carroll and reimaged it as street games, like basketball. The visual images, similar to those in *Life Doesn't Frighten Me*, are haunting and provide a very urban, contemporary interpretation of this poem.

A simple way for students to understand the power of the words in poetry is for teachers to read a single line to students and then ask them to illustrate it with whatever comes to mind. Students and teachers may be very surprised to see the variation in drawings created from a single line of poetry.

HISTORICAL FICTION

Historical fiction brings history to life for young readers through the inclusion of story about historical events. Most often, historical fiction features a child as the main character, allowing the child reader to identify with a historical event through a similar perspective. Historical fiction can:

- Increase curiosity about historical events.
- Support young readers in understanding a historical event through narrative.
- Encourage multiple interpretations of an event.
- Extend the school curriculum through reading beyond a textbook.
- Integrate curricula (Gamble & Yates, 2008).

An extensive variety of historical fiction is available to students. However, most of the topics for these books closely match popular school topics, like the Civil War or the Holocaust. The newest historical fiction books include sources of information used in the story and reprints of authentic documents. Authors are very careful to get the details correct in the informational aspects of these books.

Historical fiction picturebooks allow readers to explore an event through words and images. *Abraham Lincoln Comes Home* (Burleigh, 2008) shares the story of a young boy, Luke, who with his dad travels to witness the train carrying President Lincoln's body. In the afterword, information is shared about the assassination of Lincoln and his funeral. The illustrator, Wendell Minor, shares how he used a scaled model of the train to make sure his paintings were accurate. Within this book, there are two similar paintings of Luke imagining a conversation with Lincoln and talking to his father. Children might talk about why these images are similar and what message the illustrator was conveying. In *The Man who Walked Between the Towers*, Gerstein (2003) shares the story of Philippe Petit and his walk between the World Trade Center towers in New York, an event not often shared in classrooms but one that students will find interesting. Although students may be familiar with 9/11, they most likely don't know the story of Petit walking on a tightrope between the buildings in 1974. The book has several foldout pages that give the reader a sense of the height of his walk as the viewer is positioned on the ground looking up.

In addition to picturebooks, there are numerous historical fiction novels. Avi's most recent historical fiction series, *I Witness*, adds to a range of other historical fiction he has written. One of the books in this series, *Hard Gold: The Colorado Gold Rush of 1859* (2008b), tells the story of 14-year-old Early, who heads west to meet up with his young uncle Jesse, to help him find gold so they can save their Iowa farm. Readers follow Early and share the hardships he endured in his quest to find gold. The book is well illustrated with, for example, newspaper headlines, maps, and photographs to enhance readers' understanding of and appreciation for these times. Avi also provides a reference list for his research and for further exploration.

A second type of historical novel is exemplified by Hesse's (1997) *Out of the Dust* (Hesse, 1997). In this book, the main character, Billie Jo, shares her journal entries—all written as poems—of her life in Oklahoma during the dust bowl years and the Great Depression. Although there is a full story shared in this book, the time and setting help readers understand the circumstances of these events. Hesse created this work based on her extensive research; even the accident is an event that occurred routinely during this time.

Historical fiction has expectations surrounding it. In addition to being a good story, the history must be accurate. Authors must share their research sources so that readers can trust its accuracy and must be careful that events are appropriate for the time and setting of the story. In addition, the language must be representative of the time period. After students have enjoyed a work of historical fiction, they may want to revisit it to note items or language that are representative of the time and setting of the book.

REALISTIC FICTION

Realistic fiction features children who experience problems and opportunities. The characters represent real children living in a particular place and experiencing issues similar to the ones that other children experience. As noted by Temple et al. (2006), the value of these books is that children realize they are not the only ones experiencing problems, the book's situations and resolution allow them to ponder their own choices, and the plot line and characters allow them to feel empathy.

Realistic fiction has identified categories within it. Books center around the following topics:

- Self-discovery and growing up
- Families
- Interpersonal relations
- School
- Sports
- Nature and animals
- Adventure and survival
- Romance and sexuality
- Mental, physical, and emotional challenges
- Moral dilemmas and responsibility
- Social diversity and society
- Aging, death, and dying
- Mystery
- Humor
- Multicultural and international themes
- Magical realism (Temple et al., 2006)

Just reflecting on some of the categories within this genre, it is easy to see that many books have struggled with controversy. For instance, how explicit should authors be when the intended audience is children? What language is appropriate? Katherine Paterson (1978) was criticized when Gilly, in *The Great Gilly Hopkins*, said the words *damn* and *hell*. Paterson responded that a child, such as Gilly who had endured multiple foster home placements would use this language and she had to be faithful to her character. Likewise, Patron's (2006) Newbery Medal-winning book *The Higher Power of Lucky* was censored by some groups for its use of the word *scrotum*.

It is easy to see that this single genre has a multitude of books to represent it. I chose several picturebooks that focus on routine events in children's lives. The first, *The Hello, Goodbye Window* (Juster, 2005), presents simple activities like coloring and cooking shared by a child and his grandparents, who care for him while his parents work. In Lauren Child's *Charlie and Lola* series, the main characters find themselves in situations that every young reader can identify with: giving your friend a gift when you really want to keep it for yourself (*You Won't Like This Present as Much as I Do!*, 2009e), dropping your ice cream cone and getting angry that your friend won't share (*I am Extremely Absolutely Boiling*, 2009c), and overusing the cry for help (*Help! I Really Mean It!*, 2009b). Students will enjoy seeing these characters across books and then noticing them in other books by Lauren Child. There is also a website (*www.charlieandlola.com*) where students can extend and enhance their reading. I enjoyed watching the video of Lola and Charlie and hearing their British accents. *Pepita Talks Twice* (Lachtman, 1995), which is written in two languages, shares the experiences of a young girl as she tries to communicate in English and Spanish. Pepita is often faced with speaking for her relatives, who only speak Spanish, a situation common to many children today.

Two interesting novels that qualify as realistic fiction are *Frindle* (Clements, 1996) and *Schooled* (Korman, 2007). In *Frindle*, Nick decides to coin a word—*frindle*—that is another term for pen. He convinces his friends to use the word, and soon they all use it in and out of school. The story about his word gets reported in the newspaper and soon people in other locations are using it. Eventually, the word is placed in the dictionary. Although this all sounds positive, Nick runs into difficulty in school when he refuses to use the word "pen." *Schooled* is about a boy named Cap, who, because he lives with his unconventional grandmother, has never watched television, eaten fast food, or attended school. When his grandmother is hospitalized, Cap is sent to the local middle school. Cap learns how to handle being different.

Both *Frindle* and *Schooled* motivate readers to reflect on what it means to be different. In *Frindle*, a new word is created and with it comes success and difficulty. In *Schooled*, readers can explore the concepts of conformity and being different from the perspective of the new student. After finishing these books, students will not want to move on to another until they have had a chance to consider these ideas.

MULTICULTURAL AND INTERNATIONAL LITERATURE

Multicultural literature is an umbrella term that represents literature from around the world, literature that is cross-cultural, literature about minority cultures, and literature that intersects cultures representing mixed-race individuals (Kiefer, 2007). In this sense, multicultural literature can be representative of any genre. Through this literature, children can learn about other cultures and, in doing so, learn more about themselves (Mitchell, 2003). Multicultural literature must be carefully evaluated by teachers so that accuracy is guaranteed and stereotyping avoided. For example, *The Five Chinese Brothers* (Bishop, 1938) presents stereotyped images of Asians because all the brothers look exactly alike. A more current example, and one that is embraced by teachers, is *Ten Little Rabbits* (Grossman & Long, 1991). In this counting book, Native Americans are represented as identical rabbits, which are distinguishable by tribe only by their blankets (McCarty, 1995). Teachers must consider the following before sharing a multicultural book with children:

- Is the book of high literary value? Is the plot engaging? Are the characters well developed? Is the theme interesting?
- Does the book accurately represent the culture shared?
- Who wrote the story? Who created the illustrations?

The last question is important because readers want to be assured that the text is accurate and the people represented appropriately. Some authors and illustrators are frustrated by the expectation that they must be insiders in the culture they are writing about; however, being an outsider does present challenges in accurate presentation. Bishop (1992) argues that it is not the race of the author or illustrator that is critical but rather his or her perspective. Important for teachers to recognize is that the race or ethnicity of an author or illustrator is one factor that should be considered during book evaluation.

The good news about multicultural literature is that it is readily available. Two noteworthy authors of this genre are the poets Arnold Adoff and Eloise Greenfield. Their poetry highlights the experiences of African American and multiracial children. Adoff's *Black Is Brown Is Tan* (2004) allows children to ponder what it means to be biracial. Greenfield's poetry focuses on African Americans sharing family relationships. *Nathaniel Talking* (Greenfield, 1988) features a young boy who shares his everyday experiences in poem.

I love picturebooks that have characters who represent various cultures, races, or ethnicities. *Bigmama's* (Crews, 1991) is a joyful book about the experience of visiting a grandmother. Reading this book, it is impossible not to reflect on similar experiences in one's own life. *Please, Puppy, Please* (Lee & Lee, 2005) shares the story of two young children trying to teach their puppy to obey. Kadir Nelson paints the most beautiful images of the young children chasing their puppy as they shout, "Please puppy, please." Perhaps because I love dogs so much, I can't help giggling as the children try to control their puppy. In *My House/Mi Casa* (Emberly, 1990), readers are asked to identify things related to a house like windows and walls or kittens and dogs. All the text appears in both English and Spanish, enhancing all students' bilingual skills. When I read this book to a kindergarten class, the children who had a home language of Spanish eagerly taught me how to read the parts in Spanish! Recorvits (2003), in *My Name Is Yoon*, created a story about the difficulty of adjusting to a new life in a new country. Yoon is a young immigrant from Korea who is conflicted about living in America, symbolized by her struggles with writing her name in English. The illustrations in this book are complex, often showing Yoon in school with images of Korea in the background. Her thoughts are also represented within concrete settings such as the classroom. In *I Hate English!* (Levine, 1989), readers learn about the difficulty of moving to a different country and having to learn a new language. Finally, *How My Parents Learned to Eat* by Ina Friedman and illustrated by Allen Say (1984) is a story that emphasizes the beauty of cultural diversity and demystifies differences. These themes are explored through the eyes of a young biracial girl, who tells of her parents' love story and how they adapted to each other's culture, using the metaphors of chopsticks and forks and knives. Say's illustrations make the Japanese situations accurate. In fact, the character of Great Uncle resembles Say himself. Allen Say's books where he is author and illustrator are exemplars in multicultural literature. In *Grandfather's Journey* (1993), Say tells the story of immigration and what "home" really means. In *Erika-San* (2009), readers follow the journey of a first-generation American girl as she returns to her ancestors' homeland, seeing it for the first time. Students will enjoy exploring all the books created by Say to learn about him as an author and illustrator and how he values his home culture.

Notable among the many novels that share multicultural views are Curtis's (1995) *The Watsons Go to Birmingham—1963*, Kadohata's (2004) *Kira-Kira*, and Park's (2001) *A Single Shard*. In *The Watsons Go to Birmingham—1963*, readers learn about Byron, Joetta, and Kenny in their everyday lives and then follow them on their special trip to Birmingham, where discrimination is rampant. *Kira-Kira* features Katie and Lynn, two sisters who move with their family from a Japanese community in Iowa to the South. Through

Katie's eyes, readers experience what it means to be different, to struggle financially, and to handle a family member's illness. *A Single Shard*, set in 12th-century Korea, is the story of a young orphan who struggles to survive and fulfill his dream of becoming a master potter. This book reads as an adventure story while providing information on life in ancient Korea and the historical significance of pottery to this culture.

International literature is just that—literature created by an author or illustrator who resides outside of the United States. J. K. Rowling, Mitsumasa Anno, Mem Fox, Anthony Browne, and Robert Munsch are each prominent authors of this genre, having created books that resonate with an American audience. Mem Fox has created beautiful books like *Possum Magic* (1991) for younger readers. Robert Munsch also writes for young readers. In *Stephanie's Ponytail* (1996), he explores the concept of individualism: Stephanie's classmates copycat her different hairstyles, and allow themselves to be pushed to the furthest limits.

Several Internet sites are available to help teachers select and evaluate multicultural children's literature. A WORLD OF DIFFERENCE Institute's website (*www.adl.org/bibliography*) provides bibliographies of books organized by genre and topic. Teachers can find books about cultural and religious groups, families and friends, and customs and traditions. The Cooperative Children's Book Center (*www.education.wisc.edu/ccbc/books/detailListBooks.asp?idBookLists=42*) identifies 50 multicultural books, grouped by age, that every child should hear or read. The International Children's Digital Library (*en.childrenslibrary.org*) has an extensive collection of international books available in audio and written formats. The United States Board on Books for Young People (*www.usbby.org/outstanding_international_books_list.htm*) lists the best international books by year, organized by grade level. Teachers who use these sites can be confident that the books they select to share with their students have been vetted as appropriate and meet the high standards of evaluation.

POSTMODERN PICTUREBOOKS

Postmodern picturebooks push beyond the traditional structure and content of picturebooks. Nikolajeva (1988) wrote that contemporary children's literature exhibits "the most prominent features of postmodernism, such as genre eclecticism, disintegration of traditional narrative structure, polyphony, intersubjectivity and metafiction" (p. 222). Pantaleo and Sipe (2008) further identified six characteristics of postmodern picturebooks:

1. Blurring the categories of traditional genres and the boundaries among author, narrator, and reader.
2. Undermining the traditional distinctions between the story and the outside world.
3. Explicitly using intertextuality.
4. Providing multiple meanings, ambiguity, and open-endings.
5. Playing with the reader in response to the book.
6. Drawing the reader's attention to the text as a text through its construction. (p. 3)

Postmodern picturebooks demand that teachers engage in meaning making with students, as their interpretation is not literal or straightforward. Their illustrations and text, and the intertwining of the two, require reflection and result in multiple interpretations. In many cases, they feel like puzzles waiting to be solved and, once solved, require the reader to see if there are alternate solutions.

Many postmodern picturebooks are available, and this genre is gaining in popularity among authors and illustrators. In this discussion I offer three of the most notable. *Black and White* (Macaulay, 1990) begins with a warning on its cover flap acknowledging that it might be a single story or perhaps four individual stories. Each double-page spread is broken into four separate illustrations with accompanying text that varies for each. Unlike many titles that reveal the storyline within, for this book the connection between title and content is not readily apparent, and can be the focus of lively discussion among students and teachers.

In *Voices in the Park*, Browne (1998) shares the experience of going to the park from four different perspectives. Similar to *Black and White*, each voice is identified by a unique font. However, Browne's illustrations offer much for the viewer to pause to consider. For instance, why do the trees change from fall, to spring, to winter, to summer? Is this changing significant to the story? Are the shadows important? Why are Santa Claus and King Kong in the illustrations? Is how Browne breaks a page with a pole or uses it for framing important? This book offers students more than a simple reading of text.

The third book, *Chester* (Watt, 2007), is a humorous battle of wills between an author and Chester the cat who tries to upstage the author by editing and revising her work to his own liking. Throughout the entire book—from cover to cover—Chester uses his red marker to rewrite and reillustrate the work in progress. As the book continues, there is more rewriting text and images from the real author, whoever that may be. Eventually, the author (Watt) messes with Chester and rewrites his story. This engaging book challenges children to decide who an author is and to consider how they too can rework a story in a humorous way.

GRAPHIC BOOKS

The term *graphic novel* is generally used to describe any book in a comic format that resembles a novel in length and narrative development. Comic books, comic-style books, and graphic novels all use sequential art to present a story, stories, or other content. For teachers, the idea of sharing graphic novels, or what they perceive as comic books, may be difficult; however, readers are enamored by them. Graphic books can represent any genre, from fantasy to nonfiction. For instance, Avi (1993) wrote a fantasy, *City of Light, City of Dark*, about New York's first inhabitants in a comic book style. Hosler (2000) wrote *Clan Apis*, about the life of a honeybee, as an informational book with fiction elements in graphic format. There are also adventures in graphic format, and not surprisingly, they are often written in a series. The *Bone* series (Smith) is representative of this genre, with more than eight books in the series already. Perhaps most familiar to teachers are those by Kinney in his *Diary of a Wimpy Kid* series, where a middle schooler, Greg, shares his adventures.

Because this genre is so new, teachers may want to use Internet sources to help with book selection. At About.com: Children's Books (*childrensbooks.about.com/od/graphicnovelscomics/f/comics_faq.htm*), visitors can access overviews of graphic novels and books, articles about graphic books, and techniques to share them with children. Most importantly, this site offers lists of quality graphic books on the Sidekicks page. The American Library Association (*www.ala.org*) also provides lists of outstanding graphic books and offers suggestions for teachers and librarians regarding potential challenges.

Teachers of reluctant or struggling readers may want to provide access to these books. Because of their visual emphasis, boys, in particular, are drawn to them, perhaps because they resemble comic books.

SCHOOL-BASED LITERATURE

I pondered including this genre, but I believe there are special ways to refer to books that, are for the most part, available only in schools. However, these genres are being picked up by publishers, and they are now found in bookstores, arranged, for instance, by levels: emergent, early fluent, and fluent readers. Therefore, I thought it was important to briefly share these overarching ways to categorize books that might include any genre because they are familiar to teachers, parents, and students.

Leveled Text

Leveled text is organized by its complexity and is written to match the reading skill level of young readers. The simplest text might have just one word on a page with a corresponding illustration, offering visual support with decoding. Originally predominantly of the fiction genre, leveled text is now often nonfiction. In *Orangutans* (Marchetti, 2001), for example, children see a chapter organization in learning about orangutans. The text reads simply "Orangutans are apes. They have red hair" (p. 2). In *School* (Berger & Chanko, 1999), children explore what it means to go to school. The first page reads "In a school, people work together."

Decodable Text

These books are designed to reinforce a phonics element that the teacher has recently taught (Reutzel & Cooter, 2008). For instance, after learning about short-*a*, children read a book filled with short-*a* words, like *cat*, *bat*, and *can*. These books serve a very specific function—to allow children to practice decoding—and are not known for their great plot line. They often sound like:

The rat sat.
It sat on a mat.

Predictable Text

Predictable text is also written for young, novice readers. In these books, authors repeat text so that it includes rhyme, rhythm, and repetition. A classic example of predictable text is *Brown Bear, Brown Bear, What Do You See?* (Martin, 1970). Children quickly memorize this text and feel like proficient readers as they read it.

ENGAGING STUDENTS

Throughout this chapter I have provided numerous ways to engage students with the genres of narrative. To close the chapter, I share two more ways.

1. *Poetic dialogue.* Poetic dialogue involves students responding to a poem. A teacher selects a poem and reproduces it, allowing space between each line. After reading each line, students write what comes into their mind. By doing this for each line in a poem, a new poem is created. Students can either read their poem in its entirety or several students who have responded to the same poem can share together, with each reading, one after another, his or her response to a line, repeating this process until they get to the end of the poem. Following is a brief example from Angelou's *Life Doesn't Frighten Me.*

   Shadows on the wall

   I think it is scary when I see shadows on the wall.

   Noises down the hall

   If I see shadows and hear noises, I know I am going to jump and yell.

2. *Combining genres.* Students create a personal narrative during writers' workshop. After they are satisfied with their narrative that tells about an event in their lives, they add another genre to their piece. They might include a poem or a short graphic illustration to enhance their personal narrative. More sophisticated writers may take their personal narrative and rewrite it as fantasy or science fiction.

At the end of this chapter, it is time to take a few moments to reflect on the ideas shared:

1. What genres in children's literature are most familiar to you? Why might that be?

2. What described genre is new for you? You might visit a library and become more familiar with books that fit this genre.
3. Visit one of the websites identified in this chapter to learn more about a specific genre.

RECOMMENDED READING

After reading a chapter, there is always more to learn. The following are a few references to extend your journey.

Mikkelsen, N. (2005). *Powerful magic: Learning from children's responses to fantasy literature.* New York: Teachers College Press.

This book features specific fantasy picturebooks and novels and offers techniques to support students' interpretation of them. It enriches one's understanding of fantasy and its meaning potential.

Sloan, G. (2003). *Give them poetry!* New York: Teachers College Press.

This book has recommendations for quality books of poetry. It is filled with ideas to share poetry in effective ways with students.

Young, T. (Ed.). (2004). *Happily ever after: Sharing folk literature with elementary and middle school students.* Newark, DE: International Reading Association.

This book offers a more extensive exploration of folk literature. Many chapters focus on subgenres within folk literature like tall tales and legends. There are also chapters that help teachers bring this genre into their classrooms.

Student Voices

Stone Fox
(Gardiner, 1992)

"The book, *Stone Fox*, is sad because I have a dog, and I wouldn't want my dog to die. I see the relationship between the dogs and their human owners and it really touches me. And the relationships are why it is so sad and why I cry. The part that is happy is when Stone Fox wins every race."—Isabella, a third grader

CHAPTER 4

Exploring Nonfiction/ Informational Genres

> Regardless of a child's area of interest, whether rocks, horses, dinosaurs, medieval weaponry, outer space, or art, nonfiction books can fuel this curiosity. These are the books that answer children's questions about the universe—about the people, places, and things children encounter in their daily lives.
>
> —BARBARA MOSS, *Exploring the Literature of Fact* (2003, p. 1)

Moss's words are important in that they show informational text to be as exciting and emotionally charged as narratives. Informational books respond to the basic need of children—to learn why or more about something. Today's teachers are fortunate because informational text is readily available and of high quality (Moss, 2003). Moreover, students like to read and own informational text, as demonstrated in a survey by Mohr (2003): When asked what book they would like for their own, 84% of first graders chose informational texts.

Reading aloud and providing time for students to read informational text results in several positive outcomes for students:

1. Support students in their success in school, especially in later grades, where informational texts are prioritized over narrative.
2. Support students in engaging in extracurricular reading, especially reading on the Internet.
3. Appeal to the unique interests of students.
4. Allow students to answer questions.
5. Engage students in learning about their physical and social worlds.
6. Build vocabulary, especially that targeted to specialized fields (e.g., social and physical sciences).
7. Expand opportunities for home–school connections.
8. Support students in developing different reading strategies, such as skimming and scanning. (Duke, 2004)

Teachers wonder about the differences between the terms *nonfiction* and *informational text* (Duke & Bennett-Armistead, 2003). Nonfiction is an umbrella label and includes texts that have factual information. Duke and Bennett-Armistead view informational text as a type of nonfiction that includes features like headings and technical vocabulary and shares information about the natural or social world. Based on their definition, biographies or how-to books would not be considered informational; rather, they would be classified as nonfiction. Within this chapter, I share nonfiction texts such as biography, memoir, and how-to books. Beyond these genres, I focus on informational text targeted to social studies, mathematics, art, music, and science. The informational text category also includes book-based genres, such as encyclopedias, all-about books, photo essays, and life-cycle books. I end the chapter with a discussion on multigenre books, which offer collections of genres within a single text.

The overarching genre of nonfiction or informational literature is as varied as fiction. There are important criteria to consider when choosing informational text: The book must be accurate, well organized with lengthier text separated into chapters and sections, appealing in format and design, and written in a style that is clear in presentation.

Informational text is processed in uniquely specific ways (Duke & Bennett-Armistead, 2003). When reading informational text, students are not expected to process text linearly; rather, they may view maps or figures, read text, and then reconsider the maps or figures. This reading is recursive in that it takes no direct path; it moves forward, allows for rereading, and takes advantage of multiple features that extend or clarify reading. It supports students in skimming and scanning to find the information they are most interested in. Features include:

- Headings
- Labels or captions
- Index
- Glossary
- Diagrams
- Tables
- Charts
- Maps
- Photographs
- Sketches
- Sidebars
- Table of contents

Taking time with students to investigate more thoroughly the graphic displays typical of informational text supports students' comprehension and enjoyment. Illustrators of informational text use a wide variety of graphic displays within a text. Figure 4.1 highlights many of the categories and types of graphic displays that students encounter. It is important to notice that each display highlights different information that supports students' comprehension; moreover, many texts include more than one graphic display. Students must be comfortable with reading graphic displays so they engage with them rather than ignore them.

To help students learn to enjoy reading graphic displays teachers can engage them in the activity called "What Does It Say and What Does It Not Say?" Students view a graphic display from one of their books, perhaps a textbook so that all students have the

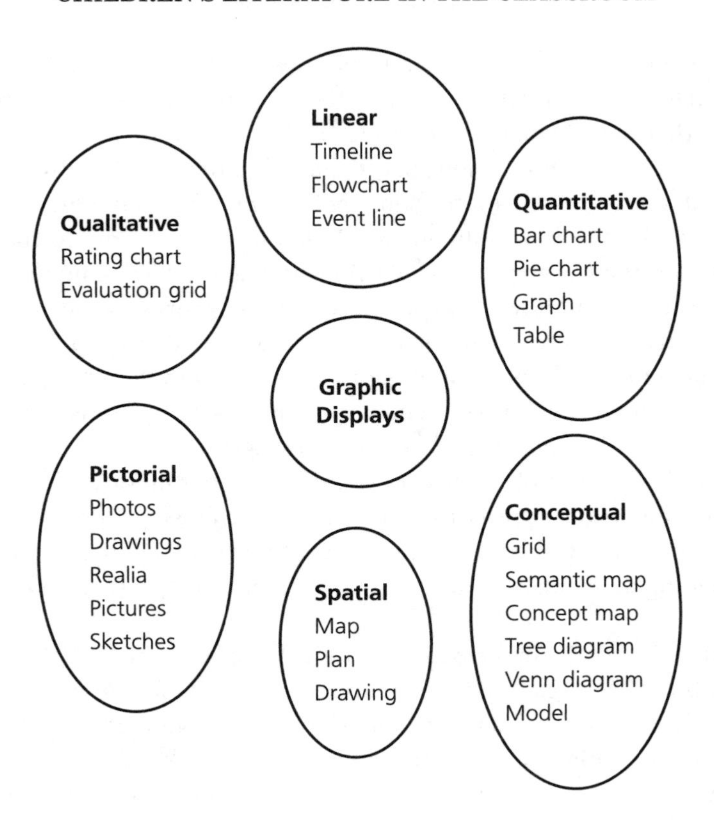

FIGURE 4.1. Graphic displays.

same display. Working with a T chart and a partner, they decide what they learn from the display and what they don't learn. Figure 4.2 is an example of this activity.

In addition to these features, informational text is structured in different ways than narrative text (Purcell-Gates & Duke, 2003). Informational text often begins with an opening statement about its topic, includes specialized vocabulary, and uses a timeless verb construction. Moreover, informational text is often organized through description, cause–effect, timeline, or compare–contrast (Read, Reutzel, & Fawson, 2008). Although one of these categories may describe the majority of text, many informational texts include several organizations where description can lead to compare–contrast, for example.

Introductory lessons that focus on organization help students become aware of these structures. Teachers might share a simple informational text to draw attention to the various structures. The following books will facilitate this process:

- *Description*. In the insect book *Super-Size Bugs* (Davies, 2007), most pages have an oversized illustration of a bug accompanied by descriptive text. For instance, the text for praying mantises reads "Praying mantises are carnivorous insects. They come in all shapes and sizes, some have spooky, alien-like heads while others look just plain

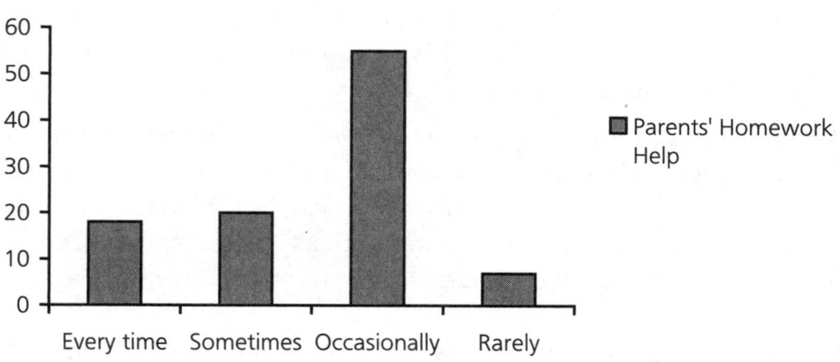

Parents' Homework Help	
What it says	*What it does not say*
Most parents (55%) only help their children with homework occasionally.	When parents help their children with homework.
The fewest parents help their children with homework rarely (8%).	How they help their children with homework.
Fewer than 20% of parents help their children with homework all or some of the time.	If their children learn a concept when their parents help them.
	If children like their parents helping them.
	What subjects parents help their children with.
	How old the children are who are being helped.

FIGURE 4.2. "What Does It Say and What Does It *Not* Say?"

goofy" (p. 14) and teachers need to allow for this before focusing on the text organization. Students will invariably become very vocal about how disgusting many of these bugs appear in the magnified images. To reinforce learning, students can create a bubble map to record information as the teacher reads, with each bubble representing a different bug.

- *Cause–effect.* In the book *When Bugs Were Big, Plants Were Strange, and Tetrapods Stalked the Earth* (Bonner, 2003), the author shares how plants grew in coal swamps and evolved into more familiar plants, how oceans divided, how insects grew, and how dinosaurs became extinct. Each chapter focuses on a set of causes and the effects noted in the environment. This book lends itself to student discussion and writing about cause–effect events.

- *Timeline.* Sandler's (2008) *Lincoln Through the Years* is a perfect book to explore time sequences. Each page is rich with photographs that document events in the life of Abraham Lincoln. Teachers might share this book over several days, with students creating timelines to help remember important events.
- *Compare–contrast.* I know students will love interacting with *Living Color* (Jenkins, 2007). Each page highlights a color and the way it shows up in various animals. For instance, on the red page readers learn about jellyfish, blood-red fire shrimp, the scarlet ibis, and other red animals. In a related activity, students, with teacher support, can identify differences across the animals sharing the same color.

Teachers often use graphic organizers to support students in understanding these organizational structures. A bubble chart works well for description where each circle contains information about the item being described. Cause–effect organizers are also effective and typically have two columns with an arrow leading from a "cause" entry in the first column to an "effect" entry in the second. Timelines can be used to plot significant dates or events and add additional pertinent information. Often younger students work with paper folded into six or eight blocks, and use each box to add details for a time sequence. The segmented paper offers an easier way for students to record information. When working on compare–contrast activities, students often utilize T charts or Venn diagrams to record important information.

NONFICTION GENRES

Biographies

Biographies are books about people—historic or political figures, sports figures, media artists, visual artists, and musicians—and can be written in various forms. A *complete biography* covers the whole life of the featured individual. Examples include *Benjamin Bannecker* (Welch, 2008) and *Benjamin Franklin* (Editors of TIME for Kids, 2005). Each of these books is organized by chapters and presents the subject's life history and other related events. They are filled with primary source documents to support text. These two books make wonderful companion texts because both Bannecker and Franklin created almanacs.

In contrast to a complete biography a *partial biography* focuses only on a single or small but important facet of a person's life. For example, *Snowflake Bentley* (Martin, 1998) focuses on Wilson Bentley's discovery of the uniqueness of snowflakes. The picturebook has an interesting format, relying heavily on illustrations to record Bentley's life's work and sharing scientific information and Bentley's techniques and observations in narrow borders. From one such border entry, readers learn how Bentley used a camera to record the variations of snowflakes.

A third type of biography focuses on multiple individuals who share a common characteristic. In *Americans Who Tell the Truth* (Shetterly, 2005), for instance, each page features two or three famous Americans who are known for telling the truth. The portraits are the dominant image on each page. At the end of the book, more detailed descriptions of each individual are shared. Some of the people featured in this book are Muhammad Ali, Rachel Carson, and W. E. B. Du Bois.

Teachers can include biography in their classrooms as it connects to their content curricula or as a focus during reading and writing. Students enjoy learning about important people, and they can supplement the information they discover during book reading with Internet resources.

There are several book series that focus on biographies. Books in the *History Maker Bios* series target inventors, like George Washington Carver and Marie Curie; company founders, like Henry Ford and Levi Strauss; and leaders who have changed the world, like Harriet Tubman and Eleanor Roosevelt. The books within this series are easy to read, and thus able to support struggling readers in the intermediate grades, and provide rich detail about each person's life. Moreover, the people featured in this series are also the subject of other books and Internet reports; thus, students can take advantage of multiple sources for additional information.

Aladdin's *Childhood of Famous Americans* series is noteworthy because the biographers do not just share information about an individual's life but also contextualize it in history. Thus, readers are able to learn, for example, about political issues that affected the individual. A good example is Kudlinsky's (2005) *Dr. Seuss*. These books target the famous person's childhood and supplement facts by adding imagined conversations that could have taken place. For an activity, students can create charts as they read about Dr. Seuss to better understand his world and to compare it to today's world. See Figure 4.3 for an abbreviated example of a student chart.

This kind of chart supports students as they learn about the United States and Europe during the first and second world wars. The hardships that families faced become real. I believe it also helps students understand a person, in this case Dr. Seuss, and perhaps why his books like *The Sneetches* (1961) and *The Butter Battle Book* (1984) were written.

Dr. Seuss Personal Event	Historical Event
1914 Dr. Seuss's family struggles because families and businesses are not ordering German beer.	Germany is attacking countries in Europe. U.S. citizens distrust Germans. Prejudice is rampant in the U.S. Whites did not talk to Blacks. Blacks attended their own schools.
1921 Dr. Seuss attends Dartmouth. No fraternities ask him to join because they think he is Jewish.	Height of German–American hatred.
1925 Dr. Seuss attends college at Oxford.	He sees the rampages of war in England.

FIGURE 4.3. Dr. Seuss chart.

Another biography I found that captivates students is one about Walt Disney: *Who Was Walt Disney?* (Stewart, 2009). The author of this book includes a timeline of Walt Disney's life with a complementary timeline of world events. Readers learn that Walt Disney was the class clown as an elementary school student. He also played Peter Pan in a school performance and had his brother hook him to wires so he could fly; unfortunately, the wires broke and Disney landed in the audience. One chapter focuses on Walt Disney, his new company, and how the Great Depression affected him.

The Walt Disney book or others in this series that ask "Who was . . . ?" are perfect models for students to use to explore a famous person. The question itself—"Who was . . . ?"—begs a response that is created during reading. Students can enjoy learning about a person and the historical context of his or her life. As students read and learn, they can create quizzes for the other students in their class. For example:

> Write true of false for the following statements about Walt Disney:
> He was born in California.
> His first movie was *Steamboat Willie*.
> Walt Disney fought in World War I.

In my experience, students love playing teacher and stumping their classmates. Creating a simple quiz highlights events in a person's life; it does not deal with the emotional concerns they may have experienced. These richer understandings of a person are best developed through ongoing conversations.

Another activity that makes the person in a biography come alive is for students to write about him or her in the first person. *Theodore* (Keating, 2006) serves as a model for this type of work. For instance, the first page begins:

> My mother named me Theodore, but everyone remembers me as Teddy.
> I grew up to be big and broad and strong. As a man I led a nation to greatness. Some said that I was born to greatness.

Once students have learned about a person, they can write a book as if they were the person. This first-person narrative allows students to explore the feelings of an individual as they ponder the facts of his or her life. An example of this writing comes from a fifth grader writing about Benjamin Franklin.

> What a shocking discovery! One more point for me—Ben Franklin. I guess since my birth in Boston on January 17, 1706, I've been this and that for the benefit of mankind. . . .

The biographies I have shared focus on scientific and historical figures. Students also enjoy reading biographies of sports figures, artists, and popular artists, which are readily available.

Memoirs

Memoir might seem to be an unusual genre to include for children's literature, but there are many memoirs by authors who write for children. Reading an author's memoirs enhances the reading of his or her book.

Tomie dePaola has created numerous picturebooks that share episodes within his life. *The Art Lesson* (1989) shows his experiences with drawing as he has pictures posted at home, at his father's work, and other places. So Tomie is excited that he will have an art teacher in school; however, the art teacher has rules that result in an unpleasant experience. In *Tom* (1993), dePaola shares a story about his grandfather, who is a butcher. His grandfather shows him the tendons in a chicken leg, without the chicken attached. Children will giggle at what happens with the chicken leg and enjoy sharing the experiences of Tom and his grandfather.

Another author who shares memories of her childhood in picturebooks is Patricia Polacco. In *The Keeping Quilt* (2001), she tells of the importance of a quilt to her family. Polacco explains the origin of the quilt and its use for generations until it was given to her. At a recent presentation, she showed the quilt to the audience and talked about where each piece of fabric originated. In *The Lemonade Club* (2007), Polacco tells the story of her child's best friend, Marilyn, who was battling cancer. The story is a positive one, reflecting Marilyn and her teacher's simultaneous determination to survive. Polacco has included photos of the real people featured in the story in the back of her book.

Although picturebooks most often share one memory from childhood, novels share many more. The following is a list of some of noteworthy memoirs available:

- *Childtimes* (Greenfield & Little, 1979). The authors engage readers with stories from three generations of the Greenfields' family.
- *Guts* (Paulsen, 2001). Paulsen shares the stories behind what happened in *Hatchet* and other Brian books. Readers learn that Paulsen has lived in the woods since he was a child, and many of the adventures written in his books are based on real life.
- *My Life in Dog Years* (Paulsen, 1998). Paulsen writes of the many dogs that have been a part of his life.
- *Knots in My Yo-Yo String* (Spinelli, 1998). These stories of Spinelli's childhood read like a novel. Readers learn that the author loved playing baseball, reading comics, and staying in the lines.
- *A Girl from Yamhill* (Cleary, 1988). Cleary tells what it was like growing up in the

1920s. Cleary reveals her process of learning to read and her refusal to open a book, among other memories.

- *Looking Back* (Lowry, 1998). In this book, Lowry presents quotes from her books accompanied by related personal memories.
- *The Dragon's Child* (Yep, 2008). Readers gain a deeper appreciation of Yep by learning about his father's entry in the United States.
- *Knucklehead* (Scieszka, 2008a). Scieszka shares stories about growing up with his five brothers. Each chapter tells about an adventure enriched with actual photos.
- *More about Boy* (Dahl, 2008). Roald Dahl's young life is presented through photos and vignettes. Text boxes throughout the book share interesting informational tidbits, such as Dahl's description of adenoids or directions from Cardiff to Weston-Super-Mare.

If teachers read these memoirs, or snippets from them, to students, they gain a deeper understanding of the novels or picturebooks written by these authors. For instance, when I reread Cleary's Ramona books, I could see where Ramona and Beverly Cleary had similar experiences, and I understood Cleary's focus on spelling in so many of the books.

Additionally, these serve as models for personal narrative, a genre that students are expected to write throughout school. Mrs. Schneider masterfully engaged her fifth-grade students in writing personal narratives by having them identify one event in their lives that was important to them and writing about it. She then asked them to focus on one small part of the event and writing about it. For instance, one student wrote about a time he won a soccer game. His first draft included details about the whole game. For his second draft, he just wrote about what happened before the game, how he was nervous, how he kept looking at the players on the other team, and how he finally took some deep breaths and hoped for the best. Through writing about small moments, students became aware of how to fully describe an event, including physical and emotional feelings.

How-to Books

Libraries carry an extensive inventory of how-to craft books for children. In *How to Make Pop-Ups*, Irvine (1991) shows students how to make pop-up books. I enjoyed this book because I could immediately see connections between this book and projects for students. Students could choose one of the pop-up forms and then complete it with a visual and written connection to another book. In *Crafts from Your Favorite Fairy Tales* (Ross, 1998), students can learn to create projects that are connected to fairytales. For example, students are shown how to make sleepy dwarfs from *Snow White*, or they can make a Little Red Riding Hood puppet. *Kites for Everyone: How to Make and Fly Them* (Greger, 2006) shows students how to make kites. What is wonderful about these books is that students learn that they must follow directions exactly, or the product won't be just right. How-to books strengthen comprehension skills.

Other how-to books center on drawing or sketching. Students enjoy books that show them how to sketch. *How to Draw Sea Creatures* (Soloff-Levy, 2002) offers step-by-step directions for drawing sharks and other sea creatures. Soloff-Levy also teaches students how to draw flowers and pets. For students who love popular culture, there are books on drawing Pokémon characters. Alfano (2008), for instance, provides easy-to-follow, clear sketching tips that will ensure students' success. *How to Draw: Bakugan Battle Brawlers* (Scholastic, 2009) is a favorite among young boys with easy instructions and diagrams for drawing these colorful characters. Drawing books help students become aware that they can draw and also to appreciate the skill of illustrators and other artists.

How-to books are available that teach students the rudiments of sports. Converse offers a series of books that explain games like baseball and football. I read *Converse All Star Football: How to Play Like a Pro* (Converse, 1996) and I learned about snap counts and offensive blockers. Gail Gibbons (2000) has written several how-to books about sports. A perfect companion to the Converse book is *My Football Book*. She shows students various football plays for them to practice. I can't imagine that boys would not love these books. More than talking about sports, they share specifics on how to play the games.

The rewards of reading comprehension are immediately evident when students become involved in how-to books or activities. Once accustomed to following step-by-step instructions, students are able to easily participate in other hands-on activities, such as simple science experiments and cooking. Students can also create their own how-to books centered on a favorite sport or activity.

INFORMATIONAL TEXT GENRES

In this section, I focus on the specific genres of encyclopedias, all about . . . books, photo essays, and life-cycle books. I then highlight books for the content areas of science, social studies, math, art, and music. There are many beautiful and concept rich books to expand these areas of the curricula.

Encyclopedias

Today's students most often use online encyclopedias like Encyclopedia.com (*www.encyclopedia.com*) for information. If students have specific questions, they might also use Ask Kids (*www.askkids.com*) or Yahooligans (*www.squirrelnet.com/search/yk/yahooligans.asp*).

Beyond Internet encyclopedia resources, DK Publishers has created a series of encyclopedias for children that focus on a wide spectrum of topics, including first animals, the human body, space, and nature. Using the *Encyclopedia of Dinosaurs and Prehistoric Life* (DK Publishing, 2008) as an example, the book is well supported with visuals, including photos, charts, and drawings. Although this book wasn't intended to be read from cover to cover, readers will find it difficult to put down. I found it interesting to discover that large dinosaurs had two brains, a small one near their head and another near their hip that controlled the hind limbs and tail. Students will enjoy becoming investigators to discover unusual information about dinosaurs that they can share with others.

Encyclopedias are packed with information and rich in visual support. They serve as excellent resource material for students. They open up topics to students that they may not have even considered before.

All about . . . Books

All about . . . books share information on a specific topic (e.g., the human body, insects, sharks). Based on my experience, there are several in particular that have intrigued students and nudged them to further exploration. One is *Extremely Weird Spiders* (Lovett, 1991), the title alone is sufficient to draw in students! Lovett's book begins with a fascinating taxonomy chart that highlights the kingdom, phylum, class, order, family, genus, and finally species of spiders. This chart by itself can be the source of enthusiastic discussion by students. Subsequent pages contain illustrations of weird, little known spiders, like the Lucky Shamrock, which gets its name from a clover-shaped spot on its abdomen. These spiders are weavers and spin complex geometric webs. The overall text is dense, and struggling readers may be satisfied with the small text boxes on each page.

Another All about . . . book is *1001 Unbelievable Facts* (Otway, 2008). The book is organized into chapters that target body facts, food facts, history facts, animal facts, science facts, world records, and random facts. All readers, no matter their level, can enjoy this book. And students have fun trying to stump adults with facts they've learned. For instance, I learned that the body is made up of more than 50 trillion cells, it is the shape of hair follicles that determines straight or curly hair, and tooth enamel is the hardest substance in the human body. Impressive!

Authors often utilize an alphabet structure for all about . . . books. For instance, Jerry Pallotta has written more than 25 alphabet books alone (*jerrypallotta.com/alphabetman_mybooks.html*), and many support classroom learning (e.g., books on flowers, bugs, and desert). In his *The Extinct Alphabet Book* (1993), Pallotta shares information about extinct animals. In addition to the illustrations and text, this book also includes images of Pallotta himself and, in an unusual twist, Elvis. While I enjoyed learning about extinct animals, I was left wondering why Pallotta included seemingly random images, like Elvis, in this book. I wonder what students would think.

Another interesting alphabet-organized book is *Oh, Yikes! History's Grossest, Wackiest Moments* (Masoff, 2006). Again, how can you not want to read this book, especially when the cover shows a boy screaming, eyeing in disbelief the fat rodent that

is perched atop his head? While I have read numerous history books, I never learned from them that during the Renaissance—men and women alike—loved clothing and fashion. The fashions trends from centuries ago seem bizarre by today's standards. For example, men put pillows around their middle so they looked big but then wore tight leggings to accentuate skinny legs. One unusual fashion design for women of that time came about because a queen sought to hide her pregnancy. The solution? Adding birdcage frames around the hips (p. 84). The book is filled with snippets of information and wonderful visuals, like that of a knight in full dress with details about his clothing. All readers, regardless of skill, can appreciate this book.

I believe that all about . . . books provide the perfect opportunity for students to learn tidbits of information that they might use in further explorations. They excite students to learn more about a topic. A fun activity to complement all about . . . book learning would be to have students create a comic strip format where they share their newly learned facts. This combination of informational text and comic book format will result in creative learning and will be especially appealing to boys. A comic strip download is available at Comic Life (*www.comiclife.com*) and allows students to select a format. Once the format is selected, students can add small pieces of information in each shape. They can also drag images to their comic and use speech bubbles to enrich its presentation (see Figure 4.4 for an example). The process is easy, and students enjoy using a novel format to share information.

Photo Essays

I find the *Letters Home from* series an amazing model for photo essays. Books in this series cover a range of destinations, including the U.S. national parks and countries such as Italy, Egypt, and Zimbabwe. In *Letters Home from Italy* (Halvorsen, 2000), a young girl describes her visits to many of the major cities in Italy. Each city is shown through photographs with text explaining them. There are photos of the Colosseum, the Pantheon, and the Spanish Steps from Rome. The text is also in first person, so readers feel they are sharing in the travels of a friend. Students can easily simulate a photo journal using PowerPoint where they can include photos and provide text. Certainly, photo essays work for learning about places, but they can also be used to share information about other topics like space, animals, and famous people.

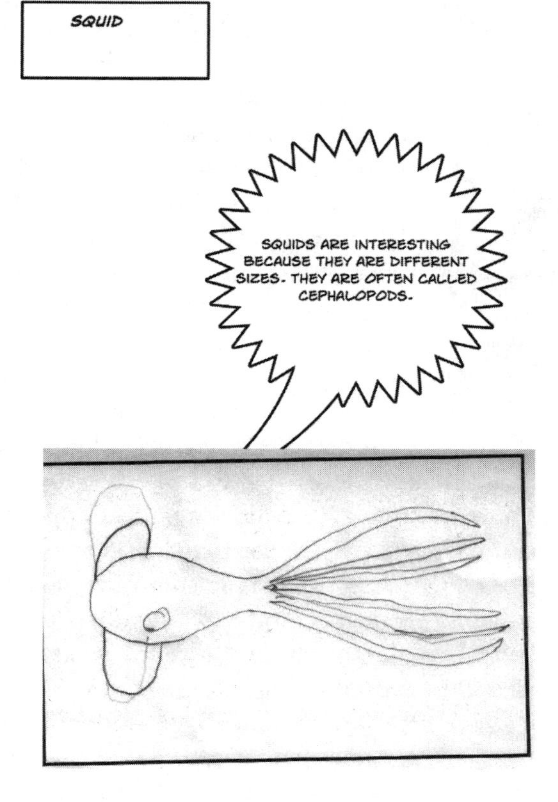

FIGURE 4.4. Comic with informational detail.

Life-Cycle Books

Life-cycle books focus on scientific life cycles such as the water cycle or the life cycles of insects or animals. I share here two easy-reader books centered on life cycles. The first, *How a Seed Grows* (Jordan, 1992), shows the life cycle of seeds, trees, and flowers. In simple terms, readers learn how seeds grow into flowers or trees. The book is written with a how-to focus that provides instructions for planting seeds in empty egg shells and watching them grow.

A second life-cycle book, *Ladybugs and Other Insects* (Jeunesse & Peyrols, 1989), describes the life cycle of a ladybug. The illustrations show the ladybugs' eggs on a leaf, the eggs turning to larvae, the larvae attaching to the leaf and becoming pupae, and the ladybugs' emergence from pupae.

For supplemental learning young students can observe the life cycle of insects by hatching butterflies from caterpillars or observing tadpoles become frogs. For teachers who are reluctant to bring insects or tadpoles to the classroom, simulations are available on the Internet. The YouTube library includes a short video showing the metamorphosis of a tadpole to a frog (*www.youtube.com/watch?v=jUrRrA5PZpw*), for example. Whether the life cycle is observed in the classroom or via the Internet, students use logs to record, sketch, and describe the changes they notice on successive days. Through this process, they learn to record information just as a scientist would. See Chapter 8 for additional website suggestions.

INFORMATIONAL BOOKS IN THE CONTENT AREAS (SCIENCE, SOCIAL STUDIES, MATH, ART, MUSIC)

Science

A plethora of science books are available for children all ages. Books series such as *Rookie Read-About Science* (Scholastic) target the youngest children. *Astronauts* (Bredeson, 2003) uses photos of astronauts and simple text to explain what readers are viewing: for example, "Astronauts are men and women who travel into space" (p. 3). In *Butterflies* (Neye, 2000), children explore paintings of butterflies supported by clear, simple text. Building from these simplest texts are Level 2 books, such as *Super Storms* (Simon, 2002), which teaches children about powerful, damaging storms.

Some science books guide children by posing questions, a very engaging way to share scientific information. As students read, they are looking for the answers to a question and their reading is focused to accomplish this goal. In *Science at the Aquarium* (Jerome, 2004), each page is organized by a question, for example, "Have you ever been to an aquarium?" or "Why don't jellyfish look like fish?" Similar in format is *Amazing Animals Q&A* (Burnie, 2007), where each page poses multiple questions and the questions are more complicated. For instance, the author asks, "Are eight eyes better than two?" and "What helps a snake to see in the dark?"

To truly engage students with science picturebooks, teachers can group books around topics. For instance, I watched as a teacher grouped books by Seymour Simon that targeted extremes. Students explored earthquakes (*Earthquakes*, 2006) and extreme storms (*Super Storms*, 2002). After these investigations, they explored regions such as deserts (*Deserts*, 1990). Figure 4.5 shares other Seymour Simon books for student exploration.

There are incredible books—in terms of both fascinating text and mesmerizing illustrations—that target animals. *Ape* (2007) by Martin Jenkins, for instance, can be considered a science book as well as a work of art. Readers learn about apes and are emotionally connected through the illustrations. The book reads like a story, but is filled with details about primates, such as orangutans, chimps, and gorillas.

Storms (1992)	*Hurricanes* (2007)
Weather (2006)	*Mountains* (1997)
The Sun (1989)	*Icebergs and Glaciers* (1999)
Lightning (2006)	*Oceans* (2006)
Tornadoes (2001)	

FIGURE 4.5. Seymour Simon books. All are published by HarperCollins.

Steve Jenkins is an author/illustrator who brings excitement in learning about animals. In *Actual Size* (2004), readers can see the actual size of animals. In *Living Color* (2007), readers learn about animals grouped by color. In *What Do You Do with a Tail Like This?* (2003), readers are enthralled with the beauty of the illustrations while learning interesting tidbits, like the fact that lizards can grow new tails.

Finally, I share two other science picturebooks that are just too good not to share with students. In the first, *Slither and Crawl* (Arnosky, 2009), readers come eye to eye with reptiles. I don't know about you, but this possibility sends shivers down my spine; however, many students would definitely respond differently. Many of the pages in this book fold out so that viewers can see the actual size of lizards and snakes. The most unnerving page perhaps is the one with a Burmese python staring right at the reader. Nightmares for sure.

The second book, *Planets: A New View of the Solar System* (Aguilar, 2008), offers information about all of the planets, with text boxes that describe their connections to Roman gods. Aguilar talks about how Pluto is no longer considered a planet, and the last chapter shares information about Eris, the largest known dwarf planet, and the Kuiper Belt. The photographs of the planets are amazing.

There are so many incredible science picturebooks available for students that it will be difficult for teachers to narrow their selections. Gill (2009) writes that this newer nonfiction genre—the nonfiction picturebook—"delights teachers and students alike" (p. 261). I can't imagine students not engaging with these books and discovering lots of information, both visual and textual, to share with others.

Social Studies

In contrast to historical fiction books, which are grounded in information supported by narrative, social studies books just target information. These books do a great job of extending the traditional social studies textbook. One such book is *Lincoln Through the Lens* (Sandler, 2008), which allows readers to learn about Abraham Lincoln from a unique perspective: photographs and paintings that vividly portray his life.

Another book, *So You Want to Be President?* (St. George & Small, 2000), presents interesting facts about presidents. I learned that six presidents had the name of James, presidents can come in all shapes and sizes (Abraham Lincoln was the tallest; James Madison, the smallest; and William Howard Taft, the fattest), and a president can be anything before being president.

Students can't help but enjoy the process of creating their own books with little-known facts about the presidents. Students might provide sketches to enrich their books, or they could cut and paste drawings obtained from the Internet. For a simpler project, students can create a card, like a baseball trading card, with the image of the president on the front and facts on the back. Students can try to stump one another by asking questions about each president. What is tricky here is keeping students focused on the goal of this project: learning and sharing information. Students can get caught up in the hands-on process of creating (cutting and pasting, finding the best image) spending more time on the search than in thinking and learning.

So far I've introduced social studies books that focus on people, but many also target other topics. In *My Map Book* (Fanelli, 1995), children learn about all kinds of maps: for example of a child's bedroom or school, others that target the parts of a dog or person, and conventional maps. This book is a perfect source to begin a more serious study of maps.

Most elementary students participate in a study of the 50 states that make up our nation. Typically a dry, nonengaging area of study, with students just expected to memorize facts, this lesson can be greatly enriched when supplemented with a book like *The Scrambled States of America* (Keller, 1998) or *The Scrambled States of America Talent Show* (Keller, 2008). These books present the states as characters who are disobedient, have feelings, and play jokes. I giggled when all the states rearranged themselves so that Alabama and New York State were on the Pacific coast and Colorado and California on the Atlantic.

One technique for history studies that meets with eagerness and enthusiasm among students is to explore history in the context of sport, such as baseball. Students enjoy uncovering details about the history of baseball while incidentally also learning American history. I created a text set, a small collection of books, that explores baseball and provides historical information. The text set begins with *H Is for Home Run: A Baseball Alphabet* (Herzog, 2004). This alphabet book is rich in detail. For example, on the *A* page, readers learn about baseball all-star athletes. Moving from the central text, a sidebar highlights Abner Doubleday, the All-Star Game, and Hank Aaron. Building from this basic information, students can explore baseball legends, like Joe Jackson in *Shoeless Joe* and *Black Betsy* (Bildner, 2002). In its opening pages, one of the most powerful sluggers of his time, Shoeless Joe, finds himself in a hitting slump. Shoeless Joe consults with a friend, Charlie Ferguson, who made him a special bat out of hickory, which Shoeless Joe named Black Betsy. Black Betsy has since become one of sports' most fabled artifacts. Although the book is written in story form, it is filled with information that is enriched in the afterword.

With this background knowledge, students are ready to explore a lyrical book, *Home Run* (Burleigh, 1998), about famous New York slugger Babe Ruth. Each page is a poem filled with information and accompanied by a Babe Ruth baseball card that entices students to read it. For instance, one begins, "You might not believe it, but if Babe hadn't become one of the best batters of all time, he could have become one of the top pitchers!" (unpaged).

To complete the text set, I chose *We Are the Ship: The Story of Negro League Baseball* (Nelson, 2008). Just from the brown front pages alone, readers instinctively know that this book is special. It is organized into innings that feature information about players and the Negro Baseball League. On one read, I just enjoyed the quotes and beautiful illustrations. Then on a second read I was ready to engage with the text. This is a beautiful book for teachers to share with students as they learn about discrimination in early baseball and the resiliency of Black players. A noteworthy companion to this book that also explores the Negro League Baseball is *Willie and the All-Stars* (Cooper, 2008). The book showcases the relationship between two boys, one White and one Black, and their baseball dreams. Willie visits Wrigley Field and watches Satchell Paige and Josh Gibson as they play the major league team. The Negro League team wins and Willie watches as the White and Black players shake hands. The book ends with an author's note about the details of the Negro Baseball League.

Text sets like this one allow students to see that even sports are contextually set in a time period. Baseball didn't always look like it does today, and certainly it will continue to change. Students can engage in personal research that mirrors this text set. They might explore other sports and research how they changed, or they can investigate how technology has changed the world. Focusing on one topic allows students to explore historical connections.

Book text sets can be enriched with visuals or primary sources easily accessed via the Internet, creating a multimodal text set (Hassett & Curwood, 2009). Teachers can visit sites like the Library of Congress (*www.loc.gov/teachers*) and explore images related to baseball (see "Baseball Across a Divided Society"). Photos, songs, and video clips are available to enrich this study of baseball. This site also suggests ways for teachers to teach effectively with primary sources.

Like science picturebooks, social studies picturebooks are available and provide rich extensions of the social studies curriculum. They allow students to explore more fully an important person or event. They also provide teachers ways to engage students in critical learning that may have been difficult because of its subject matter, like learning about each state.

Math

A great variety of books centered on math are readily available for even the youngest children through counting books. Schwartz has written several books about contemplating large numbers. In *How Much is a Million?* (1985), Schwartz explores the concept of a million. Kellogg's illustrations make this concept understandable to children. The book ends with detailed notes about the calculations used in the book. Nagda and Bickel have written two interesting math concept books. In *Tiger Math* (2000), children view photos of T.J., a baby tiger. The book teaches about graphs as readers see charts about tigers in the wild and T.J.'s weight gain. In *Polar Bear Math* (2004), children learn about fractions as they watch two young polar bears grow in the Denver Zoo.

Math picturebooks are wonderful ways to explain difficult concepts. For instance, *Ocean Counting Odd Numbers* (Pallotta, 2005) combines information about fish and odd numbers. Because these books include visuals to support difficult concepts, students understand the concepts. To extend the mathematical ideas in these books, students might create a visual such as an odd number, fraction, and so on.

Art

Children can learn about visual artists and their work through picturebooks. *The Art Book for Children* (Editors of Phaidon Press, 2007) shares art at an entry level. Within this book are color reproductions of art from the 14th century to today. The authors provide ways for children to talk about the images and paintings and what the painter wants the viewers to experience. After going through the book, I visited websites of galleries where the paintings are displayed and saw many of them as they are today (information about galleries is provided in the book). Young readers will also enjoy *Children: A First Art Book* (Micklethwait, 2008), a collection of paintings of children during everyday activities. Students can explore what it meant to be a child at the time of the painting through the work of the artist. It would be an enriching activity for each student to select a painting and then write what people believed about children during that age. I think students would be amazed at how different their world is today.

There are art books for children that feature specific artists. In *Oooh! Picasso* (Niepold & Verdu, 2009) and *Oooh! Matisse* (Niepold & Verdu, 2007), children see a Picasso sculpture come to life and discover the paintings of Matisse. These books are for preschool and primary grade children. Building from this foundation, children can explore the series of books about various artists compiled by Laurence Anholt, among them Picasso, Degas, and Monet. All of the books are filled with color photos of the artists' work, and teachers can connect from these images to websites of art galleries to see other work by each artist.

Looking carefully at artists allows students to appreciate the illustrations in the books they read. They will become appreciative in how an impressionistic illustration evokes different feelings than a surrealistic style. They will become sensitive to line, color, and so on as they explore artists and their work.

Music

The work of musicians has been documented in books as well. I love the recent work by Lemony Snicket, *The Composer is Dead* (2009). In this mystery, a detective tries to determine who killed the composer. To solve the case, the detective must visit each part of the orchestra: the string, brass, woodwind, and percussion sections. The book ends with this resolution: "Of course," he said, "the Conductor! You've been murdering composers for years! In fact, wherever there's a conductor, you're sure to find a dead composer!" (unpaged). The next two-page spread is filled with the names of dead composers, and the last page suggests that readers visit an orchestra. While the story is fun, I love the addition of a CD with music composed by Nathaniel Stookey and performed by the San Francisco Symphony. Lemony Snicket even narrates some of the music. Another book that introduces children to an orchestra is *The Philharmonic Gets Dressed* (Kuskin, 1986). In this book, children learn about musicians' preparation before the concert begins.

A very special book unites music and visual art: Lach's (2006) *Can You Hear It?*. Lach has identified paintings and paired them with classical music. Lach offers children suggestions on connecting visual and auditory images to help them with this unique interpretation. One example of this pairing is Hiroshige's painting of *Chrysanthemums* and Rimsky-Korsakov's *Flight of the Bumblebee*. Brilliant!

MULTIGENRE TEXTS

As seen with postmodern picturebooks, authors are playing with genre and blurring its boundaries. *The Invention of Hugo Cabret* (Selznick, 2007) is just such a book. Selznick marries traditional writing through a mystery with artful illustration. The book has elements of a graphic novel, nonfiction, and film. Readers sense the book is different by the use of black page borders, black as the background on illustrated pages, and only black-and-white illustrations. In the illustrations, viewers are sometimes brought in, as when viewing the inside of the old man's hand as he shows Hugo a handkerchief. At other times, viewers contemplate a scene slightly behind Hugo. After the story ends, Selznick shares his resources for the creation of this book and pushes readers to read again to see where fiction separates from informational text.

Once students are familiar with the richness of genre, they are ready to create their own multigenre projects. The easiest way to begin is for teachers to extend social studies or science content. For instance, if the focus of a particular lesson was on individuals who made a difference in social studies, each student could select one individual to research. Once they have an understanding of this person, they are ready to choose appropriate genres to share information they have learned. For instance, a student who chose Ben Franklin might write a brief biography to begin the project. Following this piece, the student could write a book focusing on the science behind electricity, bifocal glasses, or lightning rods. They can include a newspaper article about one of his inventions and perhaps a letter that Franklin might have written to someone to describe one of his inventions. A student might also choose to re-create a few pages of Ben Franklin's notebook, where he kept sketches and details of his inventions. When all the pieces are completed, a student can reflect on what was learned, in this case the inventions of Ben Franklin. A brief synthesis piece can be written that guides readers through what they will learn in reading this multigenre project. For instance, the author might inform readers that he or she has focused on Ben Franklin's inventions to show how he changed the circumstances of people throughout the world. Through combining genres, students learn more richly about historical individuals and events.

ENGAGING STUDENTS

Providing opportunity for students to routinely experience informational text is one way to engage them with these books. Combining reading, writing, and sketching also enriches students' connections to informational books. Following are a few ways to connect reading and writing centered on informational text.

1. *Observational notebooks.* Providing notebooks to students when they are studying any informational topic allows them to behave as a scientist would. They can jot notes or draw sketches. Later in their study they can refer to these notes for informational presentations or multigenre projects. Students love the freedom of recording information that they find important.
2. *Text transformation.* For this activity, students take information they learned in one genre and transform it into another. For example, having read an informational text about magnets, students can then turn this information into a different genre: a newspaper article, a poem, or a narrative that includes a magnet.
3. *Engaging students in reading and analyzing nonfiction (RAN).* Stead (2006) described a strategy where students identify "What They Think They Know," "Yes We Were Right," "New Information," and "Wonderings." Armed with a chart with these column headings, students complete them while reading informational text, with the exception of the first column, which is completed before reading. For the "Yes, We Were Right" column, students can identify page numbers where their information was verified. The strength of this strategy is that students list what they think they know rather than what they know. If their background knowledge is incorrect, they are more willing to accept new information as it is verified in text.

At the end of this chapter, it is time to take a few moments to reflect:

1. Think about the times you have read informational text to your students. What made these events successful?
2. What projects do you expect students to complete during informational explorations? What new ideas will you bring to your class after reading this chapter?
3. Visit *www.duluth.lib.mn.us/YouthServices/Booklists/Sibert.html* to learn about the newest winners of the Robert F. Sibert Informational Book Award or *www.ncte.org/awards/orbispictus* to learn about the newest winners of the NCTE Orbis Pictus Award for Outstanding Nonfiction for Children. Once you have found an interesting book, share it with your students.

RECOMMENDED READING

For readers who would like to know about some of the topics in this chapter, the following books provide additional information.

Kletzien, S., & Dreher, M. (2004). *Informational text in K–3 classrooms: Helping children read and write.* Newark, DE: International Reading Association.

This is a practical guide to help teachers with informational text in primary grades, although the suggestions can be adapted to intermediate grades. The authors write about how to build classroom libraries with informational text, how to use them as read-alouds, and how to connect informational text with Internet resources.

Stead, T. (2006). *Reality checks: Teaching reading comprehension with nonfiction K–5*. Portland, ME: Stenhouse.

This book is rich in information to help students comprehend informational text. I think the RAN strategy is perfect for helping students learn from informational text. I like the way students tentatively write what they know and then search to confirm or disconfirm this knowledge.

Moss, B. (2003). *Exploring the literature of fact: Children's nonfiction trade books in the elementary classroom*. New York: Guilford Press.

Moss provides information about informational text genres. She also supports teachers in making informational text selections and helps them find effective ways to support student response to these books.

Student Voices

The Complete Pokémon Pocket Guide: Volume 1 (VIZ Media, 2008)

"This book tells you what all the Pokémon names are and their descriptions. It tells about how they attack and what they do to defeat each other, like Thunderbolt, who attacks with electricity. They have quick attacks where they run and head butt each other. They run up and hit each other in the head. Mewtwo is my favorite. He is like Mew but 100 times its size. He has better powers. He is kind of scary. Palkia is a Pokémon. He is like a shark. I don't know his attack. Dialga is tall, like 17 feet, and he weighs a lot. Whalelord is like 45 feet long. Giritina weighs so much, more than Dialga. He is scary because he is all black with dark red eyes. He has black wings with red fingernails hanging off. He has like a gold crown. Duskull is like a skull with two purple eyes. He has something on the back of his head that makes him look scary."—Gabriel, a second grader

CHAPTER 5

Exploring Qualities of Text

"I want my writing to be elevating," said Avon.
"Living in this tree should give you lofty thoughts," Edward pointed out.
"True," said Avon, "And I like the idea of writing being upbeat."
"So much better, " agreed Edward, "than being beat-up."
"What about writing in circles?" asked Avon.
"Writers do that far too often," said Edward.
"But I'd like to be a well-rounded writer," said Avon.
"On the whole, yes," agreed Edward, "especially since it's not good to be considered square."
"And I'd like my book to be timely," said Avon.
"True," agreed Edward. "With as many deadlines as writers face, they need to be punctual."
"Then perhaps," said Avon, "I should begin my book with Once upon a time. Would that be punctual enough?"

—AVI, *A Beginning, a Muddle, and an End* (2008a, pp. 22–23)

It would seem that Avon, a snail, and Edward, an ant, have the process of writing figured out. Throughout this entire Avi book, they contemplate what it means to write—something. Avi's exemplary qualities as a writer are showcased throughout this book. First of all, think about it: Learning about writing from a snail and an ant . . . really! And yet it works beautifully. Second, the simple plot—trying to write a story—keeps readers engaged from beginning to end, with a few adventures along the way. Third, Avi intricately weaves wordplay throughout; explore, for instance, his use of the words *elevating, upbeat*, and *well-rounded* in the quote. Fourth, the elements of the setting, Avon's house and a tree limb, are adequately described so that readers understand the smallness of this setting. Avi's style of writing allows readers to experience all of the qualities of text while never having one leap out at you. It takes pausing at places and reflecting on the book when completed to appreciate Avi's expertise in crafting it.

This chapter focuses on the elements that are identified as qualities of narrative text. I lead with *plot*, because not only are most children's books driven by it, but, perhaps more important, readers are motivated by plot during the first reading of a book: They want to know the outcome, and some even skim the final pages so that they can read through the suspenseful parts more comfortably (Nikolajeva, 2005; Nodelman & Reimer, 2003). A plot can't exist without *characters*, so the focus shifts to richly developed characters in children's literature. *Setting* is critical in some books and a backdrop in others. However, exploring setting allows readers to appreciate the narrative more fully. Because *theme, style*, and *point of view* are often more subtle to determine, I discuss these at the end of the chapter because these elements are typically focused on once there is clarity with the others. In addition, most readers do not read a book to discover its theme or message; this happens after the book is enjoyed (Nodelman & Reimer, 2003).

These narrative elements are identified so that teachers can share them with students in ways that transcend comprehension questions. Today, most core reading programs provide numerous questions that target each of these narrative elements. Students often view them as a quiz: Who is the main character? What was the plot? What was the setting? The goal of this chapter is to support teachers and students in more meaningful exploration of these elements and their importance to the story being read.

PLOT

A plot is the element of a book that evokes feelings of suspense in its readers; they want to know what happens next. "Plot is the sequence of events showing characters in action" (Lukens, 2007, p. 99). Authors can write plotlines that move from one adventure to another quickly, or they can extend an event so that readers live it for a long time. Nodelman and Reimer (2003) write:

> Plots order stories in a variety of ways, but good plots almost always provide a two-fold pleasure—first, the pleasure of incompleteness, the tension of delaying and anticipating completion; and second, the pleasure of the completion. (p. 65)

Plots have a beginning, middle, and end, although the end is not always neatly tied up and concluded. Some books leave the end open for the readers to determine, as seen in *The Garden of Abdul Gasazi* (Van Allsburg, 1979). In this story, Alan, a young boy, takes care of Miss Hester's dog, Fritz, while she visits her cousin. Alan takes Fritz on a walk and they wind up at Abdul Gasazi's home, a magician who does not like dogs. Gasazi convinces Alan that he turned Fritz into a duck, and Alan watches a duck snatch his hat and fly away. Alan returns to Miss Hester's home to find Fritz there, and Miss Hester persuades him that Gasazi could not turn a dog into a duck. But Alan's hat appears at Miss Hester's feet. So can Gasazi turn a dog into a duck? That question is left for readers to answer. Can you imagine how students will try to find a clear answer as they scan and rescan the pages of this book, hoping they just overlooked it?

For very young children, the plot is usually straightforward, with one event following another and a clear resolution. As writers create for more mature child readers, they invent more complex plots, perhaps using flashbacks or dream sequences, where the plot events are not linear and are more difficult to place into a logical order. They also leave the resolution open, enticing readers to reread the book to see whether they can determine a satisfying ending. Flashback or flashforward sequences are often challenging for readers to comprehend. To support readers, teachers can provide a simple bookmark where students can record events during one time sequence on one side and events from a different time sequence on the other side. A simple bookmark like this can scaffold a student's understanding (see Figure 5.1).

Time Period 1 (indicate time and what is happening)	**Time Period 2** (indicate whether flashback or flashforward and what is happening)

FIGURE 5.1. Time sequence bookmark.

Plots involve conflict and resolution. In children's books, conflict can occur between two characters, between a character and nature, and between a character and his or her own self (Norton, 2007). *Skippyjon Jones* (Schachner, 2003), an example of conflict between two characters, is a story about a Siamese cat who is struggling to behave in ways his mother deems appropriate. First, he sleeps in a birds' nest with a mama and her baby birds—Remember: He is a cat. His mother lectures him and banishes him to his room with this admonition: "You need to think about just what it means to be a Siamese cat" (unpaged). Skippyjon Jones does stay in his bedroom, but his imagination allows him to become a Chihuahua that speaks Spanish, not exactly what his mother told him to do. He creates a whole adventure with fellow Chihuahuas against the banditos. The book, similar to *Where the Wild Things Are*, ends with hugs from his mother and his going to sleep in a big boy bed.

An example of a story with a plotline that involves a character versus nature conflict is "Down the Hill" in *Frog and Toad All Year* (Lobel, 1976). This story begins with Frog knocking at Toad's door and begging him to come outside to explore winter. He complains that he does not even own winter clothes, but Frog thought ahead and brought Toad some clothes. They eventually go outside and sled, with many bumps along the way. Although not a serious story of conflict with nature, it humorously models this plotline. A more serious example of character versus nature conflict is found in *Kidnapped: Book Three: The Rescue* (Korman, 2006). In this book, 11-year-old Meg Falconer makes her escape after being kidnapped, an event that was revealed in the previous book in the series. Unfortunately, no sooner is she free when a major snowstorm moves in, and now Meg has to survive a blizzard to reach safety. The entire book showcases her survival in the wild and cold.

A plotline involving a character in conflict with his other own self or learning about him- or herself is prevalent in children's books. In *Olivia Saves the Circus* (Falconer, 2001), for example, Olivia tries to be unique even though she has to wear a "boring" uniform to school. Her ingenuity and creativity are evident as she accessorizes herself with ribbons, tights, backpack, and purse. These personality traits are repeated as she retells her visit to the circus to her class. Olivia sees herself as the heroine to the circus because she performs for the circus people who are sick. The entire focus of this book is learning about Olivia and how she views herself. The only conflict she faces is her teacher's disbelief at her story, and Olivia easily solves that by telling her teacher that her story is true "to the best of my recollection" (unpaged).

A second example is *Knuffle Bunny Too* (Willems, 2007). This story begins with Trixie taking Knuffle Bunny, what she thought was a one-of-a-kind bunny, to school to show her friends only to discover that Sonja has a similar bunny, resulting in jealousy and anger. At the end of Trixie's dreadful day, her teacher returns the bunnies to the girls so they can take them home. When Trixie goes to bed, she discovers she has the wrong bunny, so perhaps hers is unique in subtle ways. Trixie convinces her dad to go to Sonja's house in the middle of the night to exchange bunnies. Trixie then discovers a best friend in Sonja and the jealousy over the bunnies diminishes. The simple story explores the feelings of a young child regarding her favorite stuffed animal and how they turn negative with the discovery of a similar animal.

Plot structure also has a special vocabulary to describe its parts:

- *Exposition*: This element provides the necessary information for the reader to understand the story (includes setting, characters, and a situation).
- *Complication*: Conflict is introduced and characters begin to deal with it.
- *Climax*: This is the point of maximum tension in the story.
- *Resolution*: The problem or situation is resolved.
- *Denouement*: This is the book's closure (Temple et al., 2006).

In one fifth-grade classroom, I listened in as students identified these plot parts in a book they read. They enjoyed using this sophisticated vocabulary to describe a plot. One student told another, "I just thought there was a beginning, middle, and end. Did you know there were all these parts? I am having trouble figuring out the resolution and the denouement. Are they ever the same?" Following this question, both students returned to their book to discover the difference between the resolution and the denouement.

The *home–away–coming home* pattern is the most common plotline in children's literature (Nodelman & Reimer, 2003). *Where the Wild Things Are* (Sendak, 1963/1988) is a classic example, even though maybe Max never really leaves his bedroom physically. At the beginning of the book, Max is in his bedroom. Then he participates in his wild adventures in his wolf suit. The book closes with Max, once again in his bedroom, finding his dinner. Numerous fairytales have this same structure; for example, where the prince leaves the castle on an adventure to prove that he is brave and smart, successfully combats an enemy, and returns home to win the hand of the beautiful princess. A variation of this structure is where the child remains home while his or her parents leave. *The Cat in the Hat* (Dr. Seuss, 1957c) and *Good Dog, Carl* (Day, 1997) are examples where children engage in exciting, and sometimes dangerous activities, when their parents are away, with normalcy resuming with the return of the parents.

Other plot structures are *cumulative* as seen in stories like the *Gingerbread Man* where text is repeated and extended on each page. Authors can write using a *linear* structure, where the plot moves along logically as seen in *Edwina* (Willems, 2006). In this book, Edwina, a dinosaur, plays with children and eventually proves to Reginald Von Hoobie-Doobie that dinosaurs do exist. Plot structures can also be *episodic*, with events that can be shared in any order. Lobel's Frog and Toad books are examples of episodic stories, filled with small stories that could be placed in any order. The reader knows that each book is filled with Frog and Toad's adventures, but one adventure does not necessarily lead to the next. Finally, plot structures can be *circular*, as seen in *Rosie's Walk* (Hutching, 1971), in which Rosie ends the book where she began (Anderson, 2002).

While picturebooks offer examples of all of the plotline structures, they are constricted by the typical 32-page limit. To explore plot more fully, I have chosen the short novel *Poppy* (Avi, 1995) as an exemplar. I return to this book when discussing the other writing elements as well.

Although most students would never be expected to return to a single book to explore all narrative elements, a teacher may have them reread a book to study just one. Through this closer inspection of a single element, readers more fully appreciate the craftsmanship of a writer.

Poppy is the second book in the *Poppy* series by Avi. In this book, Ragweed (a mouse and the central character in the first book) moves from the city to the country, more specifically Dimwood Forest. Readers quickly discover that Poppy is to be engaged to Ragweed. Whereas most books begin with a quiet exposition, Poppy does not. Avi has Poppy and Ragweed on Bannock Hill, without permission from the owl (Mr. Ocax). Readers know this is dangerous even as Poppy and Ragweed argue about the need for permission but enjoy being alone on the hill. The following is a brief sampling of their dialogue:

> Poppy, hurt and wanting to show she was *not* a coward, poked her nose and whisker out from under the bark. "Ragweed," she persisted even as she began to creep into the open, "being careless is stupid."
>
> Her friend took another scrap of the nut and sighed with pleasure. "Poppy," he said, "you may be my best girl, but admit it, you don't know how to live like I do." (p. 6)

Having spied the mice on the hill without his permission, Mr. Ocax swoops in and devours Ragweed and almost Poppy too—surprisingly dramatic action in the very first chapter. With this exposition, the reader immediately knows that this book is about obeying and not obeying, the authority of an owl over mice, and the fear and compliance of the mice.

The plot's complication is revealed when Poppy returns home to tell her family what happened. They are unhappy that Poppy has angered Mr. Ocax: Because their current home cannot support them all, Poppy's family wants to move but they need Mr. Ocax's permission to do so. Poppy and her father, Lungwort, approach Mr. Ocax to seek his permission; however, not surprisingly, he refuses. The mice are in a dilemma because they cannot survive in their current home and do not have permission to move. Furthermore, Poppy feels responsible for her family's predicament. The following is some of the conversation that sets up the complication.

> "Lungwort," Mr. Ocax interrupted. "I forbid you to move to New House."
>
> "What?" Lungwort gasped, flapping the rain away from his face with a paw. The word had all but stuck in his throat.
>
> "Permission *denied*, Lungwort. You cannot move to New House."

> "But, but—why, sir"
> "Because I said so." (p. 54)

The dialogue helps the reader see that Lungwort is subservient because he has to make a request to save his family, and he uses the word *sir* when addressing the owl. Mr. Ocax, on the other hand, is dominant and a bully, proclaiming his denial without an adequate reason to support it.

The story builds to a climax as Poppy leaves home to explore New House. Readers worry for Poppy's safety, because Mr. Ocax knows she has left and is trying to capture her. A secondary fear for Poppy, a needless one created by Mr. Ocax, is that she will run into Erithizon Dorsatum, a porcupine, whom she fears will eat her. (Mr. Ocax lied to the mice, telling them that he protects them from evil porcupines that eat them. Mice are not aware that porcupines do not eat meat.) Avi writes:

> The fox stuck its nose in after her, its barking booming about Poppy like a cannonade. Trying to get away, she moved deeper into the musky dark. Suddenly she stopped. At the far end of the log she heard the distinct sound of heavy breathing. It was exactly what she had feared: Another creature was already in the log. (p. 92)

As if foxes and porcupines didn't give Poppy enough to worry about, as the story continues, Mr. Ocax finds her:

> It was while she stopped to sniff a Scotch broom plant that Mr. Ocax, out of nowhere, made a dive at her, talons flashing. (p. 118)

At this point, no plot reader is going to put the book aside: He or she is reading the pages as fast as possible. Thankfully the reader is finally able to relax a bit after reading that Poppy takes care of Mr. Ocax with the use of a porcupine quill, the resolution.

The denouement occurs as Poppy returns home and shares what she has learned, resulting in the mice being able to relocate to New House. Avi writes:

> Poppy gazed at them evenly. Then she pulled the feather, Mr. Ocax's feather, from her sash and held it aloft for all to see. "Mr. Ocax is dead." She said solemnly. "And I can tell you that New House is right next to a big field of corn that has enough to feed us all forever and ever." (pp. 158–159)

The reader can feel satisfied because Poppy met the challenges of her quest and then returned safely to her home and family to share her good news.

Although readers do not have to label each of these parts of the plot to understand the story, by going back to the story and identifying them they can see how Avi constructed his narrative. Children will enjoy this process and feel quite sophisticated when they can name all the parts of a plot. This knowledge will also support them as they write their own narratives. It allows students to move beyond just considering a beginning, a middle, and an end. Teachers can create planning sheets where each part of the plot is identified and students draft their own plots (see Figure 5.2).

Name ____________________   **Story Title** ____________________
Exposition
Complication
Climax
Resolution
Denouement

FIGURE 5.2. Planning sheet for plot.

CHARACTERS

Characters, whether people, toys, or animals, are essential to a story because they carry out the plot. Nodelman and Reimer (2003) suggest that authors reveal information—or in their words, "kind of gossip" (p. 59)—about characters either explicitly or implicitly through their behavior. Readers learn about the personality of characters by repetition of a personality trait, how they behave, how they relate to other characters, how they talk, what they look like, what other characters say about them, and narrator comments (Lukens, 2007).

Characters in a story are identified as either round or flat. *Round characters* are dynamic; they undergo a change throughout a narrative. For example, they are not always good or always evil; they are more complicated. Typically, they are the protagonists, or the central characters. *Flat characters*, in contrast, usually are not the most important character to a story, and they remain static from beginning to end. Often, they are stereotypes, possessing one dominant trait (Anderson, 2002; Lukens, 2007). The flat character often represents the antagonist, or the person at the center of the conflict.

In *The Escape of Marvin the Ape* (Buehner & Buehner, 1999), readers learn about Marvin implicitly. Marvin, an ape, lives in a zoo, but he slips out when the zookeeper is feeding him. What is interesting is that Marvin already had a suitcase packed and the zookeeper did not notice it. Through illustration, the viewer learns that, although when in the zoo Marvin looks like a typical ape, once out of the zoo he wears clothes, knows how to travel on the subway, and can read books. Marvin goes to a restaurant and orders from the menu, visits a museum, goes to the movies, and visits a toy store. Most interesting is that Marvin always behaves and dresses appropriately for these events. At the end of the story, readers understand, through Marvin's actions, that he is quite intelligent and understands culturally appropriate ways of behaving. The text never hints at these traits; rather, it just shares simple descriptions of his adventures, for example, "At the ball game Marvin caught a pop-up foul" (unpaged).

In *Officer Buckle and Gloria* (Rathmann, 1995), readers learn about Gloria through her interaction with Officer Buckle. Officer Buckle is clearly the flat character, because his only worry is safety, he is boring, and he is unaware of Gloria's antics. Gloria, on the other hand, is anything but boring. She obeys Officer Buckle's commands when he is looking; but when he is not, she mimics him and extends his message. Through this interaction, readers learn that Gloria is smart, entertaining, sensitive to Officer Buckle's feelings, and his best friend.

Temple et al. (2006) identify common roles of characters in traditional literature (fairytales and folktales):

- The hero: the central character who drives the plot.
- The rival: the person who tries to thwart the hero.
- The helper: the person who helps the hero reach his or her goal.

Although these roles are clearest in traditional literature, they also show up in more current writing.

In Avi's *Poppy*, several characters can be identified: Poppy, the protagonist and hero; Mr. Ocax, her rival and antagonist; Poppy's father, Lungwort, a flat character; and Erethizon Dorsatum, the helper. Mr. Ocax is revealed to readers first. Avi describes him with these words:

> Mr. Ocax's eyes—flat upon his face—were round and yellow with large ebony pupils that enabled him to see as few other creatures could. Moonlight—even faint moonlight—was as good as daylight for him. (p. 1)

Avi does not leave readers puzzled about the nature of Mr. Ocax. Quickly, they learn that Mr. Ocax sees himself as dominant and a predator, not the kind of character most mice would want to encounter.

Readers next learn about Poppy through her interactions with Ragweed:

> "Ragweed," Poppy replied as she sniffed tensely in all directions, "you promised we'd dance when we got here. We can't do that in the open. Besides, I want to answer your question. So will you *please* get under here with me." (pp. 2–3)

Through this brief conversation, readers know that Ragweed convinced Poppy to come to Bannock Hill with the promise of a dance. Now that she is at the hill, she is afraid to come into the open because Mr. Ocax may be watching. Avi, through his narration, which combines the physical and the emotional, lets readers know that Poppy is a small, timid mouse and is tense in this situation.

This description is unusual for a character who is the heroine of a story. Readers learn more about Poppy's personality when she faces Mr. Ocax and asks permission for her family to move. After Mr. Ocax refuses, Poppy is faced with a dilemma: She can either stay a timid, fearful mouse or find the courage necessary to try to rectify the situation. Her developing personality is revealed when she says, "'If I'm the one who caused this mess, it has to be me who sorts it out" (p. 71). In this one sentence, she positions herself as a responsible, solution-driven mouse, unlike her passive personality seen earlier.

Poppy's father, Lungwort, remains the same from beginning to end. He is the leader of the extended mouse family, realizes that their current space is too small to support them, but allows his search for a solution to be restricted by Mr. Ocax's rules, to the detriment of his family: When Mr. Ocax refuses to let the family move, Lungwort meekly accepts the decision. There are other indicators of Lungwort's weak personality, beyond his blind obedience, foolishly gullible, believing Mr. Ocax when he says he is providing protection. "That owl, " he pointed out, "has incredible vision. And hearing. He can hear or see anything, even in the dark. And a food thing, too. Porcupines prowl at night" (p. 13).

Finally, the helper, Erethizon Dorsatum, enters the story. Ereth describes himself as a "grump" (p. 93). Soon after Poppy and Ereth's first encounter, she learns from him that, contrary to Mr. Ocax's warnings, porcupines do not eat meat. Ereth has an interesting way of talking, as clearly demonstrated in his response. "Eat mice!" Ereth exclaimed. "Hit the puke switch and duck! Meat disgusts me. Nauseates me. Revolts me. I'm a vegetarian, jerk. I eat bark" (p. 100). Ereth helps Poppy get to New House with the promise that, in return, she will get him salt that is on a tall pole, beyond his reach. Readers learn that Ereth is a helper but he also expects something in return.

By considering each character separately and then their interactions, readers understand them more deeply. They also learn that characters like Mr. Ocax, Lungwort, and Ereth are static characters with no personality change throughout the story. In contrast, Poppy morphs into a very different character with a complex personality. Her personality and its shifts are what make the plotline interesting.

Exploring characters and how they support the plot allows children to appreciate the character nuances shared by writers. Although children may have an idea of what they think or feel about a character, rereading to note how an author shared these personality traits is revealing, as was shown in the previous example. Children will appreciate how a writer creates a round character and subtly enriches his or her personality throughout a narrative. To supplement this lesson, students can identify a character trait and then ponder its different meanings. An example is shared in Figure 5.3, where a student explored being elegant.

FIGURE 5.3. Exploring a trait.

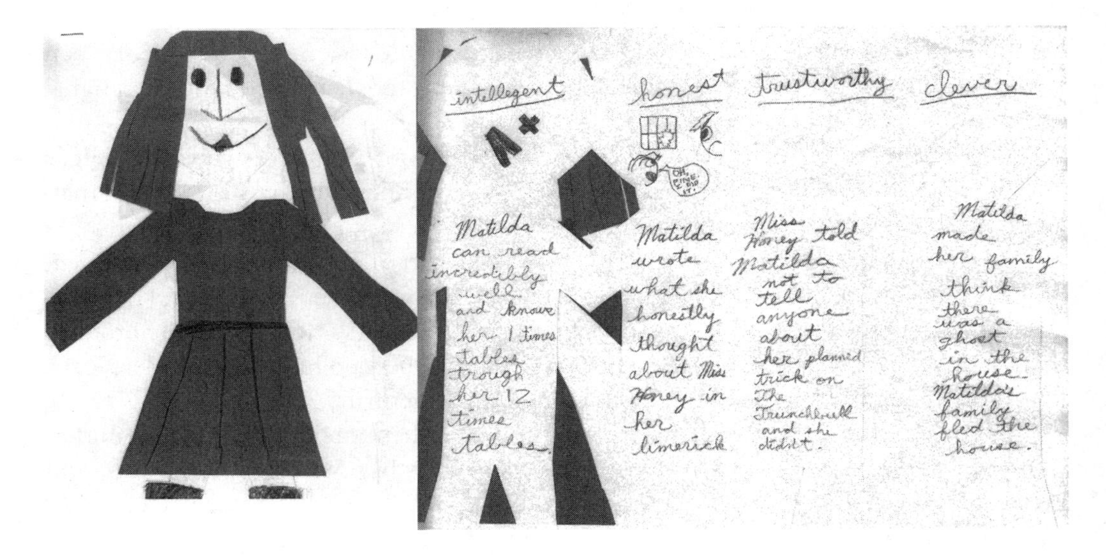

FIGURE 5.4. Exploring the character of Matilda.

There are many other ways that students can explore characters. One simple strategy is to have students who are reading the same novel each choose a character to focus on. As they read the book, students record details about their specific character in one of two ways. First, they can record the information they learn based on what their character says and does and what others say (see Figure 5.4 for an example). This information can be easily written on a form with each category heading a column. In a second strategy, students use a form divided into as many boxes as there are chapters and, for each chapter, record what they learned about their character. Through this process, students will recognize how their character is developed throughout the book.

An equally valuable strategy is to have students focus on the dominant personality trait of a character. Students form a book club and each chooses a character from the book the group is reading. On the basis of both their personal reflection and their conversation with others in their book club, each student identifies a single trait for their character and writes about it. Figure 5.5 shares Kennady's thoughts about her selected

> Self
>
> She brushed through her thick, flowing hair, fixing it in a different style for the fourth time that morning. Sticky hairspray began to fill the bathroom and fog up the mirror in front of her. She reapplied her goopy, bright eye shadow and winked at her reflection as she strutted out.

FIGURE 5.5. Student writing.

character, the evil queen in *Snow White*; Kennady chose the word *self* to acknowledge the evil queen's fixation with her beauty.

The ReadWriteThink website (*www.readwritethink.org*) offers another option for helping students. In the lesson, *Book Report Alternative: Character and Author Business Cards*, students create a business card for a character. Students write a short text about the character and insert images that represent the character. The online lesson has templates to help students create their business card.

SETTING

Characters act and the plot occurs in a setting. In some books the setting is critical to the story and in others it is in the background (Lukens, 2007). Unlike fairytales, where the setting is once upon a time someplace in the world, most often resembling Europe, there are both picturebooks and novels where setting is crucial to the story's plot. For instance, in *The Hunger Games* (Collins, 2008) the setting and the changes within it are critical to the fantasy. If readers do not pay attention to the setting, they cannot understand the feelings or circumstances of the main characters.

I believe one of the most beautiful picturebooks with a major emphasis on setting is MacLachlan's (1994) *All the Places to Love.* The book begins with the birth of a baby, Eli, who is the narrator of this story, and on the very next page, he tells about what his grandmother let him see:

> She held me up in the open window.
> So that what I heard first was the wind.
> What I saw first were all the places to love:
> The valley,
> The river falling down over rocks,
> The hilltop where blueberries grew. (unpaged)

The remainder of the book shares the places Eli sees or visits on the farm, which are complemented with the illustrator's paintings.

The entire storyline of *Bats at the Library* (Lies, 2008) rests on the setting, a library, which is visited by bats when the window is left open. It is clear that the bats have been here before as they locate books they have previously read. As the bats read, Lies changes the setting to match the one in the book the bats are reading. This would be an interesting book on which to base a discussion of setting, as it is so integral to the story and it changes to match what would be appropriate in other stories. Setting is also critical in *How Do Dinosaurs Go to School?* (Yolen, 2007). The sole focus of this book is about going to and being in school; the twist is that dinosaurs are the students. Through the dinosaurs' antics, children explore the rules and expectations of school.

For teachers who want to pursue one very special setting, the book *Home* (Rosen, 1992) is perfect. This book is a collection of artwork and writing from numerous authors and illustrators about what home means. For example, Brandenberg created a two-page spread about a child's bed, and Yep shared the importance of the light well that was part of his grandmother's apartment.

Picturebooks aren't alone in their focus on setting and how it is critical to plot. I have chosen three novels to highlight setting, but there are many more that could have been included. Spinelli shares an amazing character, Maniac, in *Maniac Magee* (1990), but the plot revolves around his location, either in East End where kids are black or West End where kids are white. In *Hatchet* (Paulsen, 1987), Brian survives a plane crash in the remote Canadian wild and must learn how to survive. The entire story centers on his existence and survival in this environment. Finally, in *The Fear Place* (Naylor, 1994), Doug is forced to confront his scariest place, "a narrow crumbling path six hundred feet above a canyon: The Fear Place" (p. 5). This whole book is unified by Doug dealing with this fear: fear of a specific place.

For further exploration of setting, I return to *Poppy*, where the primary setting is the mice's home at Gray House. Avi provides a full map of the Dimwood Forest region to help readers with setting and focuses on setting from the very beginning:

> A thin crescent moon, high in the sky, shed faint white light over Dimwood Forest. Stars glowed. Breezes full of ripe summer fragrance floated over nearby meadow and hill. Dimwood itself, veiled in darkness, lay utterly still.
>
> At the very edge of this forest stood an old charred oak on which sat a great horned owl. (p. 1)

The important part of understanding setting is not merely being able just to describe it, although that is certainly a place to begin. Most readers, because they first read to understand the plot, let the setting move to the background of their concern, unless, of course, the setting is essential in understanding the plot. However, after this initial reading, readers can ponder how this setting connects and enhances the story. What is important to know about this place, and how are the characters affected by it? Through this exploration, children learn when setting is a critical element of text and when it is not.

For books where the setting is important, teachers may ask students to quickly sketch what they perceive the setting to be. They can even reread carefully to get all the details correct. When the setting changes, they can create another quick sketch. These sketches help students visualize the worlds the characters inhabit.

A new opportunity to explore setting is available at Google Lit Trips (*www.googlelittrips.org*). Using Google Earth, a free download, viewers can "visit" the settings of several books. In *Make Way for Ducklings* (McCloskey, 1941), for example, each place that the ducks went is identified with a title and a balloon. A click on the balloon leads to a photo of the location along with details and questions. For instance, when I clicked on the public garden, I saw a picture of the boats on the pond and the question, "What are some concerns that Mr. and Mrs. Mallard have about raising a family?" Although the number of books in the Google Lit Trips library is limited, more are added almost daily. I found this site to be an amazing way to give students insight into settings, particularly those that are often unfamiliar to them.

THEME

In one of my first research studies (Barone, 1990), I asked primary grade students to write after they read independently, and I collected samples throughout an entire year. Most students constructed retellings or summaries. More proficient readers noticed personal connections or text-to-text connections. And a few—very few—students targeted theme. For example, after reading, *Danny the Champion of the World* (Dahl, 1975), one student wrote this thematic response:

> I like this book a lot because of Danny and his adventures in poaching but I would never poach. It's stealing and I don't like stealing.

This response showed the student stepping back from the text and noting that it was about poaching or stealing. He connected all the details of the story and determined that the author wanted the reader to ponder stealing.

Applebee (1978) wrote about thematic responses or generalizations: "Readers begin to generalize about the meaning of a work, to formulate abstract statements about its theme or message" (p. 25). What is particularly interesting about theme is that it is abstract and requires readers to step back from the details of a text and decide what it was all about, as happened in the prior response to *Danny the Champion of the World*.

The theme of a story is the central idea that connects the plot, characters, and setting (Norton, 2007). Theme, being abstract, can be difficult to determine. Plus, some narratives have explicit themes and others implicit themes (Nodelman & Reimer, 2003). For instance, the theme may never be overtly mentioned, but the author may share it implicitly through the actions or conversations of the characters. A tricky part with theme is that students might get the idea that all stories teach a lesson, and this is certainly not true. Although a book may explore a theme that resonates with readers, theme needs to be treated as more than a lesson provided by a writer. In sharing a few books that highlight theme, I suggest possible ways to discuss theme with students. The conversation suggestions are open ended and allow for a variety of interpretations.

Golem (Wisniewski, 1996) is a picturebook that explicitly centers on theme, although there is more than one to consider. The story is about the Jews in Prague about 400 years ago and how a rabbi brought clay to life, in the form of Golem, to save the Jews. As children read and reread this book, they consider religious persecution, the use or abuse of power, and justice. Golem saves the Jews, but he does so with violence. Children might discuss whether violence is a reasonable and just solution to the situation. They can also consider the issue of power and how it can be used and abused. This

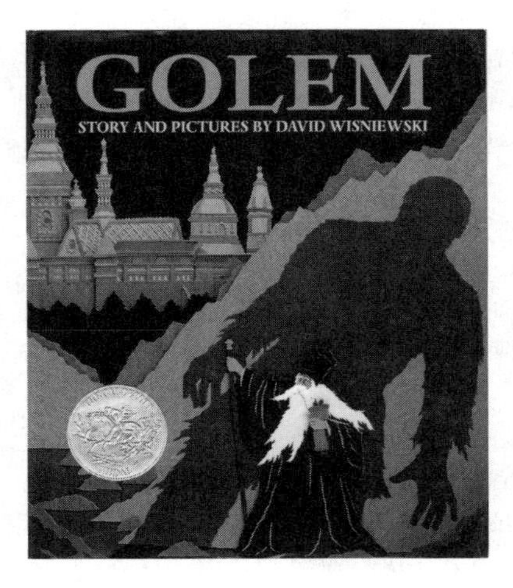

is a book that requires rereading so that children can enjoy its visual, textual, and thematic components.

Ella the Elegant Elephant (D'Amico & D'Amico, 2004) is a story about an elephant who is worried about attending a new school. When she does go to school, a bully makes fun of her hat and trips her. Ella has to deal with the unfamiliar in a new school and with a bully. The book ends happily, but children will certainly want to explore bullying and the feelings surrounding it and what it means to experience change, like going to a new school or beginning school for the first time. Teachers may initially use this book to deal with coming to school or to a new classroom and the feelings that result. Later, when students engage in discussion about power, and in particular the power that a bully feels, this will be a good book to revisit.

A book that very explicitly shares its theme is *It's Hard to Be Five* (Curtis & Cornell, 2004). The subtitle, *Learning How to Work My Control Panel*, leaves the children who are being read to with no doubt about the book's theme: self-control. This reminds me of earlier books in children's literature where the sole purpose was didactic. Children are expected to understand that this book is about self-control and how to gain it, because the message is explicitly shared throughout the entire book. Although it has been a best seller, I wonder what children think about the explicitness of the message; clearly, they know that whoever chose to read it to them is worried about their behavior. I suspect that it will not be one of their favorite books.

Children's novels, especially realistic fiction, are often grouped by theme: for example, survival, friendship, being different, growing up, and abandonment. *Wringer* (Spinelli, 1997) is about growing up, bullying, and conformity. In the dominant theme about growing up, Palmer, the main character is expected to wring the necks of pigeons when he turns 10. He does not want to do this but is conflicted between doing what is expected versus refusing. This issue is complicated, however, as Palmer befriends a pigeon that lives with him, unknown to his parents or friends. Certainly, this theme will provoke student discussion about right and wrong: from keeping a pigeon without parent consent to the act of wringing pigeons' necks. There are other subthemes in this book. Palmer has a best friend who is a girl; but he and his friends torment her. However, just as Palmer and his friends mistreat Dorothy, they are likewise the victims of bullying by an older child. Bullying is a frequent theme in children's literature, but in this book, it is complicated because Palmer is both the bully and the bullied.

In *No More Dead Dogs* (Korman, 2000), Wally, a hero on the school football team, has to write a book report about Old Shep, My Pal. Wally struggles with this report and writes a simple paragraph that is not accepted by his teacher. His teacher puts him on detention until his report is complete and acceptable, and until then he can no longer play football. Although most students would quickly write a report so they could get back to playing football, Wally doesn't. He winds up spending time with the drama club. The story's plot is engaging, and readers want to know what will happen to Wally. Moving beyond the plotline, children can consider what it means to be compliant with a teacher's requests and the consequences when they don't. Students can also consider what it's like to be someone who moves away from traditional cool activities like sports to participate in the drama club. They can talk about identity and the friendships triggered by Wally's experiences. They might also consider loyalty to a team and how Wally's behaviors affected the team. Within the story, destructive things happen to the drama club's props, and readers wonder who is doing this. These events lend themselves to another theme of trust. There is no way that students can read this book and not come away with interesting discussions focused on the main and supporting themes. It will be important to take time to talk informally about the book or to write about the thoughts the book triggers.

Returning to Avi's *Poppy*, when students discuss the theme in this book, they will first want to talk about obedience and when it is appropriate to move beyond complete obedience. The entire book focuses on Poppy and her breaking rules: first by going to Bannock Hill without permission and second by leaving home to check on the suitability of another without permission. I wondered why the first instance of leaving without permission was met with disdain by her father but the second instance was accepted, albeit unhappily. Why were these two events, both undertaken without permission, viewed differently? Within this theme, students might also explore overcoming fear as Poppy had to contain her fear, as she traveled to New House.

Although teachers want students to understand the thematic qualities of books, they are not always easy to discern. Additionally, teachers must be careful not to lead students to believe that every story is a fable, with lessons to be learned. Teachers, in providing time for conversation about the book when it is completed, open spaces for these more complex discussions, discussions that don't result in tidy endings. Rather, students explore similar themes in other reading and build connections from one reading event to another, deepening their understanding of multifaceted, complicated ideas.

STYLE

Style is the way the author arranges words, or how words are shared rather than their message. They can appeal to the senses, make readers afraid or calm, or help readers visualize a concept or situation (Lukens, 2007; Norton, 2007). Writers use word choice, images that appeal to the senses, metaphors, sounds of words, voice, and mood to create style (Temple et al., 2006).

Although all authors use words, some have a knack for choosing particularly interesting words to share details about characters, setting, or plot. Throughout *Old Mother Bear* (Miles, 2007), special words chosen with care illuminate the story. In the following examples, I have italicized the focus word:

> Overnight her *drowse* deepened. (unpaged)
>
> Every day, the cubs nursed, napped. Grew stronger, and *squabbled*. (unpaged)
>
> *Desperate*, she drew up tall and roared. (unpaged)

Each highlighted word provides information about details or emotions that support meaning, and the word is a perfect choice to help readers to clarify their understanding.

Creech in *Love That Dog* (2001) uses poetry in journal entries to share her narrative. For example, on October 10, Jack writes:

> What do you mean—
> Why does so much depend
> upon
> a blue car?
>
> You didn't say before
> that I had to tell why.
>
> The wheelbarrow guy
> didn't tell why. (p. 5)

Creech's word style reduces text to its key words as only poetic form can share.

Images that appeal to the senses are created by authors to enrich their narratives. For instance, in *The Good Little Bad Little Pig* (Brown, 2002), readers are provided with a rich visual image of the pig.

> He lived in a muddy old pigpen with four other little pigs and a mother sow. He was a little pink-and-white pig, but with mud all over him, he looked only partly pink. (unpaged)

Readers might even move beyond the physical description of the pig to sensing what it might feel like to live in mud, all oozy and yucky.

In *Who's Afraid of the Big Bad Book* (Child, 2002), readers experience the smells and tactile feelings associated with Herb, who eats as he reads. Child writes, "Herb reads his books everywhere. This was why many of the pages were stickily stuck together, soggy around the edges, and usually had bits of banana, cookie, and the odd pea squashed between the pages" (unpaged). I doubt Herb had many requests from friends to read his books; the visual image of his books is enough to put any reader off.

Metaphors and similes describe one thing in relation to another thing. Funke in *Inkheart* (2003) uses metaphors and similes throughout her book, for example,

> The night swallowed him up like a thieving fox. (p. 73)

Although many authors use metaphor or simile or specific words to enhance meaning, others use the sounds of words. For instance, in *Dooby Dooby Moo* (Cronin & Lewin, 2006), there is repetition of sounds for each animal. Farmer Brown is worried that his animals are planning something because they have done so in the past, so he listens to them at night. He hears,

> Dooby, dooby, moo . . . the cows snore.
> Fa la, la, la baaa . . . the sheep snore.
> Whacka, whacka quack . . . duck snores. (unpaged)

These sounds repeat throughout the book, even when the animals are not sleeping, and are fun to read.

Voice is the way the author shares his or her story in a formal to casual way. *John Henry* (Lester, 1994) has a casual style because Lester writes directly to his audience. He begins, "You have probably never heard of John Henry. Or maybe you heard about him but don't know the ins and outs of his comings and goings. Well, that's why I'm going to tell you about him" (unpaged). A more formal style appears in *A Wrinkle in Time* (L'Engle, 1962). The author begins, "In her attic bedroom Margaret Murry, wrapped in an old patchwork quilt, sat on the foot of her bed and watched the trees tossing in the frenzied lashing of the wind" (p. 3). Lester used more informal language like "I'm," "that's," and "don't," while L'Engle ruled her readers in with precise language and long sentence structures. Readers have different expectations for each narrative by the voice given to the narrator and characters.

Finally, mood is the "overall emotional feeling conveyed by the book—by what the characters say and do, the author's voice, what the book adds up to" (Temple et al., 2006, p. 59). The goal of the writer is to influence the reader's mood as they engage with the book. Immediately upon opening *Alexander and the Terrible, Horrible, No Good, Very Bad Day* (Viorst, 1972), readers knows that Alexander is angry. Viorst begins this book with:

> I went to sleep with gum in my mouth and now there's gum in my hair and when I got out of bed this morning I tripped on the skateboard and by mistake I dropped my sweater in the sink while the water was running and I could tell it was going to be a terrible, horrible, no good, very bad day. (unpaged)

Readers quickly emphasize with Alexander and perhaps connect to similar days they may have had and the angry feelings that resulted.

Anderson (2002) suggests using the following questions to help students determine an author's style:

- What kinds of words did the author choose to tell the story?
- Was there any distinctive words or sentence constructions? What mood did these words or sentences create?
- What effect does the author want to create? (p. 34)

Other questions that can focus students to an author's style are

- What images did you see, hear, or smell as you listened to the author's words?
- What sounds did the author use to enrich his or her story?

To facilitate appreciation of an author's style, a simple blank bookmark can be given to students as they begin a new book. During their reading, they can pause to jot down interesting or confusing words or phrases that stimulate their senses. When the book club convenes, students can share these words or text that triggered their emotions or senses. They might also record some of these words or images in a writer's notebook, where they can refer to them during their own writing. In this way, students can gain an appreciation for the writing craft of an author and can imitate this craftsmanship in their own writing.

Avi also used style when he wrote *Poppy*. Most of the story is crafted through conversation. Each character speaks in a unique way, thus offering insights about each personality. For instance, Ragweed sounds like this: "Well old lady, if them there porcupines are so huge, and we're so small, and if this dude owl has such amazing sight, how come he might confuse us mice with them there dude porcupines? Know what I'm saying?" (p. 14). Lungwort replies, "Ragweed, for your information proper grammatical usage is 'those porcupines,' not 'them there porcupines'" (p. 14). There is no doubt that Ragweed is a younger mouse who loves to talk informally, while Lungwort is older and quite proper. Avi is also quite precise in his word choice. For example, when Mr. Ocax is attacking Poppy, Avi writes, "Mr. Ocax, who had plummeted to a spot not far above and behind Poppy . . . " (p. 21). The word *plummeted* certainly provides a specific image of the flight of the owl. There are numerous times when Avi creates images that appeal to the senses. In one example, Poppy is gazing into the forest before she enters: "All she could make out was a great mass of dark trees. No wonder it was called dim, she thought and shuddered" (p. 16). Readers have a visual image of how dark and scary the trees are in this forest, and this image adds to the fear that is felt for Poppy.

POINT OF VIEW

Point of view is the way the author chooses to share his or her story. Who is sharing the story? Authors can choose to have a character be the teller (first-person narrative), have varying viewpoints where different characters tell the story, or have a narrator tell the story (third-person narrative; Anderson, 2002).

In *Pssst!* (Rex, 2007), a young girl is the teller of the story. The young girl leaves a subway station to visit the zoo. While there, the animals talk to her and tell her what they need: The gorilla wants a new tire and a javelina wants trash cans. Most of the story happens through dialogue between the girl and animals, so that readers understand her concerns and solutions.

Shannon uses David's mother as the narrator of *No, David!* (1998). Although the images are all of David and his antics, the mother's directives are the text of the book.

An interesting point of the illustrations is that the mother is never fully represented. This book would be particularly interesting to share with children on repeat occasions. During a first read, they would just enjoy it. On subsequent reading, teachers could focus student discussion to the way David and his mother are represented, in both text and illustration.

In *Do Not Open This Book!* (Muntean, 2006), the narrator is the main character, a pig, who talks directly to the reader. He begins, "Excuse me, but who do you think you are, opening this book when the cover clearly says DO NOT OPEN THIS BOOK!" (unpaged). Readers quickly discover that the text of this book includes direct conversation with the pig.

Unlike the previous stories, *The View from Saturday* (Konigsburg, 1996) has multiple narrators. The four students, Nadia, Ethan, Noah, and Julian, each share a part of the story about how they became the Souls and won the Academic Bowl. *Inkheart* (Funke, 2003) also has multiple narrators: including Meg, her father, and other characters. The use of multiple narrators allows readers to understand a single plot from several perspectives.

One way to help students appreciate different interpretations through the voices of various narrators is to have them write about a simple, familiar event in school, like forgetting homework, from several perspectives: as a student, as a parent, and as a teacher. Students enjoy this writing and quickly see how a story changes depending on who is telling it.

Third-person narrations allow readers to absorb the story without the emotional or intellectual connections that a character as narrator would share. In *Dear Juno* (Pak, 1999), the story of a young boy writing to his Korean grandmother is shared through the narrator's voice. The book begins, "Juno watched as the red and white blinking lights soared across the night sky like shooting stars, and waited as they disappeared into faraway places" (unpaged). *Frindle* (Clements, 1996) also begins with a narrator's voice, someone who appears to have been in Nick's class. Rather than someone reporting on events, this narrator, although unnamed, seems to have been there. The book begins, "If you asked the kids and the teachers at Lincoln Elementary School to make three lists—all the really bad kids, all the really smart kids, and all the really good kids—Nick Allen would not be on any of them. Nick deserved a list of his own, and everyone knew it" (p. 1). The narrator's voice in this book is more personable than the narrator in *Dear Juno*, who seems much more distant.

Exploring who the narrator is allows students to understand how the author positioned them as readers. For instance, in *Pssst!* readers participate with the main character, whereas in *Dear Juno* readers are observers. In books like *Do Not Open This Book*!, readers are essential as co-creators of the plot.

Returning to *Poppy*, Avi chose a third-person narrator as the teller of this story. The narrator began the story with a description of the night: "A thin crescent moon, high in the sky, shed faint white light over Dimwood Forest" (p. 1). Most chapters begin with a brief description of the setting to ground the readers in Poppy's current location and time of day. Avi used an interesting structure to tell this story in that the narrator provides the background and important details for the story, and characters' dialogue reveals emotions only each one could experience.

Throughout this chapter, the qualities of writing have been shared. This exploration allowed the readers to understand why some books are more appealing than others because of the author's careful crafting. After readers have had the opportunity to enjoy a book, they may similarly enjoy rereading to discover these qualities.

ENGAGING STUDENTS

1. *Anticipating the book through inspection of its cover.* Students often view a cover of a book to decide what it might be about and whether they want to read it. They can be asked to view a cover to determine which element of a book is being featured: plot, character, setting, theme, or mood. Based on its cover, the plot of *A Book* (Gerstein, 2009) appears to involve a menagerie of characters chasing a young girl, whereas in *Hook* (Young, 2009) an illustration of a bird takes up the entire cover. One can conclude that *A Book* will be filled with action, and *Hook* will focus on character. Students can view their book cover and then complete the form in Figure 5.6.

THE BOOK COVER

The book cover highlights this narrative element:

Plot   Character   Setting   Theme   Mood

This is why I think so:

What clues in the cover hint at what the book might be about?

FIGURE 5.6. Using a book cover to determine narrative elements.

2. *Graphing the plot.* Using a paper with blocks for graphing, students first identify each aspect of the plot. Typically, I have students record these aspects in sequential order and they are numbered. Then they can convert these elements to a chart, as in Figure 5.7. Graphing plot action allows students to visually see how the plot developed and was resolved.
3. *Note taking throughout reading.* After each reading episode, students add notes about reading guided by the headings shown in Figure 5.8. Following the completion of a book, students can use the note-taking sheet to provide details about a narrative element like character.
4. *Characters and social issues.* To extend a lesson on book characters, students can engage in discussion using the following questions:
   a. Gender
      - Are characters treated differently because of their gender? How do you know?
      - How are male and female characters portrayed?

   b. Race
      - Are characters treated differently because of their race? How do you know?

   c. Power
      - Which character or group of characters are the most powerful? How do you know?
      - How do the characters respond to the power structure shared in the book?

10					
9					
8					
7					
6					
5					
4					
3					
2					
1					
	Event 1	Event 2	Event 3	Event 4	Event 5

FIGURE 5.7. Graph of plot.

Story	Words or Phrases I Like
Details about Author	Author's Craft
Messages Shared in Story	Connections

FIGURE 5.8. Note-taking sheet.

At the end of this chapter, it is once again time to take a few moments to reflect:

1. Choose a favorite picturebook that you enjoy sharing with students. Read it again just to savor it. Now reread to focus on the following qualities:
   a. Plot
   b. Characters
   c. Setting
   d. Theme
   e. Style
   f. Point of view

   What did you discover?
2. Now repeat this process with a novel. What did you discover?
3. Choose two picturebooks about the same topic like friendship, getting over one's fears, or an adventure. Compare the qualities of text between these books. What new insights do you have about each book?

RECOMMENDED READING

For readers who would like to know about some of the qualities of text, I recommend the following books:

Lukens, R. (2007). *A critical handbook of children's literature* (8th ed.). Boston: Allyn & Bacon.

Unlike many other children's literature books, Lukens focuses on the quality of writing. She has full chapters on character, plot, theme, setting, point of view, style, and tone. Readers can more fully explore each of these characteristics.

Nikolajeva, M. (2005). *Aesthetic approaches to children's literature: An introduction*. Lanham, MD: Scarecrow Press.

Nikolajeva's book is a more theoretical look at the qualities of writing. She provides more thorough descriptions of each element and offers activities for students to apply this information.

Student Voices

Because of Winn-Dixie
(DiCamillo, 2000)

"*Because of Winn-Dixie* grabs my attention because there are a lot of interesting characters and things going on between them. The dialogue between the characters helps you understand their personalities. The different settings in the book help you visualize the action. I felt like I was a character in the book."—Macey, a fifth grader

CHAPTER 6

Exploring Qualities of Visual Representation

> Look at a child's face as you read an illustrated book to him. He is utterly lost in the picture, his mouth is open, his eyes are wide, it's as if his mind has left his body. It's as complete an immersion into a work of art, as a human being can ever hope for. It is pure seeing.
> —CHARLES ZORA, "Tumbling into Wonderland" (2008, p. 15)

Take a moment and read the above quote again and ponder the visual image stirred by the words. I'll wait. Thinking about that child's face as he or she is immersed in a narrative or informational picturebook acknowledges the importance of the image, the emotions and ideas stimulated just in its viewing. Viewers first notice the picturebook as a whole and gain a general appreciation of the artwork. Then they engage in looking at each image carefully, moving from one to another (Arizpe & Styles, 2003). Picturebooks, unique in their complementary use of art and text, are a child's first link to literacy and art.

Readers may be wondering why I spell picturebook as a compound word. In discussing the possible options for its spelling—picturebook as picture book, picture-book, or picturebook—Lewis (2001) argued for the compound spelling because it focused readers on appreciating the whole of the book rather than just each part. This argument resonated with me, and for this reason, I follow Lewis's preference.

When reading a picturebook, readers move from text to illustration or from illustration to text. Lewis writes that, as readers, "far from leaving behind the meaning or effect of one medium as we enter the other, we carry with us something like semantic traces that colour or inflect what we read and what we see" (p. 35). Moreover, "A picturebook story is never to be found in the words alone, nor in the pictures, but emerges out of their mutual interanimation" (p. 36). So a picturebook is a very impressive form of art that requires readers/viewers to have an understanding of textual and visual elements. Text requires readers to pay attention to the conventional signs in picturebooks that narrate and are linear (left to right and top to bottom), while images are complex, iconic signs that describe or present and are nonlinear (Nikolajeva, 2005).

Although teachers are often familiar with the textual elements of books, they are less familiar with the visual. Kiefer (1995) wrote that the picture part of a picturebook is often neglected, especially as it relates to visual literacy. She described this event:

> Children live in a highly complex visual world and are bombarded with visual stimuli more intensely than most preceding generations. Yet few teachers spend time helping children sort out, recognize, and understand the many forms of visual information they encounter, certainly not in the same way teachers deal with print literacy. (p. 10)

This chapter provides a foundation for teachers as they explore the visual aspects of picturebooks. Teachers will become familiar and comfortable with terminology and how to engage in visual interpretation with their students.

PRAGMATIC CONCERNS WITH ILLUSTRATION

The author/illustrator or illustrator alone has many choices and pragmatic issues to consider when creating the picture part of a picturebook. Often the text comes first, and the illustrator uses the words as a stimulus for the artwork (Nodelman, 1988; Robinson & Charles, 2008). In many cases, the publisher matches an illustrator with an author's work without one knowing the other, so although the picturebook results in a unified whole, each part is often created separately. When scanning picturebooks, check to see whether the author and illustrator are the same person or different people. You might also view numerous books by an author or illustrator to see whether they partner up for multiple picturebook creations. For instance, Eric Carle is always the illustrator and writer for his books, as are Allen Say, Anthony Browne, and Mo Willems. Molly Bang, a well-known illustrator, creates her own books where she is writer and illustrator and also illustrates for other writers, like Victoria Miles in *Old Mother Bear* (2007). Finally, there are author–illustrator partnerships like Jon Scieszka and Lane Smith (*The Stinky Cheese Man and Other Fairly Stupid Tales* [1992]) and Doreen Cronin and Betsy Lewin (*Dooby Dooby Moo* [2006]), who always work together.

There are numerous pragmatic issues related to illustration. First, if the words are printed in black, the art must stand in contrast so that it shows up when a child is being read to before bedtime in a low-lighted room. If the words are a lighter color, then contrast is also an issue, because the words have to be visible within the illustration. The size of the book is another consideration. Anthony Browne often uses large square shapes for his books, while other illustrators choose a rectangular shape, although it may be letter or landscape in orientation and larger or smaller. Typically, a picturebook has 32 pages, and the illustrator must decide which words are on each page so that the turning of a page heightens the readers' excitement (Sipe & Brightman, 2009). Robinson writes, "The placement of each page turn is crucial to the pacing and overall dramatic effect" (Robinson, 2008, p. 21). Nikolajeva and Scott (2001) suggest that the "pageturner in a picturebook corresponds to the notion of a cliffhanger in a novel" (p. 152).

Additionally, the illustrator has to decide on how initial single and end pages are constructed as well as double-page spreads. Double pages can be illustrated as one single vision or as two separate but related illustrations. Double-page spreads present a major challenge when used for a single illustration: Double-page artwork is not seamless because of the gutter, where the pages are bound together, and as a result eliminates some of the artwork. For instance, the artist may want a straight line running across the page, but the line may lose this when some of it is lost to the gutter. Moreover, most visual artists can focus their work on the center of a piece, but this focus is more difficult for picturebook artists because the artwork in the middle may be interrupted. When appreciating a beautiful picturebook, viewers should step back and consider the text, art, and design and how they are combined to create this work.

To help students appreciate the elements of a picturebook, teachers can conduct a picture walk, a familiar activity. In this picture walk, teachers explore the cover and front and back flaps and engage students in why different elements, like color, offer information about the book. From this discussion, students can talk about the front and back end pages and the title page, sharing what they discovered about the book from these pieces. Following this conversation, teachers and their students can view each illustration to note those that are constrained to a single page or part of a page and those that cover a full two pages. As they view these images, students can ponder how they contribute to the narrative or informational book.

ANATOMY OF A PICTUREBOOK

I just discussed some of the considerations that illustrators face before creating the art for a book. Each picturebook has an anatomy that, once learned, helps the viewer appreciate the subtleties of the art (Gamble & Yates, 2008). The following are the elements of a book, or its anatomy:

Book Shape and Opening Orientation

As previously described, the size and shape of the book are important and contribute to its overall appreciation. *Pat the Bunny* (Kunhardt, 1940) is almost square and small so that a young child can hold it. *Leonardo the Terrible Monster* (Willems, 2005) is an oversized rectangular shape, allowing ample space to illustrate the story of Leonardo and much empty space, which contributes to the telling. *Wabi Sabi* (Reibstein, 2008) has a more unusual opening orientation: Square in shape, it opens from bottom to top. Each page thus appears to be a scroll representing the artwork of Japan and provides the perfect backdrop for haiku poetry, which is part of the story.

The size of the book allows for different illustrator interpretations. Small books typically have subtle illustrations, similar to those created by Beatrix Potter for *Peter Rabbit*. Larger books allow for larger effects and more energy in the illustrations; for examples, see books by Dr. Seuss. Thus, something as simple as the size of a book sets expectations for readers and viewers (Nodelman, 1988).

After reading a book, teachers may focus their students to its shape and/or orientation. They can discuss how this structure connects and supports the text and illustrations within.

Endpapers

Endpapers appear in the hardback edition of a picturebook. In *Leonardo and the Terrible Monster*, the endpapers are brown and ground the story. In *Where the Wild Things Are* (Sendak, 1963/1988), the endpapers are the plants that appear in the land of the wild things and hint at the adventure within. Young, in *Wabi Sabi*, created different endpapers for the front and back. The front endpaper is dotted with brown watercolor as if it fell on the paper, almost showing the preparation for the art within. The final page is a collage that appears to be predominantly sand with a branch and a leaf and the paw prints of a cat, as though Wabi Sabi is embarking on a new adventure. Exploring the endpapers prepares readers for what lies within.

Borders

Jan Brett's artwork always includes intricate borders that extend the text and visual content on the page. For instance, in *The Mitten* (1989), the main illustration on one page shows a grandmother knitting a mitten; her conversation indicates that if you knit a white mitten, you could lose it in the snow. The border has the outline of a mitten with a wintery scene within. On other pages, the scene within the mitten in the border predicts the content of the next page.

In *Where the Wild Things Are*, Sendak used borders in very interesting ways to extend the meaning of his book. Early in the book the illustrations are framed in small boxes on each page; and as the action increases with each turn of the page, so do the sizes of the illustrated spaces, sometimes filling more than a single page. When Max reaches the land of the wild things—the height of action—the illustration covers a full two-page spread with no room for text. As the adventure wanes, illustrations become smaller and more contained. Illustrations that extend beyond a fixed space are described as *bleeding* over their boundaries.

Single- or Double-Page Illustrations

Picturebooks most often begin with a title page that is a single-page spread, and the first page of the story is often a single page. Illustrators then have two-page spreads until the end of the book, with a final single page for closing. Illustrators have many choices in how they use the two-page spreads. In *Old Mother Bear* (Miles, 2007), Bang created single illustrations that cover the entire page for most of the two-page spreads. Lewin, in *Dooby Dooby Moo* (Cronin & Lewin, 2006), used these pages in a variety of ways. For some, text is on one side with illustration on the other. A few pages have a single illustration covering both pages, with white as the background and the illustration appearing as a cutout, placed on top of the white. On other pages, two separate events are illustrated on one page and one event on the facing page. However, the illustrator carefully constructed each page to contribute to the reading and meaning gained from the picturebook.

Framing

A feature similar to borders, frames are used to separate illustrations on a page. Macaulay (1990), in *Black and White*, illustrated most pages with four separate but related illustrations and used black or white lines to frame each. Framing is especially evident in graphic picturebooks and novels where illustrations and text are contained within boxes or rectangles.

Gutter

The gutter is the book center where the pages are bound. It is most noticeable on double-page spreads that contain a single illustration covering both pages, and where, as mentioned earlier, a portion of artwork can be lost. In *Black and White*, the gutter was not problematic because there were four separate illustrations on each double-page spread. In *Old Mother Bear*, Bang circumvented this issue with her use of landscape. She purposely placed the focal point of her illustrations on either the right- or left-hand page, with grass, plants, or dirt filling the space near the gutter.

Text

Illustrators place text on a page, positioning it within or next to illustrations. In books like *The Stinky Cheese Man and Other Fairly Stupid Tales* (Scieszka & Smith, 1992), the text becomes part of the illustration as it is reformatted in size and font type. It is impossible to appreciate this book without also noticing the artistic representation of text. Similarly in *Princess Hyacinth: The Surprising Tale of a Girl Who Floated* (Heide & Smith, 2009), the text changes shape, color, and placement because it is an artistic element. When Princess Hyacinth is floating, the words float off the page. In other picturebooks, the text may appear to be separate from illustrations and not intertwined in any way. In these cases, the text complements the illustrations rather than being an artistic element in its own right.

Students are certainly expected to write narratives in elementary school. Sometimes they also support their narratives with illustration, an event seen more in the primary grades. However, rarely do students, especially in the intermediate grades, ponder how their text (format and font) can be an artistic element of their writing that supports meaning. As they prepare their narrative, students can play with the representation of text and illustration to convey meaning. Lane Smith's illustrations provide models for this activity, as do the illustrations in *Alphabeasties and Other Amazing Types* (Werner & Forss, 2009). Although *Alphabeasties* is an alphabet book, each page represents an object created with type; for example, an alligator created with the letter *A*. The book plays with different fonts and the emotions they can emit like a lazy *l* or a jolly *j*. Be forewarned, however: Students will spend long periods of time exploring this book, because each page is rich in detail with the placement of fonts. This book also provides a model for student imitation.

INTERPLAY OF TEXT AND ILLUSTRATION

When thinking about picturebooks, readers understand that the text and illustrations complement one another: Text may reveal parts of the story not shared in illustrations and vice versa. Illustrators have many choices in how they create their artwork for the textual aspect of a book. Golden (1990) and Nikolajeva (2005) identified some of the ways that illustrations and text pair up:

- *Symmetrical:* Text and illustrations tell the same story; they are redundant.
- *Complementary:* Text needs illustrations for clarification and illustration needs text to complete narrative.
- *Enhancing:* Illustration enhances the story.
- *Counterpointing:* Words and illustrations tell different stories. Both are critical to understanding.
- *Contradictory:* There is tension between text and illustration; often the story is ambiguous and open to multiple interpretations.

Although this list of categories is helpful, illustrators are always pushing to new, higher levels of ingenuity, when they create artwork for picturebooks. Careful viewers appreciate these novel ways to illustrate once they recognize more traditional matchups.

Teachers can explore the following books to note how illustration coordinates with text.

- Symmetrical: *The Dot* (Reynolds, 2003)
- Complementary: *Thump, Quack, Moo* (Cronin & Lewin, 2008)
- Enhancing: *All God's Critters* (Staines, 2009)
- Counterpointing: *How to Be a Good Dog* (Page, 2006)
- Contradictory: *Come Away from the Water, Shirley* (Burningham, 1977)

In this process of exploration, students will be surprised at what they discover about illustrations and text. Although they may have noticed these relationships before, they did not have the vocabulary to explain them fully.

ART MEDIA

Before the boom in electronic technology, picturebook illustrators were limited to using media that could easily be reproduced. Most illustrations were black and white drawings or woodcuts, and only a few included colors (Kiefer, 2007). In *Blueberries for Sal* (McCloskey, 1976), for example, most of the illustrations are black and white and a few have yellow and blue added. The addition of only just a few colors makes sense because the process of printing in color was both tedious and very expensive. Today, color processing can be done easily and inexpensively using computer programs. Computer programs can produce watercolors or pastels (Marcus, Curley, & Ward, 2007) and vivid colors, such as those in *Bad Kitty* (Bruel, 2005), where the colors are especially vibrant against the white background.

Although many illustrators describe their media techniques on the back book cover, when in doubt I visit their website to find this information. Tomie dePaola (*www.tomie.com*) is just one of many artists who share the details about their creative process on the website.

Illustrators may choose almost any media for the artistic work within a picturebook (Serafini & Giorgis, 2003). Some choices include:

- *Watercolor.* Watercolor often results in a softer effect. Peter Reynolds (2003) not only uses watercolor in *The Dot*, but he has the character Vashti, a young girl in an art class, use this media as well.
- *Crayon, colored pencil, and markers.* In *Hondo & Fabian*, McCarty (2002) used

pencil on watercolor paper to create his illustrations, resulting in a soft, muted effect. In *Chester*, Watt (2007) used watercolor, pencil, and markers for illustrations that are assembled digitally. Unlike the effect that McCarty rendered in *Hondo & Fabian*, the illustrations in *Chester* are brighter and have a layered effect.

- *Pastels*. Pastels are chalk that are oil or chalk based. Judy Schachner's (2003) images in *Skippyjon Jones* appear smudged, which is an effect from pastels. They allow for opaque and more translucent images.

- *Oils*. Some artists create paintings with oil paint that become the illustrations within books. Kadir Nelson paints his illustrations. In *Please, Puppy, Please* (Lee & Lee, 2005), each illustration is an oil painting showcasing two children and their puppy.

- *Woodcuts and scratchboard*. In *Snowflake Bentley* (Martin, 1998), Mary Azarian used woodcuts with watercolor. The use of woodcuts adds to the setting because it evokes a sense of the past. Beth Krommes, in the *House in the Night* (Swanson, 2008), used scratchboard and watercolor. Scratchboard is a technique where the artist starts with white cardboard and layers it with black wax, chalk, or ink. Then he or she uses a sharp tool to draw, cutting through to the white. The illustrations are various shades of black and white with gold tones throughout. Children will want time to explore these illustrations because their complexity is subtle.

- *Cut paper*. Many engineered books are created through imaginative uses of paper (see visual of *Trail* in Chapter 3). Other illustrators use paper in a two-dimensional format for their representations. In *The Paper Crane* (1985), Molly Bang created each illustration through cut paper that was photographed. The cover of her book shows the effect of this technique.

- *Collage*. Illustrators often use a collage technique, where different pieces of art or objects create a whole illustration. Mo Willems (2007) in *Knuffle Bunny Too* uses hand-drawn sketches and photographs for his artwork. Often his characters are in the foreground while a photograph is used for the background. For instance, when Trixie finds her bunny at the laundromat, there is a photo of clothes dryers in the background. Using a very different collage technique, Simms Taback, in *Joseph Had a Little Overcoat* (1999), chose watercolor, pencil, and ink and placed his pieces in a collage. Each piece stands out against its background as if it had been dropped on a canvas.

The list just presented is merely an overview of the media that illustrators might choose for their picturebook artwork; many other media choices and combinations are available, including computer-generated art using Photoshop or similar programs. This use of technology adds creative opportunities for illustrators.

Readers who want to become more expert at viewing might explore the Caldecott Medal winners, books that have been honored for their exemplary artwork. The list of winners appears at the American Library Association website (*www.ala.org*). After this initial review, viewers may want to visit individual artists websites. Figure 6.1 is a partial list of these websites.

Illustrator	Website	Comments
Portfolio of Illustrators	*www.childrensillustrators.com*	I love this site because it features illustrators, so you can see a variety of one illustrator's work. The style and medium gallery allows viewers to see the differences in each medium.
Portfolio of Illustrators	*www.readingrockets.org*	Among the many valuable resources at this site are video interviews with illustrators.
Portfolio of Illustrators	*www.childrenslit.com*	This site provides links to numerous authors and illustrators.
Molly Bang	*www.mollybang.com*	Bang provides details about many of her books.
Jan Brett	*www.janbrett.com*	Brett's site offers videos showing how she gets her ideas and how she draws her illustrations.
Eric Carle	*www.eric-carle.com*	Carle shows how he paints tissue paper and uses it in his illustrations. Viewers can see him creating his collages.
Lauren Child	*www.milkmonitor.com*	Viewers can see images of Child and her characters and learn how she created the illustrations for *Princess and the Pea*.
Gail Gibbons	*www.gailgibbons.com*	Visitors can learn about the author's informational books and view some of the original artwork. Visitors can also learn about making maple syrup.
Ian Falconer	*www.oliviathepiglet.com*	Falconer shares information about his creation of Olivia, sets and costumes, and his *New Yorker* magazine covers.

(cont.)

FIGURE 6.1. Illustrator website information.

Illustrator	Website	Comments
Steve Jenkins	*www.stevejenkinsbooks.com*	Jenkins shares information about his informational books and his process of making books, which includes an interesting video.
Ezra Jack Keats	*www.lib.usm.edu/~degrum/keats/main.html*	Viewers can see how Keats created many of his picturebooks. There are even dummy layouts to view.
Steven Kellogg	*www.stevenkellogg.com*	Kellogg shares his favorite characters.
Dav Pilkey	*www.pilkey.com*	Not surprisingly, Pilkey has many activities at his site. At the Boring Grown Up stuff page, visitors can see the cat that was the inspiration for his books.
Patricia Polacco	*www.patriciapolacco.com*	Polacco provides details about her illustrations.
Allen Say	*www.houghtonmifflinbooks.com/authors/allensay*	Visitors can listen to an interview by Say and learn about him and background information about many of his books.
Brian Selznick	*www.theinventionofhugocabret.com*	Visitors will enjoy watching the opening illustrations and seeing the models for the characters in the book. Selznick also shares the slides he used for his research.
Seymour Simon	*www.seymoursimon.com*	Simon presents many of his books and offers his list of highly recommended science Internet sites.
Lane Smith	*www.lanesmithbooks.com*	Visitors will enjoy the video of Smith and Willems creating a mural and can also view sketches and their final product.
Chris Van Allsburg	*www.chrisvanallsburg.com*	Visitors will be enthralled listening to the interviews about many of the books that Van Allsburg has written and illustrated.
David Wiesner	*www.houghtonmifflinbooks.com/authors/wiesner/home.html*	Wiesner shares many details about each of his books. Visitors will especially enjoy the thumbnail sketches and dummies used for *Tuesday*. Visitors can also see how these rough drawings turned into the final watercolor paintings.
Mo Willems	*www.pigeonpresents.com*	Willems shares details from all of his books. At Grown-Up Stuff, visitors can watch interviews and see him working in his studio.

FIGURE 6.1. *(cont.)*

Often, when thinking about illustrators, readers ponder individual names, even those shared in Figure 6.1. However, when I read *Pass It Down* (Marcus, 2007b), I discovered families of illustrators. For instance, Donald Crews, his wife Ann Jonas, and their daughter Nina Crews are all illustrators. When reading about this family, I learned that Donald Crews created the movement of the trains in *Freight Train* (1978) using an airbrush, similar to what manicure technicians use to paint nails. There are stories of how these families of illustrators learn from each other and sometimes collaborate. Other illustrator families are the Hurds, Myers, Pinkneys, and Rockwells. Children may want to explore the similarity and differences created by each member of an illustrator family in their artistic representations in picturebooks.

Knowing about an illustrator and his or her favorite artistic techniques offers students the opportunity to create in a similar style. During a lesson focusing on an illustrator, students can be asked to respond to the artwork within a book by creating a similar illustration. For example, students can identify a character from a narrative they have read and then use the medium used by the illustrator for their artistic response featuring the character. They can then add words that describe this person or animal.

ARTISTIC REPRESENTATIONS

Like writers who use literary genres for their writing, illustrators draw from artistic traditions for their work. Teachers may need to remember past art classes or recent trips to museums to help with artistic representations. Teachers with limited knowledge about artistic styles may want to begin this exploration with *Willy's Pictures* (Browne, 2000c). This book has Willy sharing many of his favorite paintings. On each page, Browne creates a painting with images from famous paintings. At the end of the book, Browne shares the original paintings and a brief description of each. This book will stimulate students to further explore artwork and the styles used by artists. It is also a comfortable beginning book for teachers to use when they first explore artistic styles.

Although there are many specific artistic traditions noted among artists, I share only a few major ones for teachers to review: realism, impressionism, expressionism, surrealism, folk art, and cartoon art.

In *realism*, a style often easy to recognize, the artist represents things as they appear (Kiefer, 2007). The works of Norman Rockwell are notable examples.

Although Anthony Browne uses many styles in his work, his illustrations also include realistic detail. His representations of the gorilla in *Little Beauty* (2008) are filled with accurate details. The cover of this book shares much of the detail used for the gorilla and kitten. On close examination, readers can see the lines from the gorilla's nostrils to his mouth, details surrounding his eyes, and the detailed representation of his fur. They may want to reach out and touch his fur, it appears so realistic.

In informational books like *Deserts* (Simon, 1990), the illustrator uses photos or illustrations that are as realistic as possible. Simon used photos, black line drawings, and paintings to represent the desert accurately.

Unlike realism, *impressionism* evokes an emotional response among viewers with its interpretation of the beauty of a constantly changing world (Nodelman, 1988). Artists who worked in Paris in the late 1990s were leaders of this style (Kiefer, 2007). Works by Paul Cézanne, Edgar Degas, and Claude Monet are representative. These artists used broad and visible brush strokes and emphasized light and its ability to show movement (*www.ibiblio.org/wm/paint/glo/impressionism/*).

A children's book that uses an impressionist style is *Lon Po Po* (Young, 1989). The illustrator's images are emotional, and he uses large brush strokes with an emphasis on light. His style in many illustrations appears similar to that of Monet.

Unlike the often subtle, muted colors used in impressionism, *expressionism* includes shockingly bright colors and images that may be out of proportion (Kiefer, 2007). For instance, a child may appear larger than the wall behind him or her. The works of Gauguin, Bosch, Modigliani, and Van Gogh are representative (*www.ibiblio.org/wm/paint/glo/expressionism*).

dePaola (1991) offers a perfect book to explore expressionist painters. In *Bonjour, Mr. Satie*, Mr. Satie takes his niece and nephew to Paris. While there, they study the work of Picasso and Matisse. The book is filled with replicas of many of these artists' paintings. Another example of this style is seen in *When Sophie Gets Angry—Really, Really Angry* (Bang, 1999). Bang uses bright, almost iridescent, colors, with images often outlined in red or purple. She also manipulates size, with Sophie appearing disproportional in size—either larger or smaller—to other objects near her.

Surrealism includes unusual images placed together, sometimes appearing as dream images (Kiefer, 2007). Artists like Magritte, Chagall, and Miró are representative (*www.artlex.com/ArtLex/s/surrealism.html*).

I believe that Anthony Browne is an illustrator who is most consistent in his use of surrealism. His books often have interesting, yet confusing images. For example, in *Voices in the Park* (1998), a viewer notices trees that change seasons and also turn into flames, clouds that change shapes, paintings like *Mona Lisa*, and images of Santa Claus and Romeo and Juliet. These images support open-ended understandings of this book, and it is often difficult to reconcile an illustration and its connections to text.

Two other examples are *The Dangerous Alphabet* (Gaiman, 2008a) where somewhat realistic images appear with supernatural images as though they belong together. For instance, one page shows floating eyeballs, creatures fishing, children trying to gain candy from weird adults, and a bird standing guard over her nest. In *My Name Is Yoon* (Recorvits, 2003), Swiatkowska includes unusual perspectives, for example, an illustration viewed through a doorway. Similar to other surrealistic styles, there are bizarre images within pictures; for instance, when viewing the teacher and classroom, there are three cats on the chalkboard where the word *cat* is written.

Folk art is known as the art of the common person because it often lacks conventions like perspective (Kiefer, 2007) and is considered to be "pleasant and harmless" (Nodelman, 1988, p. 88). The work of Grandma Moses is representative of this style (*www.artlex.com/ArtLex/f/folkart.html*).

The folk art style always calls to my mind dePaola's work, because it typically has many folk art qualities. dePaola uses repeated motifs, like hearts that resemble shapes appliquéd in quilts. He also outlines most of his images with black, resulting in a flat appearance. His style is easily recognized because he uses it consistently in his books. The cover of *The Art Lesson* (1997) is representative.

Cartoon art is art framed as a cartoon and drawn in the style of cartoons, with black outlined images and watercolor overlays (Kiefer, 2007). Many current picturebook illustrators are using cartoon art for illustration. In *There's a Wolf at the Door* (Alley, 2008), each fairytale involving wolves is retold using a cartoon strip format. Each frame leads to the next to move the story along. Rex, in *Pssst!* (2007), uses a comic book style for one page of the two-page spreads. The complementary page is a full-page illustration. The whole-page illustration serves as a transition to the story shared within the comic frames.

Each style chosen by an illustrator contributes to the visual meaning attached to the story. Students and teachers can evaluate the style and how it contributes to meaning. Through this exploration, they also learn about styles in art outside of picturebooks. To extend this study, students can record the titles of books they have read or heard on a chart or in a notebook organized by the artistic style. Once a category like impressionism has several book examples, students can discuss what they notice about impressionism across these books. Once they have created a list of characteristics, they can illustrate one of their narratives in an impressionistic style. This activity can be repeated with other artistic styles

ARTISTIC ELEMENTS

Artists, like writers, begin with a blank piece of paper or a blank screen on the computer. They know the story's narrative or informational book's text, and now it is time to create the illustrations. Similar to writers, artists have a variety of artistic elements that can be utilized for illustration. Although artists have many decisions to make in creating their artwork, some of the most fundamental include line, shape, color, texture, and perspective.

Line

Line is just that—line—and can be vertical, horizontal, diagonal, circular, wavy, thin, thick, or chaotic (Doonan, 1992; Serafini & Giorgis, 2003). Each of these types results in different interpretations. For example, wavy lines can represent continuous movement (Lewis, 2001). The following are other possible interpretations of line type:

- Horizontal—peace
- Vertical—stability
- Diagonal—movement
- Circular—safety
- Chaotic—frenzy
- Thin—fragile
- Thick—emphasis (Serafini & Giorgis, 2003).

Viewers can see on the cover of *Dawn* (2002), for example, that Bang has used a strong vertical line for the boat's mast and diagonal lines for the sail and frame. The horizon is marked with a subtle blue, shaded line. The viewer gains a calm, stable feeling from the composition of the lines within this illustration.

A fun activity to facilitate students' understanding of line combines construction paper and color. Students are given two sheets of construction paper of different colors. One sheet serves as the background and the other is cut into both thick and thin lines. Students create calm, fragile, or active illustrations just by placing the lines or folding them on the background sheet. When their artwork is complete, students share the qualities of line that resulted in an emotion. From this experience, students are ready to consider how an illustrator used line within a book.

Shape

When illustrators connect lines, they create shapes. Like line, different shapes and their positions can create emotional responses. Shapes with sharp edges create tension or movement, circular shapes are calmer (Kiefer, 2007).

Molly Bang in *Picture This* (2000) helps viewers understand the importance of shape and its placement. She starts with a red triangle and shows how this shape represents Little Red Riding Hood. She then attempts to represent her mother using a larger, red triangle. She explains that when she does this the mother becomes a more important character based on size, so she reconfigures the mother to be an amorphous circular shape. She continues to build her illustration by including trees that are black and triangular shaped; she dismisses this shape and replaces it with vertical, varied-width rectangles. Now the small triangle for Little Red Riding Hood can hide behind them. Bang continues this process until she creates an illustration with a very scary wolf represented solely by shape.

Bang (2000) shares her principles related to shape:

1. Smooth, flat, horizontal shapes provide stability and calm. She compares these to the floor, sea, or prairie (p. 42).
2. Vertical shapes are active and are opposed to gravity. They reach to the skies. "Vertical structures are monuments to kinetic energy of the past and the future, and to potential energy of the present" (p. 44).
3. Diagonal shapes imply motion or tension. She highlights that triangles placed on a flat base indicate stability while a triangle placed on point indicates movement.
4. Shapes placed in the upper part of an illustration indicate freedom or happiness.
5. Shapes in the bottom half of the picture are heavier, sadder, and constrained. They are also more grounded (p. 56).
6. The center of the page is the "center of attention" (p. 62). A viewer's eyes are drawn to the center, and then he or she takes in the surrounding illustration.
7. Viewers feel more comfortable looking at rounded shapes and are anxious when viewing pointed shapes.
8. The larger the object, the stronger it appears.

When observing the cover of *Kitten's First Full Moon* (Henkes, 2004), the viewer can see Bang's principles in action. There is a sense of calm as the viewer's eyes first settle on the kitten in the middle of the illustration. From this point, the viewer can move downward and notice a field of flowers, all created with circular lines and shapes, continuing the calm feeling. The viewer then might move up and consider that the kitten is resting in a full circle, the moon, completing the calm, quiet emotional response to this illustration.

Shape is great fun to explore with students, and many projects complement this lesson. One in particular is especially engaging. For this project, each student needs two sheets of construction paper, white and other colors, that will serve as backgrounds; three sheets of construction paper—one black and two of varying colors—that they will cut; and a scissors. Similar to Bang's placement of shapes, students will create an illustration for *The Three Pigs* just using shape and color. Students cut thick and thin rectangles from the black construction paper and place the rectangles on their white background sheet to create a calm or scary forest. They then repeat this process with their other colored construction paper as a background. Once they decide on a favorite, they are ready to add shapes to represent the pigs and the wolf. Teachers can encourage students to play with shape sizes, the shape chosen, and placement. Students then explore which shape, size, color, and placement best reflect their vision of a scary wolf in relation to their rendering of the pigs. Most students will be excited to give the wolf scary teeth. Students who are seated in small groups or with a partner will learn from others as they assess the progress of their projects.

Color

Color draws the viewer in and establishes the mood for the text. It is the strongest of any element that an artist might use (Bang, 2000). Artists can use a limited palette, as shown in Henkes's (2004) *Kitten's First Full Moon*. Although it appears that Henkes just used shades of white, gray, and black, he separated his colors into magenta, cyan, blue, and black. When the book was printed in color, it gave his black, gray, and white images an increased feeling of warmth (Kiefer, 2008).

Other color choices that are well known to artists include complementary colors (colors opposite each other on the color wheel), analogous colors (colors next to each other on the color wheel), and tertiary colors (colors created by mixing two secondary colors, e.g., green and purple; Serafini & Giorgis, 2003). Colors are also sorted into warm (yellow or orange) and cool color (blue or green) palettes.

Bang (2000) shares a few expectations for color:

- White backgrounds feel safer than dark backgrounds. Because humans cannot see well in the dark, the dark often represents danger (p. 68).
- Red is a color that excites the viewer. It is often associated with blood and fire.
- White is associated with light and snow.
- Black is associated with darkness.
- Yellow is associated with the sun.
- Blue is associated with the sea and sky.
- Viewers associate similar colors more strongly than similar shapes. For example, the viewer associates the wolf's eye and Red Riding Hood's cloak because they are red (p. 76).

Serafini and Giorgis (2003, pp. 23–24) provide additional thoughts about color:

- Red is an attention-getting color that can signify excitement and happiness or danger and courage.
- Yellow is the color of the sunshine, which makes it a happy color.
- Blue is a restful color. It can convey calmness and tranquility. It can also indicate coldness and sometimes sadness.
- Green is a color we associate with nature. It is sometimes viewed as a restful color.

- Orange is often associated with the fall season. It is a warm and cheerful color.
- Purple is a mixture of blue and red and is linked with royalty. It can be viewed as a color that suggests power and importance.

When considering the emotional effects of color, it is important to remember that there are cultural as well as gender, age, and geographic differences in how color is interpreted. For example, most boys will not choose pink as a favorite color and often see it solely as a girls' color. Culturally, red is worn by brides in the eastern hemispheres and is a color of mourning in South Africa. Colors take on different meanings based on geography and/or culture (Kiefer, 2010).

In addition to thinking about color as a single classification, colors can be modified by artists through hue, tone, and saturation. *Hue* refers to the different colors on a color wheel and how one can distinguish one from the other. For example, green is differentiated from red or blue, although the differences can get blurry when black, white, or other colors are added. *Tone* refers to brightness or darkness of a color. An artist typically creates tone through the addition of black or white paint. Finally, *saturation* refers to the intensity of a color. Primary colors, without the addition of black or white, are radiant with intensity (Sipe, 2008).

Two books that demonstrate the power of color are *My Friend Rabbit* (Rohmann, 2002) and *Free Fall* (Wiesner, 1988/2008). Rohmann uses red, yellow, and blue—primary colors—for his cover. His use of line indicates action and his color choice parallels this. In contrast, Wiesner uses muted colors. The viewer guesses that his book is a dream sequence through the use of green for the ocean with a light brown leaf on which the boy travels. Each artist has used color in important ways to suggest meaning to viewers and readers.

Color is always a delight for students to explore. One way to easily do this is to have students create a simple drawing using black marker or black crayon only. When their drawing is complete, photocopy it so each student has three copies. Then students select three color palettes: one soft with muted colors, one vibrant with primary colors, and one dark with only dark shades. Students provide color for each copy of their drawings based on the palettes described. When complete, students discuss the different moods created through the use of different color palettes and the same drawing.

Texture

Texture represents the artist's craft in making an image appear soft, hard, rough, or smooth. Anthony Browne in *Willy the Dreamer* (1997) offers the viewer many textures to consider. The clouds appear soft and translucent. Willy has smooth hair that is neatly combed. You can almost feel the gel he has used. He has a sweater that appears to

be knitted and somewhat rough. His pants look like corduroy and have a grooved texture. The chair that he is sleeping in has two textures, one soft and one hard. The top of the chair seems to be upholstered in soft fabric while the bottom of the chair looks like stone that is rough. These textured effects stimulate the viewer's curiosity. For example, why is his chair constructed in this way? Why would a stone chair be able to fly? Does the construction of the chair have anything to do with the narrative?

Texture is an element that is often missing in student drawing. They draw and then fill in a shape. Students can take one of the images they plan on using to illustrate one of their written projects. Once the illustration is complete, they can use a black marker to add texture. Don't be surprised if they get carried away on this first venture. As students explore texture in more illustrations and play with it in their own work, they will become more accomplished.

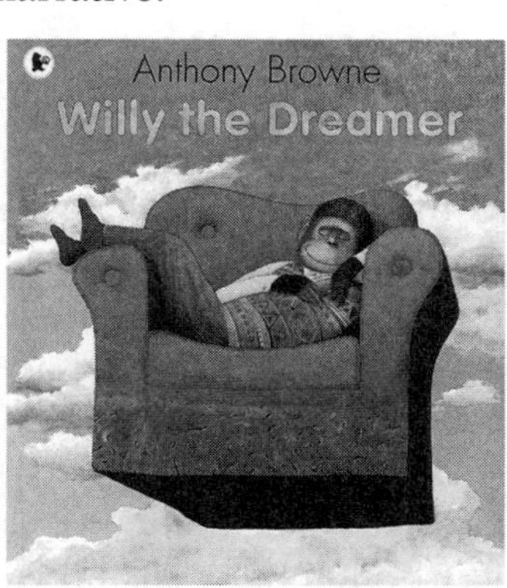

Perspective

Perspective is the way the illustrator positions his or her work for the viewer. For instance, a character can look at you directly or be looking at something or someone else. The character can be close to you or placed in the background of the illustration. Following are a few ways that artists can use perspective:

- *Bird's eye view.* The viewer looks down, as if he or she was flying over the illustration.
- *Worm's eye view.* The viewer is looking up at the illustration (see *Willy the Dreamer*).
- *Foreground.* Images appear in the bottom third of an illustration for emphasis (see *My Friend Rabbit*).
- *Middle ground.* The image appears in the middle of an illustration (see *Free Fall*).
- *Background.* The image appears in the top third of the illustration and appears to be in the distance (Serafini & Giorgis, 2003).

Kress and vanLeeuwen (1996) offer two interesting ways to think about the way a character interacts with the viewer. Characters who look directly at viewers (see *Skippyjon Jones or Wabi Sabi*) prod them to respond. This approach of looking directly at the viewer is known as *demand*, because it demands a response. Counter to this explicitness, is *offer*, in which the character looks at another character or image (see *Little Beauty* or *My Friend Rabbit*). Lewis (2001) suggests that when the character is positioned as offer, the story is straightforward, and the narrative remains as imaginary. However, "the moment that a participant turns to face the reader then the narrative spell is broken and the boundary separating (imaginary) characters from (real) is breached" (p. 157).

Most students position their artwork in the middle ground on each page. They are unaware that there are many choices regarding placement and perspective. This is another artistic element that students can play with for their illustrations. Perhaps the easiest place to begin is with offer or demand. They may want a character to beg for help from a reader or participate in a joke. Following this experience, they are ready to look at the position of the illustration and experiment using a bird's eye view or a worm's eye view.

Robinson (2008) proposes, "Each book is a performance waiting to happen, like musical notes written on a page but not yet played" (p. 21). However, the image within picturebooks may never be played if teachers are not as familiar with artistic elements as they are with narrative elements. To fully appreciate a picturebook, both must be explored. Starting with just one of the elements shared previously is a good way to begin this exploration. As a teacher, you may choose artistic traditions and explore picturebooks through the styles used by illustrators. I am guessing that style may not be where you want to begin unless you have an interest in art. Instead, you may choose color and study the effects of varied use of color on the viewer. Perhaps color seems too complex; line and shape may be the best place for you. It really doesn't matter where you begin; just beginning opens up entirely new interpretations of picturebooks, interpretations that you can discover simultaneously with your students.

POSTMODERN PICTUREBOOKS

Okay, so you thought the artistic part of picturebooks was an innovative way to consider them and to extend meaning past the text part. You may even be planning how to begin now that you have recognized the visual possibilities. Maybe you will have students explore the color palette used by illustrators. I am guessing you are thinking of starting with picturebooks that are familiar to you or with an illustrator whom you appreciate. All of this planning is sounding good, and I know you are excited to begin. I also know that once you begin engaging students in visual exploration, you will want to extend your initial forays, just as you moved students from literal to inferential and critical comprehension. To help support you in these more complex journeys, I share postmodern picturebooks, picturebooks that push traditional understandings of the visual and textual aspects (Goldstone, 2001/2002; Pantaleo, 2004).

Postmodern picturebooks are the result of illustrators and authors experimenting with form, structure, and tradition (Pantaleo, 2007). In postmodern picturebooks, "authors and illustrators work against a linear story-telling pattern" (Wolfenbarger & Sipe, 2007, p. 275). Authors and illustrators ask readers to create the story with them, often moving through various time and space sequences in a narrative rather than simply from beginning to end. To accomplish this task, authors and illustrators use four elements: nonlinearity, self-referential text, sarcastic tone, and an antiauthority attitude (Wolfenbarger & Sipe, 2007).

Nonlinearity implies that the text does not have the traditional beginning, middle, and end. The story can move backward and forward. Wolfenbarger and Sipe (2007) describe nonlinearity in this way:

> This orientation to the page of a postmodern picturebook is like watching children playing on various pieces of playground equipment while also being aware that others are chasing around or playing kickball in another part of the space. All are contained by the boundaries of the playground, and all are playing—some children knowing other children and the other games they are playing—but not everyone knows the "inner life" or connected stories that are sure to be moving through the children's lives. The reader, author, and illustrator, like playground directors, have to move more closely into the "play space" to understand patterns and purposes for the player's moves. (p. 275)

Macaulay's *Black and White* (1990) is a classic example of nonlinearity. Readers have to decide whether to read all four stories simultaneously—follow one story strand, or to move between the four and determine how they are connected. This book requires multiple readings where readers participate in a multitude of reading possibilities.

Chester's Back (Watt, 2008) begins with "A long time ago, in a faraway land, lived a cat named Chester" (unpaged). Readers are familiar with this beginning and the illustration matches it. On the next page, the text repeats; however, the images are complicated with a crown and jester's hat flying, among other things, and the tail of Chester in the corner. Readers immediately recognize that this is not a traditional story. The author/illustrator and main character, Chester, are changing it from page to page. The cover of this book sets up this expectation, because Chester appears with his marker and star badge that announces him as star author, but viewers must be able to interpret the illustrations to understand this relationship.

Self-referential text shows the book being created as it is read (Wolfenbarger & Sipe, 2007). This format positions readers to be active, and not get lost in the narrative (Goldstone, 2001/2002). In *A Book* (Gerstein, 2009), readers first meet a young girl on the front flap asking what her story is. The book opens with each member of the family eating breakfast and getting ready for their day. Even the young girl's brother sets off to learn to be an astronaut. The girl, however, concerned about her own story, sets off and meets a goose, who helps her find a story. On one page, the goose tells the girl, "Oh, you'd better find it. Readers like a good story, else they close the book you know." The girl asks, "What are readers?" The goose replies that she should look up and she will see readers. She looks directly at the readers and is frightened by their faces. The readers clearly know that they are participants in this story. The characters in the book force this participation throughout. At the end of the book, the girl even tells the readers to close the book as it is time for bed.

In *Who's Afraid of the Big Bad Book?*, Child (2002) writes about Herb, who loves storybooks, although he mainly looks at the pictures. Herb falls asleep and finds himself in the middle of the story of Goldilocks. This Goldilocks is no sweet little girl, though; she yells at Herb for being in her story. For example, she says to him and the three bears, "In case you pea brains have forgotten, this story is called Goldilocks and The Three Bears not The Little Show-Off in Pajamas has Breakfast!" (unpaged). The book continues with Herb entering other fairytales. The illustrations match this text but include unconventional elements, like princesses who are contemporary and using phones, not typically seen in fairytales. Text moves around pages and on some is upside down. Some double-spread pages open to four pages, revealing highly detailed illustrations, such as a royal ball. Child adds intricate details to make her story real and engaging, for example, a ball gown made of real fabric, a window scene that is an actual photo, and "real" hair on a prince or princess. The entire book is complex and requires multiple readings, because the illustrations and text are not straightforward.

Sarcastic tone is common in postmodern picturebooks (Goldstone, 2001/2002). I shared an example in the way Goldilocks talked to Herb and the three bears in *Who's Afraid of the Big Bad Book?* and in the way the main character in *Do Not Open This Book* confronts readers.

Before the fables begin in *Squids Will Be Squids* (Scieszka & Smith, 1998), readers are told, "Because even thousands of years ago people were bright enough to figure out that you could gossip about anybody—as long as you changed their name to something like 'lion' or 'mouse' or 'donkey' first" (unpaged). Later in the foreword, readers discover that within this book "are beastly fables with fresh morals about all kinds of bossy, sneaky, funny, annoying, dim-bulb people. But nobody I know personally" (unpaged). The entire book, including illustrations and text, is sarcastic and incredibly funny.

Antiauthority attitude implies that transactions among the readers, author, illustrator, and text are not straightforward. Goldstone writes (2001/2002):

> In these new books the reader must cobuild the framework, supplying missing features of the story structure and pulling together discrete narrative strands. The reader not only enriches and supports the storyline by infusing personal emotions and experiences but also actively creates parts of the narrative. (p. 366)

In *The Stinky Cheese Man and Other Fairly Stupid Tales* (1992), Scieszka and Smith have Jack, the narrator, talk to readers and give orders on what to do. For example, in the introduction, Jack writes, "You should definitely go read the stories now, because the rest of this introduction just kind of goes on and on and doesn't really say anything" (unpaged). Rather than having Scieszka and Smith write the introduction, Jack from Up the Hill in the Fairy Tale Forest barks directions and, in so doing, is critical of the introduction's content.

Jack, the narrator, criticizes fairytales throughout the book. In "Little Red Running Shorts," he argues that after he has told the tale, it has to start with "Once upon a time." Then he argues with Little Red Running Shorts about the length of the story, saying it needs to be three pages long. Little Red Running Shorts and the wolf leave, and Jack wonders what will happen when the page is turned. The result is a blank page with the Little Red Hen questioning why and concerned that it was part of her story. Each story is related and requires readers to remember the original tale, appreciate the variant, and interweave all of the stories into one grand narrative.

Sipe and McGuire (2008) and Pantaleo and Sipe (2008) note six other major characteristics of postmodern picturebooks:

1. *Blurring*—The distinctions between popular and high culture, genres, and boundaries among author/illustrator, narrator, and reader/viewer are vague.
2. *Subversion*—Literary traditions and conventions are undermined by challenging a story's boundary with the real world.
3. *Intertextuality*—References to other texts are explicit. Characters from a variety of stories may be included within a single narrative.
4. *Multiplicity of meaning*—There is high ambiguity throughout a narrative, and often there are open-ended conclusions.
5. *Playfulness*—Readers are invited to play and participate within the narrative.
6. *Self-referentiality*—Readers cannot just be immersed in the narrative, they must participate in it.

Postmodern picturebooks require readers who have had experience with traditional picturebooks. For example, readers have to know about traditional covers and endpages to appreciate when they are modified (Sipe & McGuire, 2008). How could readers appreciate the front flap in *The Stinky Cheese Man and Other Fairly Stupid Tales*, where Jack advertises that it is "New! Improved! Funny! Good! Buy! Now!," if they were not familiar with traditional story overview cover flaps? Young readers also have had to have experience with the traditional tales of *Red Riding Hood, Cinderella, The Three Pigs*, and so on to appreciate when they appear in a postmodern picturebook. For example, in *Beware of the Storybook Wolves* (Child, 2006), readers encounter the evil fairy from *Sleeping Beauty*, the wolf from *Little Red Riding Hood*, and the fairy godmother from *Cinderella*. If children are not aware that these characters come from different stories, they cannot appreciate their co-appearance in this narrative.

To begin this process of exploration of postmodern picturebooks, Figure 6.2 shares a few titles to start your search.

You may also want to include *Seen Art?* (Scieszka & Smith, 2005) as a vehicle that connects the visual, artistic traditions in a postmodern picturebook. In this book, a young boy visits the Museum of Modern

Name of Book	Author (year)
The Jolly Postman or Other People's Letters	Janet Ahlberg & Allan Ahlberg (1986)
There's a Wolf at the Door	Zoe Alley (2008).
Voices in the Park	Anthony Browne (1998)
Into the Forest	Anthony Browne (2004)
Who's Afraid of the Big Bad Book?	Lauren Child (2002)
Beware of the Storybook Wolves	Lauren Child (2006)
The Dangerous Alphabet	Neil Gaiman (2008a)
Black and White	David Macaulay (1990)
Snowflake Bentley	Jacqueline Briggs Martin (1998)
The Stinky Cheese Man and Other Fairly Stupid Tales	Jon Scieszka & Lane Smith (1992)
Squids Will Be Squids	Jon Scieszka & Lane Smith (1998)
Bad Day at Riverbend	Chris Van Allsburg (1995)
Chester	Melanie Watt (2007)
Chester's Back	Melanie Watt (2008)
The Three Pigs	David Wiesner (2001)

FIGURE 6.2. Postmodern picturebooks.

Art in New York looking for his friend, Art. He travels through the entire museum looking for Art, along the way considering the art and what is art. Similar to dePaola's books, there are artistic renderings along the way. In the tradition of Anthony Browne, the book ends with photos of the original artwork.

Postmodern picturebooks offer students a way to consider books that have multiple interpretations (Pantaleo, 2008) and multiple paths for reading, similar to the reading expectations of the Internet. Sipe and McGuire (2008) urge teachers to engage students with these books because "they present challenging and intriguing literary puzzles to solve" (p. 287). Through this process, teachers and students come to appreciate books that are unlike the more familiar narratives they have read before. They understand that these new narratives use this base to engage readers in more intriguing, complicated stories. Postmodern narratives and illustrations provide an opportunity for teachers and students to equally engage in sophisticated conversation about possible meanings, where students often reveal ideas and emotions not considered by their teachers.

NONFICTION PICTUREBOOKS

Throughout most of this chapter, I have shared narrative picturebooks as examples. Nonfiction books include many of the visual elements described, although the relationship between image and text is more typically complementary. Artists and authors share concerns about engaging visual representation, accuracy, and reader engagement with the information (Gill, 2009) as these books are created. As I perused nonfiction picture-books, I noted that illustrators often created artwork or representations of an object or included photographs for a more realistic portrayal. For instance, Seymour Simon most often uses photographs while Steve Jenkins creates artwork.

In *Butterflies* (Neye, 2000), Broda, the illustrator, chose realistic artwork to showcase interesting information about butterflies. The image from this book shown in Figure 6.3 represents the illustrations throughout. On this page, the illustrator has created contrasting images of where butterflies live, children have to infer that these images and their colors (white for cold and brown for hot) represent cold mountains and hot deserts.

In my teaching with students, I have found that some students are confused with artistic renderings of information, because they first view them as being narrative. Even though Broda's drawings are representative of the various places butterflies are found, teachers need to support students in understanding these are facts about butterflies and not a story. Additionally, teachers may need to help students interpret that the artist is representing mountains and deserts and cold and hot geographic regions.

Beyond these issues, students can ponder Broda's use of color and placement. She has distanced the location while highlighting the butterfly. Students may find this representation particularly interesting because the facts highlight the location and not the type of butterfly. In this case, do the illustrations directly complement the text?

FIGURE 6.3. Page 7 in *Butterflies*.

Extreme Weather (Phelan, 2004), a second nonfiction picturebook, relies on photos, text boxes, and drawings. Most of the book is written so that two-page spreads carry information and support each other. For instance, on pages 20 and 21 (Figure 6.4), Phelan shares information about tornadoes and lightning. He does this through text, text boxes, drawings, and photos.

As seen in this example, the author/illustrator thought about placement of text and illustrations. For each section of text there is a text box or a visual to complement the information shared. For instance, the map shows where Tornado Alley is in the United States. One text box provided a list of tornado safety tips with—as a close examination reveals—a tornado photo as a background. The second text box provides lightning safety types and has a vivid photo of lightning as a background. The last visual is a photo of a tree split in half by lightning.

As I review just these two pages from this single book, I imagine the rich conversation it can generate among teachers and students. The author helps readers through his words, like "You may not have been in a tornado even if you live in Tornado Alley. But you may have been in many thunderstorms" (p. 21). These words are so engaging, they actually invite readers to share their own experiences. Students can talk about their experiences or share them through visual aids or through writing.

Teachers will then want to refocus students to examine how the author used visual text to support written text: Why did this author/illustrator choose photos? What do the photos reveal about tornados or lightning? Why was a drawn map used to share information about Tornado Alley? Students may have appreciated what they learned

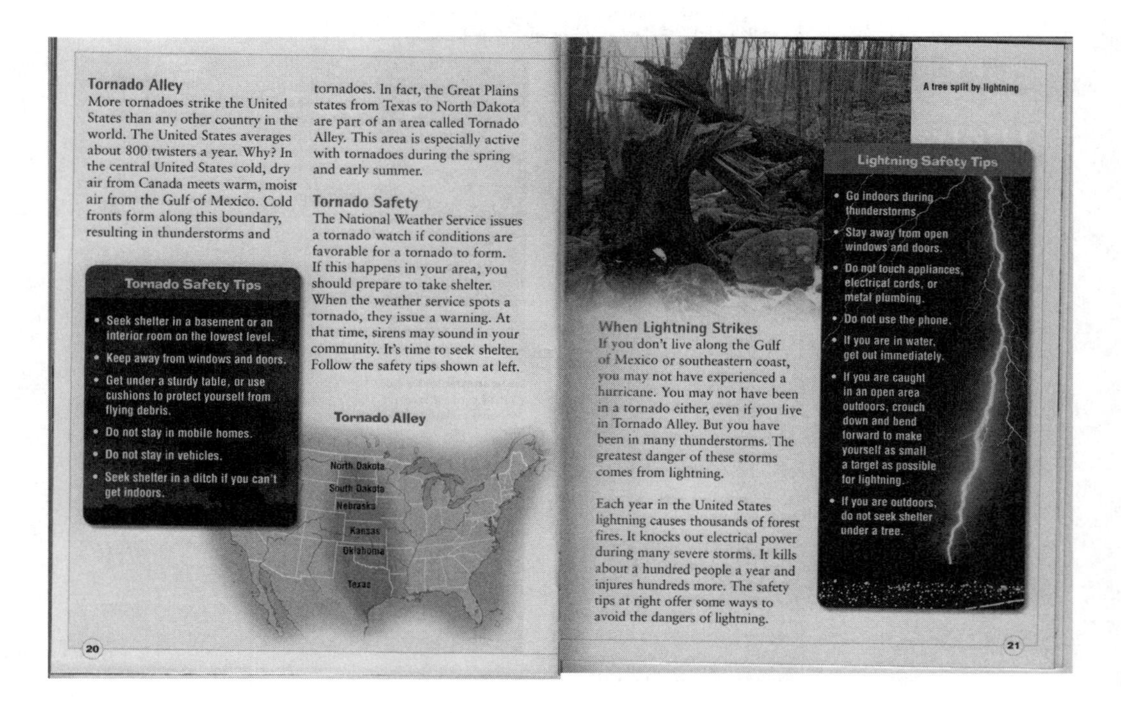

Tornado Alley
More tornadoes strike the United States than any other country in the world. The United States averages about 800 twisters a year. Why? In the central United States cold, dry air from Canada meets warm, moist air from the Gulf of Mexico. Cold fronts form along this boundary, resulting in thunderstorms and tornadoes. In fact, the Great Plains states from Texas to North Dakota are part of an area called Tornado Alley. This area is especially active with tornadoes during the spring and early summer.

Tornado Safety
The National Weather Service issues a tornado watch if conditions are favorable for a tornado to form. If this happens in your area, you should prepare to take shelter. When the weather service spots a tornado, they issue a warning. At that time, sirens may sound in your community. It's time to seek shelter. Follow the safety tips shown at left.

Tornado Safety Tips
- Seek shelter in a basement or an interior room on the lowest level.
- Keep away from windows and doors.
- Get under a sturdy table, or use cushions to protect yourself from flying debris.
- Do not stay in mobile homes.
- Do not stay in vehicles.
- Seek shelter in a ditch if you can't get indoors.

20

A tree split by lightning

When Lightning Strikes
If you don't live along the Gulf of Mexico or southeastern coast, you may not have experienced a hurricane. You may not have been in a tornado either, even if you live in Tornado Alley. But you have been in many thunderstorms. The greatest danger of these storms comes from lightning.

Each year in the United States lightning causes thousands of forest fires. It knocks out electrical power during many severe storms. It kills about a hundred people a year and injures hundreds more. The safety tips at right offer some ways to avoid the dangers of lightning.

Lightning Safety Tips
- Go indoors during thunderstorms.
- Stay away from open windows and doors.
- Do not touch appliances, electrical cords, or metal plumbing.
- Do not use the phone.
- If you are in water, get out immediately.
- If you are caught in an open area outdoors, crouch down and bend forward to make yourself as small a target as possible for lightning.
- If you are outdoors, do not seek shelter under a tree.

21

FIGURE 6.4. Pages 20 and 21 in *Extreme Weather.*

from text and visuals, but they may never have critically thought about the decisions an illustrator makes. These discussions provide a backdrop of information that students will use as they engage with other nonfiction picturebooks, thus deepening their understanding and appreciation of this genre.

ENGAGING STUDENTS

Students learn to appreciate the artistic qualities of picturebooks when they explore the visual elements used by artists for illustration.

1. *Responding visually.* Most students are familiar and comfortable writing about their reading, whether it is a picturebook, a novel, or an informational text. Students can be asked to respond visually to their reading and then provide text to explain their visual connection. They will be surprised at how their visual responses provide new understandings of their reading.
2. *Playing with perspective.* Using one of their recently written narratives or informational texts, students select a portion that they wish to illustrate. Rather than just creating an illustration, students experiment with sketches from multiple views, for instance, a worm's eye view, a bird's eye view, and a middle ground. Once these sketches are complete, they can choose their favorite to add to their text.
3. *Illustrating poetry.* Choose a poem, preferably one that does not have illustrations accompanying it. Separate each line or stanza and write each on separate pages. Students then illustrate each line or stanza of the poem, paying close attention to the mental pictures created by the poem. This activity allows students to experiment with line, shape, texture, color, placement, and perspective.

At the end of this chapter, take a few moments to reflect upon the following:

1. Choose a picturebook, perhaps one of your favorites. Look through this book and then answer the following questions:
   a. How do the illustrations support the meaning of the text? Review the Interplay of Text and Illustrations section and determine how they correspond to each other.
   b. What medium did the illustrator use? How does it support the mood of the narrative?
   c. How has the illustrator used line, shape, color, and texture?

2. Choose a book by an illustrator, read it, and then visit his or her website. What did you discover about this illustrator that helps you interpret his or her work? Make sure that students choose illustrators of narrative and nonfiction picturebooks.

3. Choose three books by the same illustrator. View each carefully. What did you discover about similarities and differences in his or her work?

RECOMMENDED READING

For readers who would like to know about some of the topics in this chapter, the following books provide additional information.

Bang, M. (2000). *Picture this: How pictures work*. New York: SeaStar.

This book allowed me to understand how the shapes and color within an illustration create meaning. Bang carefully takes readers through the experience of understanding these influences. Her book ends with activities to support students in learning about color and shape placement.

Pantaleo, S. (2008). *Exploring student response to contemporary picturebooks*. Toronto: University of Toronto Press.

Pantaleo shares her research on children's responses to postmodern picturebooks. Teachers can read the conversations that first and fifth graders had about these books. In one of the last chapters, readers can see the stories that fifth graders created using the characteristics evident in postmodern picturebooks.

Sipe, L., & Pantaleo, S. (Eds.). (2008). *Postmodern picturebooks: Play, parody, and self-referentiality*. New York: Routledge.

This edited volume shares a variety of perspectives on postmodern picturebooks. Each chapter enriches one's understandings of the qualities of postmodern picturebooks. I especially enjoyed the chapter by Susan Lehr that focused on the illustrations of Lauren Child.

Student Voices

20,000 Leagues Under the Sea (Verne, 1869/2005)

"In *20,000 Leagues Under the Sea* I like the creatures and scenery. The action also makes me like it. I learned a lot of stuff from it because it is science fiction. I can picture myself in the story. There is hard vocabulary in this book. When I hear it, I match it to the action going on so I know what it means."—Michael, a second grader

CHAPTER 7

Children's Views of Children's Literature

> I must quickly add that I'm not professing that young people should read only books specific to themselves. I shudder to think what a horrible, bland, confused world that would make. (I shudder even more when I think what that would do to the sales of my books!) I'm suggesting that if a book is to attain the lofty level of being "touching," as a bookworm would define the word, there has to be something in it to which he or she can relate on more than just a superficial level.
>
> —CHRISTOPHER PAUL CURTIS, "The Literary Worlds of Bud, Kenny, Luther, and Christopher: Finding Books for Me" (2008, p. 158)

Christopher Curtis shared that when he visits schools to showcase his books, he typically gets the same questions from students. However, on one visit a young girl asked, "Mr. Curtis, what books really, really touched you when you were a kid?" (p. 156). Unprepared for this unusual question, Curtis had to think long and hard about his response. He recalled that as a kid he read comics, magazines, and *Mad* magazine, none of which answered the question. Further, he remembered books he was assigned to read at school and the infamous SRA reading comprehension kits he had to complete, which involved reading a short passage and answering questions. Reflecting on his struggle to respond to this question, Curtis expressed his hope that the books he has written about young African American boys may help today's children find a book where they see a child like them within the narrative. Curtis's experience points to the fact that many students, both boys and girls, complete their education without having read a single book that really touched them.

Data from reports about reading support Curtis's personal observations. In *To Read or Not to Read* (National Endowment for the Arts, 2007), it was noted that students who read for pleasure, score higher on reading assessments, although these students are in the minority. Moreover, they discovered the following:

- Less than 33% of American 13-year-olds read daily.
- On average, each day Americans ages 15–24 watch television for 2 hours and read for 7 minutes.
- Fifty percent of Americans ages 15–24 do not read for pleasure.

In an earlier report from the National Endowment for the Arts (2004), it was noted that only 4% of adults were considered avid readers and over 54% of adults were nonliterary readers.

One could assume from the reports that most adolescents and adults do not find reading pleasurable. Finding time to read could be an issue—after all, everyone is busy—but adolescents and adults are able to devote 2 hours each day for television, rendering this argument invalid. Further, a Kaiser Foundation (2006) report (*www.kff.org/entmedia/entmedia052406nr.cfm*) based on a national survey documented that parents often rely on electronic media, not books, to keep their children occupied. Among their specific discoveries:

- Among children younger than 6, 83% watch about 2 hours of television daily.
- Among this same category, 33% have a television in their bedroom (this rate increases to 43% for children ages 4–6).
- Among children younger than 2, 43% watch television every day.
- Among children 6 and under, 43% use a computer several times each week.

It is apparent that children as young as 2 watch television more than they engage in reading. In a broader scope, the Kaiser Foundation reported that 8- to 18-year-olds spent, on average, in a single day 4 hours watching television and videos; 1 hour on the computer, either on- or offline; almost 1 hour on video games; and less than 1 hour reading, either books, magazines, or newspapers.

Taking an alternative approach to the study of literacy, other researchers (Cunningham & Stanovich, 1998; Daane et al., 2005) found that students who do read frequently have higher intelligence, better decoding ability, increased vocabulary, and stronger comprehension in third to fifth grades. Fourth graders who reported that they read each day scored higher on the National Assessment of Educational Progress (NAEP) in 2002. Further, Daane et al. found that teachers who had students read more than their core reading program materials scored higher on the NAEP. Clearly, data support positive results for being engaged with reading.

Based on these results, although it is critically important for teachers to develop students' capabilities as readers, a further goal is to cultivate students' engagement with text, a thirst for new experiences that reading offers (Kelley & Clausen-Grace, 2008). Without this ability, students will relegate reading events to the bottom of their list of free-time choices, as they have a wide variety of activities to choose from. This decision will have lifelong effects, as shown in the research of Cunningham and Stanovich (1998).

So who exactly is an engaged reader? First, this is someone who gets lost in a text, who becomes absorbed in it to the point of tuning out all else. Think about summer reading on the beach: All the potential distractions—children crying, music blaring, teenagers yelling—cannot disturb an engaged reader. Second, an engaged reader is active when reading and reads for meaning. Third, an engaged reader knows a lot about books and authors/illustrators and finds books that are interesting to read. Fourth, an engaged reader shares what he or she is reading with others, encouraging them to read a particular book as well (Guthrie & Wigfield, 2000).

Teachers, however, know that it is no easy task to develop skilled and engaged readers. Kelley and Clausen-Grace (2008, 2009) describe the variation in readers in a typical classroom. They divide their descriptions into two major categories: engaged and disengaged. Engaged readers can be identified as follows:

- *Nonfiction readers.* They love to read nonfiction but may struggle with narrative. These students are complex in that they are engaged with informational text but are reluctant to read or avoid narrative genres.
- *Readers who can read but choose not to.* They read what they are expected to read and often take forever to finish a book. They have the skill and can be engaged with text, showing they enjoy reading; however, they are still developing a passion for reading.
- *Genre or series readers.* They love to read the books in a series or within a genre. They like reading in their comfort zone.
- *Bookworms.* They are addicted to reading. They read everything and everywhere.

In contrast, disengaged readers can be described as follows:

- *Fake readers.* They pretend they are reading, often taking more time to select a book than to read it.
- *Challenged readers.* They are readers who read below grade level and are frustrated when asked to read text at grade-level expectations.
- *Unrealistic readers.* These readers choose books that are too difficult. They switch books often without having completed any.
- *Compliant readers.* They read for the expected time set aside. They are not selective about their reading choices because the goal is reading to expectation, not enjoyment.

This variation in readers offers teachers challenges in developing engaged readers or bookworms (Gambrell, 1996). I am guessing that you have identified students who fit each of these descriptions, and you are most concerned with your disengaged students, especially those who fake reading. Here are a few things to help create avid or engaged readers.

1. Teachers reading aloud can interest students in reading books they may have never chosen. Students who choose a book just read by their teacher will better understand the book, because it is not a first reading. Teachers may also provide book talks about books and share a little of the text to entice students to read them. Teachers might also schedule guest readers, who can model reading for students. Inviting fathers, male authors, or prominent men in the community as guest readers can work especially well to engage boys.
2. Teachers who are readers can share their enthusiasm for reading with students.
3. Teachers and students can create a well-designed class library that has books and magazines to interest all students. The books and magazines need to be changed frequently to maintain student interest.
4. To encourage reading, teachers provide time for students to read. Creating a reading routine in classrooms supports students, especially those who are disengaged, in finding interesting books to read.
5. Students who are allowed choice in what they read are more likely to become engaged with reading.
6. When teachers confer with students or encourage reading discussions among students, motivation to read is increased.

Although the majority of these suggestions are cost-free, creating a classroom library is not. New teachers may especially worry about how they can afford to build a classroom library. First, teachers inventory the books that are currently in the classroom library. With this information, they can visit the school and public library where books can be borrowed. Often teachers can borrow as many as 40 books at a time. Librarians can also help teachers select important books for student interest or to extend the materials in the classroom library. Third, teachers should check with their principal and parent–teacher organization to determine whether funds are available to purchase books. Fourth, teachers should check with retiring teachers or parents of older children to see if they can donate books to the classroom library. Alternatively, teachers can patronize bookstores or online businesses that offer educator discounts (e.g., Amazon and Barnes and Noble). They might also use class bookclub lists where students buy books at discounted rates. When I was teaching, I asked parents to buy a book each month (among my selection of four titles of similar cost). These books were in the classroom for 1 month for student reading. At the end of the month I sent one book home with each student. The value of this suggestion was fourfold: There were new books in the classroom each month; many of these books connected to popular culture and students found them highly interesting; students owned a book at the end of the month; and I received points to be used to purchase additional books.

CHECKING THE CLASSROOM LIBRARY AND DETERMINING STUDENT INTERESTS

As mentioned in the previous discussions about building a library, teachers should first take inventory of the books or magazines that are currently in the library. A simple genre tally chart is provided in Figure 7.1 to facilitate this process. Teachers can use this chart to tally the number of books from each genre. Some genres are only pertinent to certain grade levels. For instance, first grades will have more alphabet books than intermediate grades.

Once teachers are aware of the range of genres in the classroom library, it is time to determine students' interests. Even if the library is balanced in genre, students' interests may require the addition of other selections. Young children can respond to a student interest inventory orally (for an example, see Figure 7.2), and older students can write their responses.

Once students have completed the inventories, teachers create lists of preferred topics and genres. Sometimes teachers may discover that students love graphic books or cartoons and question whether these genres are appropriate for the classroom. If these are the books that can engage compliant or fake readers and help them become avid readers, teachers must ensure that they are a part of the classroom library. By supporting students in reading materials they love, teachers can nudge them to other kinds of books through read-alouds or book talks. By denying students books that they find enjoyable, teachers make it much more difficult and perhaps impossible to create engaged readers.

Guthrie and Humenick (2004) identified four factors that contribute to reading motivation: easy access to interesting books, opportunities to read, choice in reading material, and collaboration about reading with a teacher or other students. Additionally, the incorporation of these four factors in the classroom was correlated with huge gains in students' reading achievement. Because teachers face extraordinary pressure in terms of student test performance, and may thus worry about providing time for students to read books of their choosing, Guthrie and Humenick's research should assure them that they can develop their students into skillful readers while simultaneously increasing their motivation.

EXPLORING GIRL AND BOY READERS

Boys continue to struggle with literacy, while girls continue to test higher and are even performing better in math and science. This phenomenon has been attributed to several factors, among them high dropout rates among Latino and African American males and the widespread perception among boys that reading is a feminine activity, pushing them to Internet use or video games as favorite pastimes (Lehr, 2008). Schools and teachers have begun to address this issue, asking themselves, What might we do to better to

Genre	Tallies
Alphabet Books	
Rhyming Books	
Poetry	
Nonfiction	
Mystery	
Adventure	
Realistic Fiction	
Historical Fiction	
Biography/ Autobiography	
Science Fiction	
Sports	
Fantasy	
Memoir	
Cartoon	
Graphic	
Popular Culture (Like *Star Wars* Books)	
Magazines	
Other	

FIGURE 7.1. Genre chart for evaluating a classroom library.

What are your hobbies? What do you like to do when you have free time?
What do you like to do with your friends?
What is the best book you ever read?
What is the best magazine you ever read?

Circle the kinds of books you like to read:

Magazines	Biography	History
Science Books	Animals	Sports
Historical Fiction	Mystery	Adventure
Realistic Fiction	Science Fiction	Fantasy
Comic Books	Graphic Books	Poetry
Series Books	Information Books	Joke Books

FIGURE 7.2. Student interest inventory.

engage boys in reading and thus help them succeed in school? How might we change the perception that reading is only for girls?

There is no doubt that boys and girls prefer different books. Often, because teachers are mainly female, book selection reflects their favorites. Additionally, many of the books boys prefer have not been accessible within classrooms. One would think it would be easy to create separate lists of books for boys and girls and then make sure they are available. However, their differences in preference might not be as straightforward as one might expect. For instance, a common assumption is that boys love informational text, and girls prefer fiction. However, Pappas (1991) showed that kindergarten boys and girls like both informational text and fiction; there were no gender differences evident. Teachers may be thinking, "Sure, but by fifth grade this is different and boys prefer informational text." Genuard (2005) found that boys and girls in fourth, fifth, and six grades liked informational text equally, again no gender differences.

So what should teachers do? First, they should consider the interests of students and make sure that books and magazines on these topics are available. Second, while observing students when reading, especially those who are most often disengaged, they should note the books or magazines that the students seem to especially embrace. During book talks, teachers can share others like these to nudge these students to further reading. Teachers should also include books that are known for supporting struggling or less engaged readers, including series books, comics, graphic books, and magazines (McGill-Franzen & Botzakis, 2009).

Series books are books that repeat plots and characters and typically have simple writing. Although these books have been prevalent and popular since the Civil War, with cheap fiction such as dime novels (Ross, 1995), they have been criticized for their lack of multidimensionality and thus excluded from the classroom library. As a teacher I thought this as well, but then I reflected on my own reading. I know I read series books. I love James Patterson, and I like reading books where the main character is repeated. I also like David Baldacci, especially his books that feature the Camel Club. I find these books enjoyable, and my background knowledge from my previous experiences with the characters allows me to become even more immersed in subsequent books. So would it be incorrect to support student readers with the series books they love?

A series might be a way to change disengaged readers' perceptions about reading. Students come to the second, third, and other books in the series with background knowledge and expectations about plot. They can read these books more easily because of this background, and they get to feel like a proficient reader. Figure 7.3 shares many of the series books available to students.

Other series books tied to popular culture are also interesting literature for many children (Miller, 2009; Xu, Perkins, & Zunich, 2005). Children enjoy these books because they are multimodal; they see them on television, on the Internet, and in a book. Some of these books include:

Title of Series	Author
A to Z Mysteries	Ron Roy and John Gurney
Amber Brown	Paula Danziger
Amelia Bedelia	Peggy Parrish
Arthur	Marc Brown
Bailey School Kids	Various authors
Bone	Jeff Smith
Brian Series	Gary Paulsen
Cam Jansen	David Adler
Captain Underpants	Dav Pilkey
Dinotopia	Various authors
Franklin	Paulette Bourgeois and Brenda Clark
Frog and Toad	Arnold Lobel
Harry Pottter	J. K. Rowling
Henry and Mudge	Cynthia Rylant
Julian	Ann Cameron
Junie B. Jones	Barbara Park
Little Bear	Else Holmelund Minarik and Maurice Sendak
Marvin Redpost	Louis Sachar
Nate the Great	Marjorie Sharmat
Olympian Series	Rick Riordan
Poppy	Avi
Read and Find Out Science	Various authors
Series of Unfortunate Events	Lemony Snicket
Sideways Stories from Wayside School	Louis Sachar
Starcatcher Series	Dave Barry and Ridley Pearson
Stink Series	Megan McDonald
Sugar Plum Ballerinas series	Whoopi Goldberg and Deborah Underwood
The Magic School Bus	Joanna Cole
The Magic Tree House	Mary Pope Osborne
The Riot Brothers	Mary Amato
Time Warp Series	Jon Scieszka
39 Clues	Various authors

FIGURE 7.3. Series books.

- *Thomas the Train*
- *Pokemón*
- *Spongebob Squarepants*
- *Hannah Montana*
- *Transformers*

Comic and graphic novels offer students an opportunity to explore reading through text and visual elements. Although graphic novels are finding wide support among teachers, comics are not. Comics, however, can be an especially important genre to engage boys (Smith & Wilhelm, 2002), because they love to read about Batman and Spiderman. Comic books allow them to explore all the elements of narrative text, such as character and plot.

Graphic novels have become popular, especially with the success of *The Invention of Hugo Cabret* (Selznick, 2007), which was awarded the Caldecott Medal. These books require careful attention to both illustrations and text, similar to a picturebook. I find that I am a struggling reader with books like *Hugo Cabret*, because I am learning how to simultaneously read both text and visual elements.

I did, however, enjoy *City of Light, City of Dark* (Avi, 1993). Perhaps because much of it is like a comic book, a familiar genre, I was able to feel more comfortable interpreting the illustrations simultaneously with text. Students who have experience with graphic novels and comic books can be placed in the position of expert and can instruct teachers in the nuances of these genres.

Magazines make up another medium that inspires students to read. Many classrooms do not have a wide selection of magazines because of cost. Teachers can subscribe to magazines with the help of parents and others. Parents who subscribe to magazines for their own children may be willing to loan issues to the classroom. Parents and possibly grandparents may offer to subscribe to certain magazines for the classroom if they know they are important for students. Alternatively, perhaps schools can loan their subscription magazines to classrooms. Remember to search for discounted magazine subscriptions; many are offered on the Internet. Figure 7.4 shares some of the many possible magazines available for students.

Highlights for Children	*Your Big Backyard*	*Sports Illustrated for Kids*
Ranger Rick	*Muse*	*Ask*
National Geographic Kids	*Cricket*	*Zoo Books*
Kids Discover	*Boys Life*	*Cobblestone*
Odyssey	*Girls Life*	*Kids Discover*

FIGURE 7.4. Magazines.

Boys' Choices

Hill (2009) writes that boys enjoy "gross and gory literature" (p. 6). She notes that *How to Eat Fried Worms* (Rockwell, 1975) might have been the first book to capitalize on boys' interests. She continues, "Boys like to read books filled with action and adventure. They like toilet humor" (p. 6). Miller (2009) concurs and suggests that "teachers and parents often scorn the type of reading that boys most enjoy" (p. 86). Meeting the reading needs of boys will certainly push teachers to explore books they typically pass over, books they may have felt were inappropriate for in-school reading.

Zambo and Brozo (2009) offer suggestions to teachers to support boys in becoming engaged readers, among them:

- Viewing boys' imaginations and curiosity as a resource rather than a behavior issue.
- Supporting boys' reading interests by providing access to books that push the established expectations for classroom reading.
- Providing books that have strong male characters, particularly *entry-point texts*, books that capture the imagination of boy readers and propel them to engage in other reading.

Scieszka (2005) has taken on the challenge of engaging boys in reading. In his book *Guys Write for Guys Read*, he asked authors to write about their experiences with reading. They responded with stories, memoirs, comic strips, poems, and drawings. In addition, on his website, *www.guysread.com*, teachers and parents can discover books and authors that boys enjoy. Scieszka believes that boys need choice in what they read, should be able to read more than school-selected novels, and need to know what other boys read. To accomplish these goals, he has grouped books for young readers, middle-level readers, and older readers so they are aware of choices and what other boys have found interesting.

In his contribution to Scieszka's book, "Guy Things," Gordon Korman (2005) provides a hilarious look at things that are and are not guy things. He writes:

> The following things are, without question, one-hundred percent non-guy: good smells, princesses, salad, figure skating, cuteness, bedtime, yoga, all fat-free products (except nitroglycerine), periwinkle blue, periwinkles, and three-quarters of the books your librarian describes as award winners. (p. 138)

Guy things are very different.

> Compare this to the core list of guy things: bad smells, Cartoon Network, jock itch, torque, XGames, Z-rays, XBox, underwater explosions, Monty Python, gas (all varieties), professional wrestling (including sumo), and any injury that involves something being hyperextended. (p. 138)

After reading Korman's ideas about guy and non-guy things and then reading the other chapters in this book, it was apparent that much of what teachers ask boys to read is a real stretch for them, and not necessarily one they want to make. I also became aware that most boys read comics and enjoy them, although they may hide this interest in the classroom.

Most teachers are less familiar with boys' books and authors. Figure 7.5 identifies authors who are particularly appealing to boys and may serve as a base for teachers in extending their knowledge about boys' books.

There are also some very amazing books that appeal to boys. I share a few here to spark your interest and, perhaps, make you giggle or just laugh out loud.

Don't Let the Pigeon Drive the Bus! (Willems, 2003) is about a pigeon who wants to drive a bus—a bit insane, but once you meet this pigeon it seems possible. This is a pigeon with attitude! This pigeon argues as to why he should drive the bus: He'll be careful, he'll just steer; and if that isn't convincing, he adds that his cousin drives a bus almost everyday. Then the pigeon is dejected when he isn't allowed to drive, complaining "I never get to do anything" (unpaged). Just like most kids, he recharges and resumes his argument with gusto, finding more reasons why he should get to drive the bus. Eventually, he shifts course to maybe driving a truck. Willems's experience in cartooning is clearly evident in this book and makes it entertaining in both story and illustration.

Picture Books	Novels
Chris Van Allsburg	Avi
Tedd Arnold	Andrew Clements
Anthony Browne	Christopher Curtis
Arnold Lobel	Roald Dahl
James Marshall	Jack Gantos
Brian Pinkney	Will Hobbs
Richard Scarry	Gordon Korman
Jon Scieszka	Gary Paulsen
David Shannon	J. K. Rowling
Mark Teague	Louis Sachar
Mo Willems	Jerry Spinelli

FIGURE 7.5. Authors that appeal to boys.

Another picturebook that is sure to excite boys is *How I Became a Pirate* (Long & Shannon, 2003). This book reminds me of *Where the Wild Things Are* in that Jeremy is playing on the beach when he sees pirates coming. His family does not see them, and Jeremy accompanies the pirates to their ship and plays at being a pirate. The best part is Jeremy gets to eat with his hands, there are no vegetables on board, he doesn't have to say "please" or "thank you," and he doesn't have to have a bath or brush his teeth before bedtime. The book ends with the pirates bringing Jeremy home, hiding the treasure in his backyard, and his going to soccer practice. What a wonderfully satisfying ending to a book filled with fun and adventure.

Most teachers will eagerly bring Willems's pigeon books into their classrooms as well as Long and Shannon's *How I Became a Pirate*, but will they be brave enough to bring in the *Captain Underpants* books (Pilkey, 1997)? Pilkey uses comic strips, text, and illustrations within his *Captain Underpants* series and much to boys' pleasure writes about gross things. This 10-book series features George and Harold, two imaginative boys always eager for adventure. Among the crazy adventures in this series, George and Harold hypnotized their principal, Mr. Krupp, who becomes Captain Underpants, a superhero who wears underpants and a cape. George and Harry, not the best students in their school, discover the joy of placing ketchup on toilet seats, with the expected and quite silly squishy result. The books include entertaining features like Flip-O-Ramas (pages that, when flipped, show movement and action). These books require flexibility on the reader's part as they move from cartoon, to text, to illustration, to lists, and so on. They replicate reading that is available on the Internet (*www.pilkey.com*).

Similar to the *Captain Underpants* series are the *Riot Brothers* books (Amato). In *Snarf Attack, Underfoodle, and the Secret of Life: The Riot Brothers Tell All* (Amato, 2004), the Riot brothers engage in many schemes, games, and adventures, most of which are not particularly appreciated by parents. For instance, they invented a game called Snarf Attack, where they stare at each other over dinner, trying to get each other to laugh until food spills out of his mouth. They give "annoying lessons" to classmates; for 25 cents students can learn how to annoy from experts. At the end of the book, specific directions are provided for each of their games so that readers can continue the adventures.

Informational books are perfect to entice boys. *Amazing Animals Q&A* (Burnie, 2007) provides vivid photographs and unusual facts about animals. For example, readers can learn why animals' eyes are wide set (gives them wide peripheral vision, a protective feature) or which animal has the largest eyes (giant squid). *It's Disgusting and We Ate It! True Food Facts from Around the World and Throughout History* (Solheim, 1998) entertains with facts and trivia about disgusting things people eat. *Grossology* (Branzei) is a series of books about gross stuff and covers a range of topics, from animals to humans to gross experiments. In a similar series, *That's Disgusting* (Miller), readers learn about disgusting animals, bugs, plants, and so on.

History is also a ripe subject for gross things. In *Oh, Yikes! History's Grossest, Wackiest Moments* (Masoff, 2006), students will no doubt enjoy reading about guillotines and vomitoriums. In *The Wicked History of the World* (Deary, 2006), they can learn about creepy villains like Vlad the Impaler and Attila the Hun. The *Wicked History* series (by various authors) shares stories of nefarious characters such as Genghis Khan, Robespierre, and Ivan the Terrible.

Boys enjoy books that have strong, independent, interesting boy characters. In the following, I share but a few examples. The literature includes a multitude of books geared toward boys, many written by the authors listed previously.

One author familiar to teachers is Gary Paulsen. His stories about Brian and his survival in the wilderness, *Hatchet* (1987), enthrall boys as they follow in the adventures. His books are quite authentic: Paulsen is an expert at living in the wilderness and bases his stories on some of his personal adventures. Teachers can share snippets from *Guts* (Paulsen, 2001) to help students, especially boys, see how Paulsen brought his personal experience into these stories.

In *Bud, Not Buddy* (1999), Christopher Curtis shares a character who will stay with readers long after they have completed this book, even though he was 10 in 1936. Bud, a young African American boy living in foster care, decides to venture out on his own to find the man he believes is his father, Herman Calloway, a jazz musician. Throughout the story, readers better understand Bud and his need for a family during the time of the depression. Curtis deftly adds humor to a very sensitive story.

Jerry Spinelli has numerous books that appeal to boys. In *Crash* (1996), John Coogan, aka Crash, is focused on winning in football and tormenting another boy, Penn. Boys will struggle with their emotions about Crash as he experiences loss and regret as a result of his actions. Gordon Korman is also a favorite author among boys. In *Swindle* (2008), after selling a baseball card that he found to a collector, Griffin discovers that he has been swindled (although he never really owned the card) and decides to steal the card back. Throughout the book, readers contemplate the rightness or wrongness of Griffin owning the card, Mr. Palomino's cheating, and Griffin's decision to steal it back. Boys who enjoy this book can be enticed to read the sequel *Zoobreak* (Korman, 2009), where Griffin engages in a new plan to rescue animals.

Jon Scieszka's (2008a) *Knucklehead* is also a perfect book for boys and exposes them to the memoir genre, which they are less likely to choose to read. Scieszka retells stories of his childhood with his five brothers. His tales are filled with family photos, and students are sure to laugh as they see his brothers and Jon in school pictures. He shares adventures of learning to cook, read, and terrorize his brothers, among others.

These books just mentioned are a fabulous "first stop" for teachers wanting to become familiar with books that boys love. As mentioned, there is a vast array of books specifically intended to appeal to boys. Teachers can visit libraries, bookstores, and the Internet to determine which ones would best suit their classrooms. Specifically, Jon Sceizska (*www.guysread.com*) and James Patterson (*readkiddoread.com*) facilitate this exploration on their websites with information and recommendations about books and authors.

Girls' Choices

Teachers often assume that girls like books with a strong girl character so that they can identify with her and share in the book's plot. Blackford (2004) interviewed girls between 8 and 16 years of age and learned that they often read from multiple viewpoints, not just one. Moreover, they often align with the narrator. Unlike boys who prefer action, girls appreciate the art of literature. Blackford writes:

> The girls whom I interviewed for this book taught me that literature matters because it teaches how perspective can be brought to bear on experience. It makes people see and experience worlds they would not normally see, experience, and think about in their everyday lives. (p. 1)

Further, she discovered that girls select books they think will have a good story. She found that, regardless of race, class, age, family circumstances, reading preferences or ability, girls choose books with a strong storyline, preferably not one they are themselves living. Blackford concludes, "I found girls wish to read or see fiction in order to experience something radically different from their everyday lives" (p. 6).

Girls, not unlike boys, are also influenced by mass media (Fleener, Morrison, Linek, & Rasinski, 1997; Wray & Lewis, 1993). Girls experience book talks in the TV shows they watch and movies they see, as evidenced by the popularity of the *Twilight* series (Meyer) and books about Hannah Montana or Taylor Swift.

Girls also like series books (see Figure 7.3) and graphic novels that are targeted to them (Teale, Kim, & Boerman-Cornell, 2008). *The Baby-Sitters Club* (Martin), for example, is a popular series of books that come in traditional as well as graphic novel form. Other graphic novels that are appealing to girls include:

- *Redwall: The Graphic Novel* (Jacques, 2007). A young mouse, Matthias, must save his community when it is threatened by enemies.
- *Scary Godmother* (Thompson, 1997). This book series features Hannah Marie and her encounters with her scary godmother.
- *To Dance: A Ballerina's Graphic Novel* (Siegel, 2006). This is the story of Siena as she grows from a novice to an accomplished ballerina.
- *Nancy Drew* (Petrucha & Murase). These books retell familiar *Nancy Drew* mysteries in graphic format.
- *Miracle Girls* (Akimoto). This series is about twin girls who are very different from one another but have miracle powers like telepathy and teleportation. They try to keep their special powers secret.

Beyond graphic novels and series books, there are numerous books that appeal to girls. The Flashlight Worthy website (*www.flashlightworthybooks.com*) is a valuable resource for book recommendations from third grade and up. Most of the book choices feature strong, female characters. From this list and from recommendations from girls, I selected multiple books to highlight. The books I share include a girl as main character and more intricate plots for readers to explore and enjoy.

Knuffle Bunny (Willems, 2004) is a humorous book sure to generate laughter and fond memories of stuffed animals that provided comfort. Girls will explore all of Trixie's facial expressions as clues to her feelings throughout the story.

Edwina: The Dinosaur Who Didn't Know She Was Extinct (Willems, 2006). This book is enjoyable on many levels. First, the character of the dinosaur is the antithesis of what is generally expected: Edwina is female and helpful, not male and mean. Then there is Reginald, who is sure that dinosaurs are extinct, so Edwina cannot be real. Unfortunately, when he tries to convince his classmates of this, no one listens. Reginald finally convinces Edwina that she is extinct, but she doesn't care and neither does Reginald.

The *Olivia* series (Falconer) is another favorite for girls. In *Olivia Saves the Circus* (2001), girls will appreciate how Olivia changes her boring uniform with accessories like a purse, tights, and hair ribbons. Olivia believes she is very sophisticated and an expert at pretty much everything. For example, her mother takes her to the circus and all of the circus people are home sick with ear infections. Olivia visualizes herself as a tattooed lady, an elephant rider, lion tamer, and so on. In fact, she saves the circus, or so she tells her teacher. True or false, readers must decide for themselves.

I believe that girls will delight in the books written by Lauren Child. In *Beware of the Storybook Wolves* (Child, 2006), wolves come out of storybooks and terrorize Herb, who has to persuade the wolves not to eat him. He does this by convincing them that jelly would taste better, but he has to enter a fairytale to secure jelly. As a wise reader predicts, a wicked fairy enters his world from this book. Throughout the book there is interaction between Herb and creatures from fairytales. A baby wolf winds up in a ball gown designed for Cinderella, and the wolf is so pleased he goes to the ball, leaving Cinderella behind to clean. This book, like others by Child, is incredibly clever and requires readers to have had experience with previous books, like fairytales in this case.

Girls stand to gain much in their own personal development by reading about others living in difficult situations. They can learn from characters' experience with overcoming adversity, successfully surviving, emerging even stronger. *The Great Gilly Hopkins* (Paterson, 1978) features Gilly, a bright but disagreeable 11-year-old who has spent much of her life bouncing among foster homes and is consumed with feelings of hurt, abandonment, and rejection. She believes her mother loves her and will someday come back to her, and they will have a happily ever-after ending. Throughout the book, the author brilliantly presents Gilly's raw emotions, evoking empathy among readers: for instance, "She began to cry softly into her pillow, not knowing why or for whom. Maybe for all the craziness she had tried so hard to manage and was never quite able to" (p. 127). Snippets like this allow a capable reader to gain insights into who Gilly is and why life is so difficult for her. A similar theme is found in *The Higher Power of Lucky* (Patron, 2006). Lucky fears that her foster mother is planning to leave her and return to France. Moreover, like Gilly, Lucky ponders life: "Lucky was pretty sure she'd be able to figure out the difference between the things she could change and the things she couldn't, like in the little prayer of the anonymous people. Because sometimes Lucky wanted to change everything, all the bad things that had happened, and sometimes she wanted everything to stay the same forever" (p. 8). For both Gilly and Lucky, control is an issue, as they seek control and comfort in their lives.

In *Becoming Naomi León* (Ryan, 2004), Naomi and her brother live with their great-grandmother, Gram, who believes in keeping them busy. Naomi spends time making lists, carving soap, and surviving her last name, Outlaw. The conflict in this book makes readers thoughtfully consider the mother–child relationship: Naomi's relationship with Gram is challenged when her mother returns to take Naomi away to live with her, but not Owen, who has physical challenges. Naomi's alcoholic mother left the children more than 7 years ago and wants Naomi only as a babysitter for her boyfriend's young daughter. Readers will become engrossed with each turn of events, rooting for Naomi's triumph.

Similar to Naomi is India Opal from *Because of Winn-Dixie* (DiCamillo, 2000), who, with her father, recently moved to Florida after her alcoholic mother left the family. Like *Becoming Naomi Naomi León*, this book honors relationships, this one between fathers and daughters.

Each book in this set explores the themes of home, security, identity, and changing circumstances. Young, strong, independent girls are the center of each story, and they provide opportunities for readers to discover more about themselves. The best attribute of these books is they are not preachy, they entertain while sharing powerful themes.

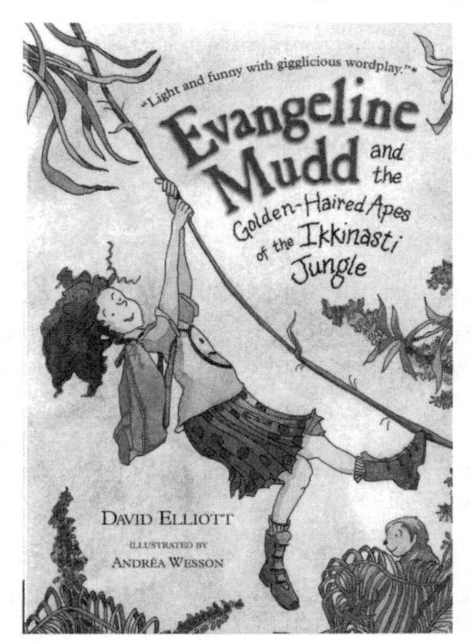

Evangeline Mudd and the Golden-Haired Apes of the Ikkinasti Jungle (Elliott, 2004) is an exciting adventure story. Evangeline is left at home as her parents go to the Ikkinasti Jungle for a scientific expedition. Evangeline's parents are experts on golden-haired apes, and she has been raised as an ape, learning to swing from branches. Naturally, in a mystery adventure, a problem arises: Evangeline's parents have disappeared, and she has to find them. The story is funny, and Elliott loves to play with words. For example, one character is named India Terpsichore and another Dr. Pikkaflee.

The View from Saturday (Konigsburg, 1996) provides the perfect opportunity for girls to interpret books based on multiple viewpoints. Four characters—Noah, Nadia, Ethan, and Julian—are part of a group competing for the Academic Bowl. They are required to answer questions quickly, and each contribute unique strengths to their team for this competition. Answers to some of the questions are offered at the back of the book, and I can see girls comparing their answers to these. Additionally, readers will enjoy the complexity of this book, because there are frequent flashbacks and four stories meld into one.

Girls also enjoy informational text. Young girls might enjoy the Animals and Their Senses series of books (Hall). I learned many interesting details about how animals hear in *Animal Hearing* (Hall, 2006): For example, when animals move their ears, they hear sounds coming from different directions. and in snakes bones send sounds to the inner ears, enabling them to hear. A book for older girls, *Leonardo's Horse* (Fritz, 2001), centers on DaVinci's attempt to create a bronze horse three times the size of a real horse. Within the book are DaVinci's drawings from his notebook. Although DaVinci did not accomplish the creation of the horse, the book describes how Charles Dent, many years later, completed this project.

Although girls and boys can enjoy the same books, wise teachers make sure that they bring books to their classrooms that target each gender. Girls can often appreciate books targeted to boys, but boys do not like books that they view as "girl books." Further, they lose interest in reading if there are no books in the classroom that satisfy their interests. Fortunately, there are many books and series that specifically address both genders. Teachers' primary task is to provide these books to the students in their classrooms and demonstrate equal enthusiasm for boys' choices and girls' choices. Not always easy to do!

ENGAGING STUDENTS

Once teachers have provided books, magazines, and other material that meet the needs and interests of their students, there are other activities that help develop student engagement in reading.

1. *Books and Authors I Might Like and Book Pass sheets.* Kelley and Clausen-Grace (2008) share forms that can be used to track student interest and to support students in reading new books (see Figures 7.6 and 7.7). Using forms like these allow students to have a voice in nudging other students to read books they found appealing.
2. *Student writing guided by gender preferences.* Boys would love the opportunity to write about information using a comic book format. They can decide on several important pieces of information about a topic of choice or related to content area instruction. Using a large piece of white construction paper folded into eighths, in each box they create a cartoon highlighting a piece of information. When complete, they will have a cartoon report with eight interesting details. Although girls will enjoy this format, they might prefer to explore character. For an example, they might pick *Matilda* (Dahl, 1988) and then write a description from several perspectives: Matilda's Ms.

Title	Author	Genre	Recommended by

FIGURE 7.6. Books and Authors I Might Like sheet.

Title	Author	I recommend because	Rating (1 = BEST; 5 = AWFUL)

FIGURE 7.7. Book Pass sheet.

Trunchbull's, her parents', and Miss Honey's. They will enjoy representing how one character is perceived differently depending on who is doing the describing.

3. *Character comparison*. After having read several books that they believe have strong, appealing major characters, students can compare those characteristics that they find attractive across characters. They can create a semantic features chart (Figure 7.8) to help with comparison. To support their decisions, students can be asked to provide a detail from the book that shows the character trait in action.

At the end of this chapter, take a few moments to reflect upon the following:

1. Visit Jon Sceizska website (*www.guysread.com*). What discoveries did you make about books that appeal to boys? Do you own any of these books? Have you read any of these titles to students?
2. Choose one of the authors that appeal to boys. Read two or three of this author's books. Why might these books resonate with boys?

Character	Brave	Kind	Humble	Friend
Matilda	X	Not sure	X	X
Gilly Hopkins	X	–	–	X

FIGURE 7.8. Semantic features chart.

3. Choose one series that appeals to boys and one that appeals to girls. Read one or two books in the series. Why might these series be interesting to boys or girls?

RECOMMENDED READING

For readers who would like to know about some of the topics in this chapter, the following books provide additional information.

Blackford, H. (2004). *Out of this world: Why literature matters to girls.* New York: Teachers College Press.

This book shares research results that complicate prevailing notions about books that appeal to girls. I learned about girls' preferred books by listening to them talk about their reading interests.

Scieszka, J. (Ed.). (2005). *Guys write for guys read.* New York: Viking.

The short chapters by numerous authors who write for boys offer teachers evidence of the importance of meeting the reading needs of boys in their classrooms. It also helps teachers find appropriate books for boys.

Zambo, D., & Brozo, W. (2009). *Bright beginnings for boys: Engaging young boys in active literacy.* Newark, DE: International Reading Association.

This book helps teachers understand the importance of bringing books into their classrooms that support the reading interests of boys.

Student Voices

Stargirl (Spinelli, 2000)

"This book is unique. It is a twisted love story—a weird girl who is different from others but finds love with a completely ordinary person. It is filled with adventure and is mysterious. I kept trying to figure out why she is so different from the others. What caused her to be that way? It is written in the first person so you feel like you get to know the character better. I can hear her thinking. I felt like I was right in the scene with her."—Kennady, a sixth grader

CHAPTER 8

Learning about Illustrators and Small Text Sets

> The Monday morning buzz in 6B was all about books. Plot lines were yammered from excited lips. Reviews were given on a scale of one to ten. Authors were measured up against each other like championship boxers. Every few seconds, someone would shout, "Yeah? Well that's nothing! In my book—" And another argument would start over which story was the funniest/scariest/saddest/most exciting.
>
> —GORDON KORMAN, *The 6th Grade Nickname Game* (1998, p. 86)

Wouldn't all teachers love to have students similar to those Korman describes? Well, these students weren't always so involved with reading. Actually, their class was known as "the Dim Bulbs" because of their laid-back attitudes about learning. However, the class gets a substitute teacher, Mr. Hughes, who is also a football coach. He is loud and cheers on his students as he would during a football scrimmage or game. Students retain their casual view toward learning even with the coaching, until they overhear Mr. Hughes will be fired because his students, the Dim Bulbs, have the lowest reading test scores in the district. The students don't want to lose their teacher, so they decide that the way to raise test scores is to read. Cassandra tells her classmates, "It's so obvious. It's a reading test! We've got books in the class, books at home; there are zillions in the media center, zillions more in the public library! How do you get ready for a reading test! By reading!" (p. 72). Because these students valued their teacher and his 110% attitude, they read and did well on the test. This book has a happy resolution for the students and the teacher, although it highlights the stress related to high-stakes testing.

The students in Mr. Hughes's class read everything they could find and talked passionately about their books, favorite authors, and genres to each other. This chapter and the next offer ways for teachers to group books so that students come to appreciate various genres, topics, and authors and illustrators. Within each grouping, there are opportunities for student choice and conversation centered on books. I have created text sets, collections of books and other material (e.g., web pages) related to a theme, topic, author, or illustrator. Each set includes a range of books, from simpler to more complex, so that all readers in a classroom can learn new information and participate in ongoing discussion and activities (Flint, 2008). Robb (2002) writes, "Multiple texts enable teachers to offer students books they can read, improve students' application of reading-thinking strategies, build confidence, and develop the motivation to learn" (p. 29).

I must warn teachers that, once initiated, this thought process regarding books is all-consuming. I can no longer go into the children's section of a bookstore and not think about how I might build a collection of books to share with students. I look at the books on my bookshelves and rearrange them into a new collection. Because of this addiction (I do admit it), this chapter features how to get started with text sets and identifies small collections of books. Chapter 9 targets larger text sets that require more time for exploration. I believe that as teachers consider the sets I have created, they will, likewise contemplate their own text sets that meet the needs and interests of students.

WHY TEXT SETS?

Text sets—collections of books, magazines, or Internet resources (Hassett & Curwood, 2009; Vasquez, 2010)—offer students the opportunity to integrate much of their knowledge about genre, topic, themes, and authors and illustrators. Moss (2000) describes how grouping books around a concept supports readers' development. Specifically, she noted that text sets:

- Allow students to experience a wide variety of literary material throughout an academic year.
- Provide opportunity for students to experience oral and written structures like narration, description, exposition, and persuasion.
- Allow for in-depth exploration of a multitude of genres and allow students to see connections among them, as they come to know each well.
- Provide opportunity for students to discover narrative, visual, and informational text elements through reading. (p. 10)

Moreover, with the use of text sets, students have multiple opportunities to share their experiences through conversation with their teacher and peers, writing, and drawing. These pairings with reading provide numerous opportunities for students to deepen their comprehension and knowledge of text.

Text sets provide opportunities for students to build background knowledge as they explore multiple books about a concept (Mangelson & Castek, 2009). After their first reading or listening to a teacher read aloud a book, students most likely will display naive knowledge about the targeted concept. However, as teachers scaffold from each reading event to another, by the end of a text set, students will have gained sophisticated knowledge about the featured concept.

An example of this growth is demonstrated through the writing of Gabriel. Gabriel's first-grade teacher decided that she wanted students to focus on characters in the books they read. After they read independently, she had students write about a character. In October, Gabriel wrote about Spencer Sharp: "Spencer Sharp was my favorite character. I liked Spencer because of how he looked." Gabriel certainly identified a favorite character and provided a reason for his choice, although his reason is not detailed. In a later similar assignment, Gabriel was able to provide more detail: "I liked Clara Jean because at the end, she made a copy of herself. I wish I could do that. She was prepared for anything, anytime, anywhere." Gabriel's growing understanding of character is certainly evident in a comparison of his responses. He started by identifying a character and a reason for selection, and as the focus continued, he provided details of his choice supported by events from his book.

Through text sets, teachers can easily extend their curriculum in literacy and other content areas to offer students free choice in independent reading that is related to the concept being explored. Students are provided choice in independent materials that is constrained only by a concept. Students who are particularly interested in the concept have multiple opportunities for exploration, and others who are not so interested can find aspects of the concept that are exciting. For instance, many students love exploring the work of a particular illustrator; others who are not so enamored can focus on the artistic style, life history of the person, and so on. Thus, even though a concept might be seen as constraining, with flexibility, students can find an aspect that interests and excites them.

Finally, text sets offer teachers ways to meet the wide-ranging literacy skills of their students. By having simple to complex texts, magazines, and Internet sites available, all reading levels are accommodated. Moreover, by accompanying reading with more open-ended response activities, all students can feel comfortable participating. For example, Gabriel was able to write freely about characters, because his teacher only wanted him to present ideas; there was no expectation that all his words would be spelled correctly. Without the pressure of correct spelling for first-draft ideas, Gabriel as well as the other students in his class could participate.

THINKING ABOUT STUDENT ENGAGEMENT

Throughout this book and in the text sets to be shared, conversation is critical to deepen comprehension or to more thoroughly learn about a concept. Conversation can be tricky, though, because often one or two students end up monopolizing the talk, resulting in other students becoming disengaged. The following are a few ways to support all students as they participate in conversation groups.

- *Labeling partners*. Having students share with a partner is a great way to get them to discuss a concept. However, it may be that only one student in the partnership talks, leaving the other to merely listen. By identifying each partner with a letter or numeral, teachers can direct Partner A to share with Partner B and then vice versa. Through this simple adjustment, all students participate.

- *Think–pair–share*. This strategy is familiar to most teachers. The adjustments that are considered here are that first teachers ask students to chat about something that requires reflection and, second, that students have time to think. For instance, students might be asked to consider a graphic organizer they have completed and what they now know based on the information recorded on the organizer.

- *Write–think–pair–share*. Students write in response to a teacher question. Once finished, students think about their response and anything they may want to add. Then the procedure follows as a pair share. Students can be asked to ponder the theme within a book. The teacher asks them to write the theme and to provide examples from the book to support their decision.

- *Four corners*. In this activity, teachers use the physical boundaries of the classroom to help students explore elements of a book. For example, to assist students in reflecting on their favorite character from a set of books, the teacher labels each corner with the name of a major character from each of the books. Students move to the corner/character they deem their favorite and then they share the reason for their preference with other students in their corner. Teachers can ask one student to report for each group.

- *Book bits*. This assignment helps students to work together and combine their knowledge to arrive at an answer. The teacher collects facts about a topic and writes one or two on fact sheets. Students assemble in groups, work together on a fact sheet to determine the topic that the facts represent. For instance, the teacher can identify characteristics of toads and frogs, and students must determine which animal is being identified. The teacher can also use this strategy for students to identify interesting words or phrases from their reading, details about a setting, and so forth.

- *Numbered heads*. Assembled in groups, all students are assigned a number. Within their group, students converse about a topic. Then students whose numbers are randomly called out by the teacher are asked to share. Through this process all students are prepared to participate because they do not know who might be asked to share.

With each of these strategies, all students participate. They move away from teachers calling on students with raised hands and allowing other students to become passive or disinterested listeners.

In addition to talk, there are many ways to engage students before, during, and after reading. The following are a few suggestions:

- *Graphic organizers*. Graphic organizers serve to deepen comprehension if students record on them as they read informational or narrative text. The graphic organizer serves as a way to collect information more systematically. It provides the support for extended conversations, either oral or written, about the more inferential or critical meaning of a text. Teachers may want to vary the graphic organizer format from a simple paper with the organizer to a foldable format to enhance student motivation. See the Catawba County Schools website (*www.catawbaschools.k12.nc.us/Teacher_Resources/Foldables/Forms/AllItems.aspx*) for several student examples showing how foldables can be used as graphic organizers.

- *Personal connections.* Students write about personal, text-to-text, or text-to-life connections they have with a text. For instance, they might write how one character is similar to another in a different text. Or they might share certain qualities that they have in common with a character (e.g., sloppy, organized). What is important with personal, text-to-text, or text-to-life connections is for students to elaborate on why this connection is important and how it helps them understand the text they are reading (Keene & Zimmerman, 2007). By examining the "why" behind the connection, students are not distracted by the connections they make; rather, they see them as enriching their understanding of text.

- *Bookmarks.* Teachers create bookmarks that are recorded on by students as they read (McLaughlin & Fisher, 2005). Students do not engage in extensive writing on the bookmark; however, they are expected to target their thinking through this reflective process. The *because* part of the bookmark helps students think about their choice, rather than just writing anything that comes to mind (see Figure 8.1).

- *Semantic maps.* Students create a cluster with a topic or important word in the center. If the topic is *snakes*, the other areas of the map might be "Kinds of snakes," "What snakes eat," "The habitat of snakes," and "Enemies of snakes" (see Figure 8.2). Semantic maps work especially well when students are providing description of things, places, people, or events. They also serve as a basic structure for writing a description or a simple report. Students whose classrooms have Kidspiration or Inspiration software on computers can utilize these programs to create their semantic webs.

- *Sketching connections.* Students create a quick sketch of their connection or a detail that is particularly interesting and then write several sentences about it. I have noticed that when teachers ask students to use pencils rather than crayons or markers for the sketch, the project remains a sketch guiding one's understanding rather than an art project.

The use of writing, drawing, and talking enriches all learning, not just the learning that centers around text sets.

In addition to these suggestions, teachers may want students to have a notebook for text set exploration. Similar to a writing notebook, students record interesting information or ideas that they ponder during an exploration. Students can refer to these during their study and add to them. At the end of a text set study, students can refer to these notebooks as they engage in culminating activities.

I wonder	The most important fact is	Something that confused me was
because	because	because

FIGURE 8.1. Bookmarks.

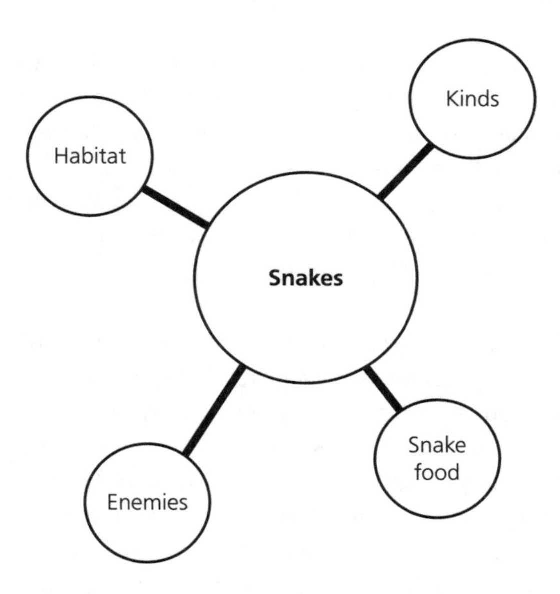

FIGURE 8.2. Semantic maps for *snakes*.

WEBSITE SUPPORT

There are numerous websites that offer teachers support as they engage students in text sets. Some, like Carol Hurst's website (*www.carolhurst.com*), have books grouped by theme or topic. Kay E. Vandergrift's website (*comminfo.rutgers.edu/professional-development/childlit*) has information that helps teachers group books.

Others websites provide ideas and resources for teachers. The American Library Association (*www.ala.org/gwstemplate.cfm?section=greatwebsites&template=/cfapps/gws/default.cfm*) provides links to numerous websites for children. The sites are grouped as follows: animals; literature and languages; science; the arts; reference desk; history and biography; mathematics and computers; and social sciences. The authors and illustrators page (under literature and languages) contains links to many authors' and illustrators' home pages. In addition, each site is coded with an age range for appropriateness (PreK, elementary, middle school, parents, and caregivers).

The Children's Literature Web Guide (*people.ucalgary.ca/~dKbrown*) provides multiple supports for teachers. They have lists of recommended books, children's book award winners, Internet discussion groups, and a web traveler's tool kit that identifies essential children's literature websites. I was thrilled to find a new list of books recommended just for girls. There were 18 recommended books with activities to support them.

Beyond general support websites, there are ones that tie to specific curriculum areas. For social studies, I found the Smithsonian's History Explorer to be an amazing site (*historyexplorer.americanhistory.si.edu*). This site has lessons, activities, media, museum artifacts, and primary source material. The opening page has a timeline that viewers can click on to focus on a particular period in history. Each lesson ties to national U.S. standards in history. The Digital History is another site that supports history (*www.digitalhistory.uh.edu*). It is remarkable because it has video, primary source documents, "virtual" interviews with participants in history (e.g., ethnic voices describing Italian immigration), and lesson plans for teachers. Another website is Have Fun with History (*www.havefunwithhistory.com*). Similar to the other history supporting websites, this one has videos, activities, and support materials for teachers.

At Extreme Science (*www.extremescience.com*), teachers and students can explore astronomy, entomology, geology, oceanography, seismology, and zoology. The site groups areas by earth science and the animal kingdom. On my last visit, I learned about giant squid. There was even a fact sheet that showed the basic anatomy of a squid. National Geographic (*www.nationalgeographic.com*) and National Geographic for Kids (*kids.nationalgeographic.com*) provide science information for students. I learned that trap-jaw ants have the fastest snapping jaw of any species. In addition to information, photos, and videos, these sites provide activities for teachers to use for science exploration.

In the arts area, the Children's Music Website (*www.childrensmusic.org*) shares music for students and resources for teachers. Visitors to the National Gallery of Art website (*www.nga.gov/kids/kids.htm*) can create an abstract painting online. I also found information about artists and how to view their work.

These websites represent a mere fraction of the Internet support that is available for teachers. I was careful to select websites that are created by reputable sources with well validated support for teachers and students.

GETTING STARTED

The preparation of a text set requires several necessary steps. Don't worry, they aren't difficult, and the preparation sets the stage for student reading and enjoyment.

1. Decide on a topic, genre, author, illustrator, or theme. This is often the hardest part because there are so many to choose from. You may consider your students' interests or state standards as a place to begin. Many teachers begin with extensions of their social studies or science curricula. Once comfortable with these extensions, it is easier to consider books that are similar in theme.

2. Once you have decided on the connecting topic, theme, genre, author, or illustrator, begin the search. I always start with a search of the class library and then the school library. I also ask students and colleagues to bring in their personal books, magazines, or website suggestions to enrich the exploration. I find that a collection is quickly gathered. Make sure the books range from easy to complex to satisfy the reading needs of all students. Where appropriate, there should be picturebooks and longer texts.

3. Visit appropriate websites or reference materials to discover additional information about your choice. For instance, when I choose an author or illustrator, I find material about who he or she is as a person to enrich students' reading experiences. Although there are several websites to support this search the Library of Congress (*www.loc.gov/bookfest/2008/toolkit/*) is likely the richest resource for information. Frequently, interviews and webcasts are available. I also explore websites that provide visual support. I want students to appreciate the strength of websites and how they share information that cannot be found in a book.

4. Gather all your materials together. Decide which book or books you will read aloud to students. Called *touchstone books*, these are the foundation for exploration (Calkins, 1994). Students return to them as they ponder a topic, theme, genre, or author/illustrator. These books serve as models to deepen students' thinking throughout an exploration.

5. Decide on books that students can use during independent reading. There should be at least one to two books for each student in the class to choose from. If possible, have a computer available with specific websites bookmarked for easy accessibility.

6. Find a place for displaying books and other material in your classroom. Teachers may want to highlight the topic or theme and what it means to students. Students' thoughts can be posted and added to as the theme or topic is explored. If an author or illustrator is highlighted, a photo of this person is important to include as a supplement to learning. Blank chart paper on which students can post ideas or facts helps contribute to learning. Teachers can title the chart and students can add to it when appropriate.

7. Decide on expectations for students. How will students share their reading? Will they have notebooks to record ideas, graphic organizers, or small-group discussion? More about these choices will be shared in each text set. Will there be specific activities used throughout the study?

8. How will the text set exploration conclude? Will there be a final discussion, PowerPoint presentation, writing activity, or art activity? Teachers need to determine closure for a text set exploration before moving on.

The important part of using a text set is to get started. With each text set, you will think of additional ways to enhance learning and offer students opportunities to expand their knowledge of genres, themes, topics, authors, and illustrators. Students will lead you in innovative ways to think about books through their reading, writing, and discussion, if they are allowed.

Because time in classrooms is so limited, I find it easiest to begin with small text sets. The remainder of this chapter shares small text sets, collections that can be quickly adapted to a classroom. The first sets presented explore illustrators, and later sets are centered on topics or themes.

LEARNING ABOUT AN ILLUSTRATOR

There are so many amazing illustrators to choose from, but I limited my choices to three: Molly Bang, David Wiesner, and Anthony Browne. Each has a unique style, and students can learn the nuances of illustration as they come to understand the connections between illustration and text from them. Exploring illustrators is often a bit difficult for students who have only focused on text, so be patient with their early understandings shared through comments. Their knowledge will develop as they observe over and over again to value and interpret the creative work of an illustrator.

For each illustrator I identify a sample of their work. Teachers can choose one or two to share with students, allowing students to investigate the others during independent reading. Or they can extend an exploration of an illustrator to a larger text set by including other books in more direct ways.

To initiate a text set focused on an illustrator, I recommend that teachers share a bit about the artist because students like knowing about personal details. If students are new to a focus on art, I suggest that one aspect of visual display be selected for each illustrator. For example, students might explore only line or color. Later, when studying a different illustrator, other artistic elements can be investigated. Through a simple focus on one element, with the addition of elements during further exploration, students become comfortable viewing a book and identifying the multiple elements used by a single illustrator.

Molly Bang

Molly Bang grew up in Baltimore with her father, a doctor and her mother, an illustrator of science texts. Bang studied language and literature and spent time in Japan as a translator. She says that her early work involved fairytales, but after her daughter was born she wrote more family-oriented stories. More recently, she has written books about science, but she says they do not sell well (*www.mollybang.com*). In addition to learning a bit about Bang's life at her website, many of the details of her books are discussed. For instance, Bang's research revealed a huge gap in children's literature: mother–daughter conflict and resolution. The finding gave birth to *When Sophie Gets Angry—Really, Really, Angry*. For this book, Bang created a child who looked like Bang did as a child with similar expressions. She discusses how she used mud-like paint for the book and colors that match Sophie's mood. Her book *Picture This* (2000) shares information about the creation of illustrations and shows how structure and color influence emotion. This is an important book to share simultaneously with Bang's picturebooks (see Chapter 6).

Teachers might choose from books illustrated by Molly Bang for a text set (see Figure 8.3).

To begin this focus on Bang's illustrations, I would use *When Sophie Gets Angry—Really, Really Angry* as the touchstone book. The text in this book completely supports her illustrations. The color throughout is vibrant—red for anger and green and blue for calm. Her illustrations convey movement—You can actually see Sophie scream, and her

Name of Book (year)	Brief Description
Ten, Nine, Eight (1991)	This is a counting book featuring a dad putting his little girl to bed.
The Paper Crane (1990)	The story is about a man, quite magical, who comes to a restaurant and creates a paper crane.
Goose (1996)	A goose egg falls out of a nest and lands in a woodchuck's den. This is an ugly-duckling type of story.
The Grey Lady and the Strawberry Snatcher (1980)	This is a story of a strawberry snatcher who tries to steal the grey lady's strawberries.
When Sophie Gets Angry—Really, Really Angry (1999)	This is the story of Sophie, who gets angry and then calms down.
My Light (2004)	A nonfiction book about light and electricity.
Living Sunlight: How Plants Bring The Earth to Life (2009)	A nonfiction book about photosynthesis.
Delphine (1988)	Delphine lives with a wolf, a guinea pig, and a lion. She learns that she has a package at the post office, which worries her. It is a bike.
Old Mother Bear (Miles, 2007)	A story about a mother bear and her cubs.
In My Heart (2006)	This book highlights how children are always in their mother's heart.
Common Ground: The Water, Earth, and Air We Share (1997)	A book about natural resources and their use.
Dawn (2002)	A story of a shipbuilder, his wife and daughter, and a goose.

FIGURE 8.3. Molly Bang text set.

scream takes on a physical shape. Bang uses outline to present each shape in a variety of ways (smooth, jagged, thick, thin). When Sophie is calm the outlines are small, but as she gets angry they get larger and change color to match her mood. Bang's placement of objects is quite interesting. When Sophie is calm, the illustration is centered, with balance; however, when angry, she is on the left, with her feelings displayed on the right. Once a teacher has shared this book, with a focus on illustration, students will clamor to view it individually and learn more about Bang's artistic work. The availability of multiple copies will further support students in these investigations.

On the first reading of this book, I would ask students what they notice about the illustrations and chart their responses so that students can use them for reference. On a second reading/viewing, I would just share the illustrations and have students think about color and how they feel. Students can record their notes on paper divided into four blocks, with a color labeled in each block, or teachers can let students label each block. During viewing, preferably on a document camera where pages can be easily viewed, students record their feelings. Then they can share their thoughts in small groups to enrich their observations.

Afterward, teachers may want to let students experiment with color. Students can draw self-portraits using black marker or pencil. Two copies are made of each drawing, and students complete one drawing using colors that reflect them as being happy or exuberant and the other using colors that represent them when they are sad. Students can then write briefly about themselves when they experience these emotions.

Teachers might stop here with this book, or they might ask students to explore outlining and how it affects an illustration. If this exploration is extended to outlining, students can use their happy and sad images and outline them with marker to emphasize the feeling expressed. When the artwork is complete, teachers can have students engage in a gallery walk, where they carefully observe other students' work. Teachers may ask students to jot notes about the feelings shared in the art as they observe each one.

Following this book, I would share *Picture This* with students. Students will hear Bang's voice as she describes the process of illustration. Teachers may choose to share just the part about shape placement and then return to *When Sophie Gets Angry* to explore this aspect. This book supports this observation because each shape is outlined and carefully placed.

Teachers may decide to engage students in a drawing where shape is explored. Students can create calm images where shapes are balanced or centered. Or they may take a risk and create an edgy work by putting shapes at angles or resting them uneasily like a triangle lying on its corner.

Before moving to other books, teachers can offer students an opportunity to illustrate like Bang. Students can tell a part of a story they wrote through shape placement, or they may choose to illustrate an emotion through color (details are provided in the *Picture This* book; see also Chapter 6 for further detail). These artistic renderings can be placed near Bang's books for students to consider as they view other books illustrated by her.

As another activity, teachers can divide the class in half, with one half exploring Bang's fiction books and the other her informational books. Students can engage in discussion about Bang's use of color and shape in these genres, because they have experience viewing and drawing in her style. Although there is more realistic illustration in her informational books, students learn that her use of color and placement are similar in both. For example, in *Old Mother Bear,* the color is dark brown when the bears are sleeping in a cave and natural sunlight seems to fill the pages when the bears are outside. In *My Light*, the background color of each page shifts to highlight the information, and there are cross-sections of plants to explain photosynthesis. Before moving on, the class divisions would change, so that all children explored both fiction and informational text.

The most complex of Bang's books is *The Grey Lady and the Strawberry Snatcher*, a wordless picturebook. By now they may be surprised that a book without words can be so difficult to understand. Students will feel comfortable with Bang's use of color and shape because they are familiar with her technique. What is new in this book is her use of foreground and background, and these representations will challenge and advance their current artistic understandings. This book is a true visual delight, full of complexity, that makes readers return to previous pages for clarification.

To conclude this book set, I would have students once again draw in the style of Bang. They might take a simple event, like recess or lunch, and create drawings focused on color or shape. These drawings can be shared as students move around the room to explore each other's work and talk about them. They can then be compiled into a class book for further reflection.

To keep this exploration small, teachers might only focus on *When Sophie Gets Angry—Really, Really Angry* and then let students independently explore Bang's other fiction and informational texts. For this smaller exploration, I would focus on either color or shape placement, not both. Through this singular focus, students come to understand one artistic element well.

David Wiesner

As a child, David Wiesner thought about the clocks, elephants, and other creatures on his bedroom wallpaper before going to bed. Later, he pursued his interest in art by studying at the Rhode Island School for Design. His picturebooks—more than 20—are often described as cinematic because they are illustrated in panels similar to comic books and reveal movement from frame to frame (*www.houghtonmifflin.com/authors/wiesner/home.html*). Teachers can learn more about Wiesner and his illustration process at his website. I found it interesting to listen to a podcast of Wiesner talking about his work (*www.loc.gov/podcasts/bookfest/podcast_wiesner.html*). He shares the story of his viewing the *Mona Lisa* and paying more attention to the background and trying to determine where it might be geographically. To view Wiesner talking about *Flotsam* and seeing him at work, visit *alfocus.ala.org/videos/david-wiesner-interview*. A list of some of his books is shared in Figure 8.4.

Because Wiesner has been so popular with children, his wordless picturebooks are easy to find. Most children are familiar with *Tuesday* but may be less so with his other books. Unlike Molly Bang, his work is often surrealistic and includes flying and dream sequences. Beyond the content of his work, Wiesner creates his books similar to movies, so viewers are captured in moving from scene to scene and in his unusual close-ups and distant focal points for his illustrations. Building on knowledge of shape and color, students will be ready to explore the detailed representations in his books and how the eye works across his pages to stimulate movement.

I took a long time selecting a touchstone text, but after reading how Wiesner's early imagination was stimulated by his wallpaper, I settled on *Free Fall*. The front cover shows a boy riding a leaf over water. He is calm, and certainly not afraid, as fish seem to

Name of Book (year)	**Brief Description**
Flotsam (2006)	A young boy discovers objects that wash up on the beach.
The Three Pigs (2001)	An interesting version of *The Three Pigs*.
June 29, 1999 (1992)	A young girl sends her plant experiments into the air.
Tuesday (1997)	Frogs fly in the sky.
Hurricane (1990)	Children watch as a hurricane comes near their home.
Sector 7 (1999)	Shares the amazing possibilities of a field trip.
Free Fall (1988)	A boy dreams of dragons and faraway places.
Chronicles of Narnia Series (C. S. Lewis & Pauline Baynes)	Wiesner illustrates this series.
Night of the Gargoyles (Bunting, 1994)	The story captures gargoyles at night.
Gonna Roll the Bones (2004)	A man leaves his family to gamble.

FIGURE 8.4. David Wiesner's books.

fly out of water near him. The front and back pages of this book are green, suggesting a calm text. This idea is partially reinforced on the first title page, where a map is shown in muted colors; however, the map appears to be moving with the folds that are represented at the top. With more careful viewing, the shapes of land also appear more like clouds than landmasses. On the second title page, seagulls fly above the map, suggesting that the map is in the air and the landforms on the map seem more stable. From these pages, the viewers move to a full-page spread with a boy holding a book, asleep in his bed. Subtly off to the right side of the page is a lamp held in place with a belt, leaving readers wondering why the lamp has to be secured. There are also cloud-like shapes on his pillow. The next page reveals a two-page spread, where the boy's book opens up showing many maps. The squares on his quilt morph into ground contours with mountains in the distance.

While there is white space on the left, the right page continues right to the edge, suggesting movement to the next image. Although Wiesner's images seem realistic, the misty clouds suggest that something unusual will appear, a contradiction in what might typically be expected with such realistic images. Immediately the careful viewer is rewarded: The next page shows a chess game with some pieces appearing human, a bit like *Alice in Wonderland*. The images are very complex throughout this adventure. Birds fly in gloves and the glove shakes hands with the boy. In the background, there is a dragon, although some viewers may miss it totally until they turn the page. Viewers who are familiar with Wiesner's other work will notice characters that appear in other books.

After teachers engage students in carefully viewing this book, which can't happen until they have seen each page at least once, they may want to focus on movement or perspective. In understanding movement, students will notice the lack of white space on right-hand pages, thus blurring the story between pages. They will observe how images like the dragon continue to the next page. Birds always fly left to right. Characters always move left to right. On one page, the forest turns into a curtain on the right through which the characters move. The next scene often begins on the left side of a previous page and then continues to the right. I know that teachers and students will discover many other ways that Wiesner creates movement.

To explore drawing with movement in evidence, students might take a personal narrative they have written and attempt to illustrate it as a picturebook. Through this process, students need to decide how much text to place on each page and then how to illustrate so that the viewer's eye is moved to the next page. As students participate in this process, they may first want to try just two pages, to learn about constructing images in this way.

Perspective varies throughout the book and adds to the story created by illustrations. When first entering the narrative, the viewer is placed at the boy's feet. On the next page, the boy is not the focus of interest; rather, the land and map are with the viewer still looking up. On the next page, the boy is placed with other characters and seems to be of the same size. However, his size changes and soon he is huge compared with the others; they seem like toys. Throughout the book the boy never looks directly at the readers. He does not seem to be concerned by his circumstances, so he is not seeking help. Rather, it appears he has had many similar adventures in the past.

Students love exploring perspective. They might first sketch a drawing of themselves reading a book. Typically, these drawings represent the image as straightforward with the viewer on the same plane as the image. Then students can experiment, sketching the same image but from the perspective of the viewer looking at the image from above or below. This shift in perspective can be challenging because students have not drawn in this way before.

Teachers may choose to end this exploration here and let students independently view Wiesner's books during independent reading. If teachers want to extend this text set, descriptions of ways to do this follow.

Before moving to other Wiesner books, students create a chart that shares what they have learned about Wiesner as an illustrator. They are sure to mention movement and focal point if these features were highlighted during instruction. They may also notice that the story takes place at night, it is a dream, there is flying, and unusual creatures appear. As they engage in other books, they may want to identify those that have similar qualities and those that are different. For instance, *Free Fall, Night of the Gargoyles, Sector 7, Tuesday, and June 29, 1999* showcase flying at night.

To continue to build on the idea of perspective, I would then share *Flotsam*. On the front page, the viewer is held at a distance looking at a boy on the beach. The title page shows items that are carefully placed, with white space surrounding each, and most likely found at the beach. The next page makes you giggle at first; it reveals a small

creature that appears to be afraid. Then when you view the background, you notice a huge eye. The next, double-page spread shows a boy looking through a magnifying glass with the bug in his hand. Wiesner uses panels of illustrations on several pages to show action, especially of the boy finding and studying objects. The viewer is close to the boy's face in some and looking at a distance in others. When the boy is swept into the waves, he looks directly at the viewer, asking for help. Then the boy finds the ancient camera, and the illustrations are in frames providing multiple details of the story. Throughout this book, the viewer is placed at a distance or up close. Images are viewed over the boy's shoulder and then close up with him. While the story is amazing, the illustrations are even better.

To extend students' understanding of perspective, I would have them return to the drawings they did of themselves reading. They have a straight-on view and a view from above or below. Now they can add to these drawings by creating an image close up and one from another angle. These four drawings can be displayed by placing them on a single sheet of construction paper, preferably black, so that all the views represented can be appreciated.

I would end this unit of study with *The Three Pigs*. Although all of Wiesner's books have surrealistic elements, this postmodern picturebook pushes students to unusual illustrations with supportive text. The book begins the story of the three pigs in the traditional way: once upon a time, the wolf watching as houses are built, and the three pigs. Soon, though, the traditional story disappears. When the wolf blows down the house of straw, he blows the pig out of the story. The pig now looks like a real pig. The storybook wolf says he ate the pig but, based on the way his arms and expression are illustrated, it is clear that he didn't and doesn't know what happened. Soon the pigs talk about what happened, and they discover they are out of the story. They fold up the scary pages and build an airplane (flying again). As they fly, there are no words, and Wiesner plays with white space; it increases in size to almost a full two-page spread. The pigs then fly into other stories that are illustrated in very different ways; the nursery rhymes appear to be illustrated by Caldecott. They enter a fairytale with the same dragon from *Free Fall*. Students will certainly notice connections from other Wiesner books, including *Flotsam*. Similar to other postmodern picturebook authors and illustrators, the words themselves become part of the illustration as they blow around on pages and are rearranged.

Students will feel so knowledgeable when they explore *The Three Pigs* because they bring sophisticated skills for viewing to this book. Even if they have experienced this book before, they will find richer understandings by knowing Wiesner's other books, his artistic techniques, and how they are combined within this single book.

As a culminating activity for this unit, students might complete the Wiesner chart they started at the beginning of this exploration and chat about their discoveries. Teachers might need to encourage students in these conversations so they don't merely label what they have viewed. Rather, teachers want students to ponder why Wiesner creates images as he does: Why does he change perspective? How does that affect a viewer? Students can choose an example and talk with their partner about how it makes them feel. What do students notice about an image that is part of a dream? What colors does the artist use?

Students might then select an animal or imaginary creature that Wiesner often represents and draw one of their own, like the frog, fish, or pig. Once they are satisfied with their image, they can create a backdrop or a setting for their image, like the ocean, sky, or maybe even a dragon. After the drawings are finished, they might use watercolor and marker to complete them. These drawings can be posted for others to see, or students can create a PowerPoint to share their images and compare them with Wiesner's work. To focus these images so there is similarity across them, teachers might ask students to represent them as in a dream-like stance, as is so often the situation in Wiesner's books.

Anthony Browne

Anthony Browne talks about how he lived in a pub as a child surrounded by storytelling. His father often told stories to him and drew images, and then taught him to play rugby and to box. He studied graphic design at Leed's College of Art. He began by designing greeting cards and then creating picturebooks as well. Once his picturebooks became successful, Browne stopped designing cards, although many of the images that were on his cards appear in his books. On June 9, 2009, he was appointed as Children's Laureate from 2009 to 2011 in the United Kingdom. Although Anthony Browne does not have a website, there is a video of him—an interview soon after he received the Children's Laureate award—that provides much information (*www.childrenslaureat.org.uk/For-teachers*). I learned that Browne loves to paint gorillas because he feels he is looking into human eyes. He also says that gorillas remind him of his dad, who was a large person.

From listening carefully to Browne, one learns of the importance he places on image within books. He believes that pictures tell more than words because they offer clues to the way a character feels or thinks. His books are complicated, with images that often relate to a character's feelings—like the painting of *Mona Lisa* who is sad—and often the relationships are difficult to determine. His books are surrealistic in style and are considered postmodern. He places paintings in many of his books, often in the background. Figure 8.5 shares some of his books.

Before beginning an exploration of Anthony Browne's artwork, students can engage in the shape game. One student quickly draws a shape, any shape. Then the next person turns it into something. Browne says there is evidence of the shape game in all of his work. These creations can be posted in the classroom's Browne display area and referred to throughout the text set.

Because the concept of shape is important to Browne, I chose *The Shape Game* as the touchstone book for this adventure. Students will immediately see the connection between drawing shapes and this book, where the reason for the shape game is explained. When

Name of Book (year)	Brief Description
Piggybook (1986)	The story of a family that turns to pigs, literally, when the mom leaves for a short time.
My Dad (2000a)	The story of a dad.
My Mom (2005b)	The story of a mom.
Willy the Dreamer (1997)	Willy's dreams are shared.
Willy's Pictures (2000c)	Willy shares his favorite paintings.
Willy and Hugh (2000b)	Willy meets Hugh.
Willy the Wimp (2008e)	Willy tries body building.
Willy the Wizard (2003b)	Willy plays soccer.
Willy the Champ (2008d)	Willy is bullied.
Hansel and Gretel (2008b)	A retelling of the fairytale.
Changes (2008a)	Objects turn into other objects.
Silly Billy (2007)	Billy is a worrier.
King Kong (2005a)	The story of King Kong.
Zoo (1994)	A family visits the zoo.
The Tunnel (1989)	Children enter a tunnel.
Voices in the Park (1998)	A single episode told in four voices.
The Shape Game (2003a)	Making shapes and turning them into art.
Into the Forest (2004)	A variation of *Little Red Riding Hood*.
Little Beauty (2008c)	The story of a gorilla and a kitten.

FIGURE 8.5. Anthony Browne text set.

Browne was a young boy, his mother took him, his father, and brother, George, to a museum. Despite anticipating that this would be a boring activity, Browne says this first visit to the museum "changed his life forever" (unpaged). The front and back pages of this book are filled with children's shape game results. The title page is a major shift, showing a white silhouette stepping from a neighborhood with a fence and tree through a caged door. On the bottom right is a part of a boy's foot walking off the page. So is the foot that of the person leaving the cage?

Does the silhouette represent Browne entering the museum and thus his world opening up? The title page pushes the viewers to contemplate what these images might mean. They demand attention as they bring readers/viewers into this book.

The next, left-page spread shows an artist at work. At first I thought it was Browne, but it doesn't look like him, perhaps it is his father. On the next page, the family drawn on the previous page in four separate images is revealed. This time you can see the artist's hand at work creating a self-portrait of Browne as a young boy. The next pages show the family traveling to the gallery. Browne holds hands with his mother as they enter the museum, framed by his father and brother. When the family views art together the father is frustrated that he cannot tell what a sculpture represents. Many of the pages allow viewers to see the art as the family does; the perspective is from behind them. When viewing a painting of a family, the mother asks her own family what it reminds them of. The next page dissects the painting, with the family commenting on various aspects of it. The following pages are like a puzzle, where viewers have to notice the differences; careful viewers also notice that the family is more interested in the paintings in the museum. Finally, while gazing at a war painting, the family imagines they are part of it and flee from it. When they see a painting with an image that resembles their father, Browne creates a whole painting in the style of Peter Blake's *The Meeting*, where an image of his father is repeated. After they leave the museum, Browne's mother teaches them the shape game.

I chose this book as the one that students will return to throughout the text set because it shows how Anthony Browne became interested in art, leading to his life work. It shares the shape game, so children see that illustration begins with the simplest scribbling. And it highlights the creativeness of Browne as an illustrator. Browne represents feelings in people, and just watching the family walk to the gallery shows how expertly he does this. The mother leads with her head held high and she smiles. Anthony is behind her with his hands in his pocket, appearing happy. Both of them have subtle color in their clothes, which is missing in his father's and George's. In the distance there is an unusual shape chalked on the wall. After this distance, readers see the dad with his hands in his pocket, slumped, looking sad. Then readers see George, hands in pocket, and looking behind him, not engaged at all. Once the family enters the museum, only the mother has color in her clothes; the others are shades of brown. As the family becomes involved and excited by the artwork, they gain color. Now that the art is exciting, objects come from the paintings and spill to the museum's floor or gallery, like blood and a lion. The book ends with inviting children to participate. The elements that Browne uses for illustration are evident in this book: color, surrealism, perspective, characters' feelings, unusual objects throughout, and his connections to real art and artists.

Students can easily experiment with representing characters. They can be asked to sketch a family, limited to four members. Once they have the basic configuration of a family, they can sketch the family but this time with one member who is angry and doesn't want to be there. Teachers can build on this by asking students to once again sketch a family with one member sad. Students can then offer ways to represent the family.

For a short text set, teachers can stop here and allow students to explore the work of Anthony Browne independently. If teachers are ready to explore the often unexplainable work of Browne, the following books and suggestions should support them.

Teachers might follow this book with *Willy's Pictures*, in which Browne replicates many famous paintings with characters that appear in his book, like Willy and Hugh. Moving to all of the Willy books and exploring feelings is a good follow-up. Teachers might also consider why Browne repeats illustrations of gorillas in so many of his books.

Students might return to their earlier family sketches and replicate one family member as an artist has done. I went to the Garden of Praise website (*gardenofpraise.com/art.htm*) to find models for this replication. A variety of paintings are shared to serve as models. There are also art suggestions for teachers to help with this project.

Family is a recurring theme in Browne's books, whether it be a gorilla family or a human family. Although many of his books are obvious in their focus on families, *Voices in the Park* is not. In this narrative, describing a trip to the park using four voices, relationships between a father and daughter and mother and son are shared. Font helps with the narratives, as does the art surrounding the words. Symbols, paintings, color, and shadow all help explore the characters' feelings. I think this is the perfect book to end this unit of study because this is one of Browne's most complex books in words and illustration.

To end this unit, teachers can have students create a single character, perhaps the one from their artist's replication or one from their family sketches. Following this initial drawing, students can create four images showing different feelings. After the person or animal is drawn, they can complete the artwork by adding details to the background that enrich the character's emotions. At the end of this project, they will have four drawings showing a range of emotions. After this experience or in preparation for it, they can choose one of Browne's books and just focus on how he illustrates a person's feelings.

Teachers might also ask students to select one event from their life—perhaps their first experience with school would prove rich for this activity—and then write about it from their perspective. They can then shift perspectives and write it again from their parents and then their teacher's perspectives. Following are some suggestions for this writing:

1. Choose an event. Briefly describe it.
2. *My perspective*—Brainstorm feelings or images from that event. Think about words you might use to describe it. Now write.
3. *Parents' perspective*—Brainstorm feelings or images that your parents might have had during this event. What words might they have used? Now write.
4. *Teacher's perspective*—Brainstorm feelings or images that your teacher had during this event. What words might he or she have used? Now write.
5. Put all your pieces together to show how each of you experienced this event. What did you learn?

A VARIETY OF TEXT SETS

Teachers may want to create text sets where groups of students read individual books and then contribute to a whole-class discussion. Teachers may focus students on a genre or an element within these books that is particularly interesting. For example, if teachers choose mystery books, while they read students might record clues that forecast what is going to happen.

The following are a few small text sets to encourage you to create your own as you support your students in their focused, independent reading.

Books about Real People or Events

For this discussion, I selected three books that reflect the range and quality of the numerous books available. As teachers move from book to book, they want to build students' understanding of each person or event. In *Henry's Freedom Box*, the focus is mainly on one event in a person's life. Students can consider what it means to want freedom. What is freedom? What would you feel if you had to follow someone else's rules whether they were fair or not? The next book, *So You Want to Be President*, shares unknown facts about presidents. Rather than a story, this is an informational text that allows students to learn about presidents. Students can model this book in writing. When they are writing about a person, event, or animal, for instance, they can include little known facts that will interest and excite readers. They might include these facts in borders surrounding other information they are sharing. Building from a focus on individuals, the next book targets the Apollo Space program. Students learn about the brave people and the amazing missions they participated in. This book serves as a model for using photos to tell a story. Students exploring a historical event or person can share information through photographs retrieved from the Internet.

- *Henry's Freedom Box* (Levine & Nelson, 2007). This beautifully illustrated book chronicles a 19th-century Virginia slave's quest for freedom. As a slave, Henry had faced much adversity, including separation from his mother as a child and the loss of his wife and children, who were sold in a slave market, never to be seen again. Henry devises a plan to escape and, with the help of an abolitionist doctor, ships himself in a wooden crate to Pennsylvania. Students will be amazed when they realize this is a true story.

- *So You Want to Be President?* (St. George & Small, 2000). This book reveals unknown facts about various presidents. Students will giggle when they learn that presidents do not take out the garbage and don't have to eat vegetables unless they want to.

- *Mission Control, This Is Apollo: The Story of the First Voyages to the Moon* (Chaikin, 2009). This book shares information about the Apollo space travel program. The photos are amazing.

Teachers can see that this collection was easy to compile, and if these books are not available others can certainly be substituted. Teachers might also decide they just want to focus on people or on events, not mixing the two.

After the three books are shared, teachers may ask students to reflect across books. For example, they may ask students to write about what they learned about bravery or how insignificant, but interesting, facts allow readers to learn more about a person or event.

Books with Puzzles

Books with puzzles challenge readers to pay attention to text and illustration and to solve puzzles within. Teachers might share one book with the whole class, while book club groups read the others.

- *Enigma: A Magical Mystery* (Base, 2008). In this book there is a mystery that is enhanced with a secret code. At the end of the book, readers open a cupboard and find directions on how to crack the secret code.
- *Chasing Vermeer* (Balliett, 2004). Another mystery, throughout this book are pentominoes that help solve it. Messages are hidden within illustrations. To check on interpretations, readers are sent to a website (*www.scholastic.com/blueballiett*).
- *The Calder Game* (Balliett, 2008). Pentominoes also play a part in this book along with Calder code.
- *The Mysterious Benedict Society* (Stewart, 2008). Four children are recruited—based on their answers on tests and challenges—to join this secret society whose mission is evil. Readers can take the tests with the characters and are challenged to work with them to uncover secrets and clues to defeat the villain.
- *The 39 Clues: The Maze of Bones* (Riordan, 2008). In this first book in a series, Amy and Dan Cahill and other family members search for clues to gain a treasure. When their wealthy grandmother dies, in her will she offers her heirs the choice of one million dollars or the chance to find 39 clues that lead to an important treasure. The family fights along the way to find the clues. Readers can solve the puzzles with the characters and learn about historical figures like Benjamin Franklin. Other books in this series are written by different authors like Gordon Korman, who continue the mystery begun by Riordan. There are also website connections where readers can find out more about the clues and join the chase (*www.the39clues.com*).

Each of these books contains puzzles to be solved. Students may explore this genre by creating puzzles within their own mysteries. To prepare students for this writing, teachers draw attention to the puzzle or code shared in the previous books so that students see how it is essential to solving the mystery. Teachers and students might create charts showing these relationships. To facilitate this writing, students engage in thinking before writing:

1. Contemplate the characters in their mystery, identifying the suspects, detective, and witnesses.
2. Determine the setting.
3. Identify the plot, which includes a problem, a mysterious event, a secret, and perhaps a crime.
4. Design a mysterious code or clue that needs solving and help solve the mystery.
5. Start drafting.

Looking-Back Books

Looking-back books can be written from a variety of perspectives: a young character investigating her heritage or a seasoned author or illustrator reflecting on his or her own youth. Teachers may model with one book while book club groups explore the others. The memoir *Knots in My Yo-Yo String* may be the perfect book to read to the class because it shares many memories.

- *Bigmama's* (Crews, 1991). This is a joyous book about a trip to Grandma's house during the summer.
- *When I Was Nine* (Stevenson, 1986). Stevenson recalls the details of a summer when he was 9, pre-World War II. He begs readers to think about their own childhood.
- *When I Was Young in the Mountains* (Rylant, 1982). Filled with beautiful images and gentle humor, this is a story of a young girl's time spent with her grandparents in the mountains.
- *Erika-San* (Say, 2009). Mezmerized by the paintings of Japan that hang in her grandparents' home, Erika decides that when she is older, she will visit the images in the paintings. Readers follow Erika as she grows and finally realizes her dream.
- *Knots in My Yo-Yo String* (Spinelli, 1998). Spinelli shares his story of growing up in Pennsylvania.

As students complete these books, teachers can have students select one vivid memory and write about it. For example, Jed, a second grader, wrote:

> My grandma is funny. She tickles me. This is why she is funny. She lets you have pillow fights and do flips on her bed.

Matthew wrote about his grandfather:

> My grandfather isn't just nice, he is better than that. He does stuff with me. He showed me how to trap a gopher.

From these recollections, Jed and Matthew were ready to prewrite and then draft a personal narrative. Students can use these books to share in mini-lessons during the writing block, so that they examine how these authors wrote about events in their childhood.

Each of these text sets is small and a good place to start. When I read children's books, I often leave notes about possible connections, like a strong main character or looking back. When I think I have a few within a single category, I try them out with small groups of students. As students read individual titles, the whole class makes comparisons from one book to another. Some of these comparisons are oral, and others are recorded on charts or in student notebooks.

ENGAGING STUDENTS

Throughout this chapter, I have shared ways to engage students. Here are a few more ideas:

1. *Character focus.* Choose three or four books that have a strong central character. Have students create a quick sketch of this character. Then have them write a few words to describe this character. They can then complete a chart like the one in Figure 8.6. Through this process, students see how a quality of a character is developed by an author. Once students are successful with one character, they can compare characters within a text set to learn more about personality qualities.
2. *Artistic responding.* When students have completed an exploration of an illustrator's style, they can choose a book by a different illustrator and respond in the style of the illustrator they just studied. For example, students might visually respond to the work of Wiesner using Molly Bang's style. Or they can respond to a novel or informational text using the style of an illustrator. For example, after reading a book about snakes, students can use Wiesner's style for a response.

Henry from *Henry's Freedom Box*—He is brave.		
What Henry says to show he is brave.	What Henry does to show he is brave.	What others say about Henry's bravery.

FIGURE 8.6. Character chart for *Henry's Freedom Box* (Levine & Nelson, 2007).

3. *Tic Tac Tell*. Peterson and Swartz (2008) share an organizer they refer to as Tic Tac Tell (see Figure 8.7). The organizer allows students to describe a favorite book and share details with other students. Teachers can certainly change the topic for each block to match how they want students to consider a book or its illustrations.

At the end of this chapter, it is once again time to take a few moments to reflect:

1. Think about a topic or theme that you are expected to teach. Now visit your library, bookstore, and the web to discover books about it.
2. Find five books listed within this book that you have not read, secure them, and just enjoy reading them.
3. Choose an illustrator, one who is new to you. Find several books illustrated by this person. Think about the artwork. What did you feel and learn?

Book title	First sentence of book	Author's name Illustrator's name
A sentence I liked	A sketch that could be the cover of the book	Three interesting words
My opinion of the book	I learned	I wondered

FIGURE 8.7. Tic Tac Tell.

RECOMMENDED READING

For readers who would like to know about creating text sets, the following resources should help.

Duke, N., & Bennett-Armistead, S. (2003). *Reading and writing informational text in the primary grades: Research-based practices*. New York: Scholastic.

The authors discuss informational text and how to share it with students and suggest ways to engage students in writing in response to their reading of informational text.

Peterson, R., & Eeds, M. (2007). *Grand conversations: Literature groups in action*. New York: Scholastic.

This book supports teachers in engaging students in critical conversations about books. Each time I read this book, I learn something new about student conversations.

Peterson, S., & Swartz, L. (2008). *Good books matter.* Portland, ME: Pembroke.

This book offers guidelines and recommendations for selecting children's books. I think teachers will appreciate the graphic organizers they share for student engagement.

Student Voices

Afternoon on the Amazon
(Osborne, 1995)

"The best part was when they came to the tree house. There were army ants marching. Jack read about them: 'When animals hear a crackling sound, they flee in panic. The sound means that 30 million flesh eating army ants are marching through the dead leaves' (p. 21). When the army ants came, they were so small and the animals went crazy."
—Micah, a first grader

CHAPTER 9

Learning about Authors and More Extensive Text Sets

> I would like to suggest that, as we thoughtfully choose our books and questions and watch children leap into new territory, new ways of knowing and structuring their worlds, we be unafraid to grow with them . . . As we set out to stretch children in their responses to the literature that we share, let's make sure that we have signed on as well.
>
> —SUSAN S. LEHR, *The Child's Developing Sense of Theme: Responses to Literature* (1991, p. 167)

Lehr's words open opportunities for teachers to explore books with their students, setting aside their current knowledge of a book to see it once again with the new views of their students. For example, while reading *Voices in the Park* (Browne, 1998) to a first-grade class, I thought they would focus on the different characters and their experiences in the park, which many students did. One student, however, asked, "How can a gorilla have a chimpanzee child?" Although I did not have a satisfactory answer for the child, this thoughtful question motivated me to reevaluate the way I look at books, to examine more carefully the subtle nuances, and, specifically in *Voices in the Park*, question why indeed did a gorilla have a child who is a chimpanzee.

Within this chapter, I share author text sets and more extensive text sets. These longer explorations allow teachers to move students beyond surface understandings to deeper, more complex thoughts about a collection of texts and, in particular, an author. My hope is that these collections will provide models for teachers in selecting texts and finding appropriate activities for students to engage in throughout longer explorations. To support this more extensive understanding, I first share suggestions for student response that foster engagement and more reflective contemplation of reading.

For initial response to a book, students may:

- Retell.
- Offer immediate responses, like "I am sad" or "It makes me happy."
- Predict the next element of a plot.
- Describe a character or setting.

As students engage in a text set and read multiple books by an author, focused on a genre or a theme, they may:

- Make text-to-text connections.
- Make text-to-self connections.
- Make text-to-world connections.
- Understand the personality of a character through his or her description, actions, and what other characters say.
- Have empathy for a character and better understand his or her circumstances.

With support from a teacher through modeling and think-alouds, students may:

- Evaluate the motives of characters.
- Deliberate why the author or illustrator made specific choices.

Critical Reading of ______________________	
Something important that I want to remember about this book	An anomaly: Something I did not expect
A question I have	A connection I have with our world is

FIGURE 9.1. Critical reading response frame.

- Critically evaluate a book.
- Consider a book's theme.

Heffernan (2004) suggests a writing response frame (Figure 9.1) to help students develop critical reading skills. His frame includes four blocks for student response.

A second strategy format, Alphaboxes (Morrison & Wlodarczyk, 2009), helps students attend to details. Using this strategy, students can share fiction or information details from the text they are reading. Figure 9.2 shares a partial Alphabox from a study of wolves

A third strategy, suggested by Peterson and Swartz (2008), supports students in building personal connections during reading. Students reply to the following prompts, or others determined by the teacher or students, as seen in Figure 9.3. This strategy form works best when students are reading the same book.

As teachers move from book to book within an exploration, they may want to think of ways to engage students in discussion that moves them from initial basic responses to more complex ones, as just detailed. The frameworks shared or other guides to promote deeper levels of comprehension help students with the shift from literal to inferential or critical understandings.

A Angry wolves have erect ears	**B**	**C**	**D**	**E**
F	**G** Gray wolves	**H** Host for rabies	**I**	**J**
K	**L**	**M**	**N**	**O** Omnivores
P Wolves live in packs	**Q**	**R** A relaxed wolf has his or her tail down	**S** Wolves use scent for marking	**T** Timber wolf
U	**V**	**W**	**X**	**Y**
Z				

FIGURE 9.2. Alphabox for wolves.

These are my personal connections to . . .
People I know
Adventures I have had
Places I have been
News events
Other stories
Feelings I have experienced
Problems I have had
Other books I have read or written
Television or movies I have seen
Internet visits

FIGURE 9.3. Personal connections.

LEARNING ABOUT AN AUTHOR

Avi is an excellent author to use as a basis for this text set because his work crosses into all genres, from picturebooks to novels. Teachers can find background information about Avi from a variety of Internet sources, among them the Avi website (*www.avi-writer.com*) or a *Book Links* interview, "Talking with Avi" (Weisman, 2009). From my search, I learned that he was born in New York City and raised in Brooklyn. As a child, he read comic books and listened to radio. He was not very good in school because he was a poor writer (he had dysgraphia) and had to be tutored. He was a playwright and a librarian. He also shares five secrets to good writing that teachers can bring to their classrooms:

1. Write.
2. Rewrite. (He rewrites a book 56 times or more.)
3. Write for a reader.
4. Listen, read your work out loud.
5. Read: The more you read the better you write.

On the Avi website, his books are categorized by genre and reading level so that teachers can easily select and arrange books to suit classroom needs.

To begin an exploration of Avi, teachers might describe his books that are displayed in the room so that students become familiar with the possibilities. Students can choose which books they want to read or perhaps the genre, and then the teacher can form small book club groups based on student selection. By the end of the exploration, students might have read three or more of his books, with the teacher reading one aloud as a touchstone book.

Once students have an understanding of Avi's books and have chosen their first to read, teachers can share the author's background. Toward this end, there are countless sources. A Google search identifies sites that have videos of Avi talking about his writing and the winning of the Newbery Medal for *Crispin: The Cross of Lead*. At *www.readingrockets.org/books/interviews/avi*, viewers hear Avi talk about writing and how it is still difficult for him, which will surprise students because he is so accomplished. He also provides pointers for the teaching of writing. At *www.plumtv.com/videos/vail-avi/index.html*, Avi talks about being proud to have his books in the library and how a writer must always consider the reader.

In addition to Avi's website and videos, I found two books that provide information about him: *Avi* (Markham, 1996) and *Presenting Avi* (Bloom & Mercier, 1997). The first book includes a chapter about his writing. Markham summarizes Avi's thoughts about his audience: "Most young people are as emotionally complex as adults. Some perhaps are more complex. He's also convinced that today's young people are aware of the harsh realities of life. Therefore, he never tries to simplify complicated situations" (p. 89). Because of his belief in the expertise of children readers, Avi writes fast-paced compelling stories that keep readers turning pages. In *Presenting Avi*, the authors identifies Avi as a storyteller, magician, historian, stylist, risk taker, truth teller, subverter, family auteur, writer, and subject. As students read some of the Avi's books, they might explore these labels and how they relate to the text.

To begin the author exploration, students can contribute to a chart that shares important facts about Avi. While reading his books, students keep an eye out for facts that show up in text or passages that reflect Avi's personal experience and make notes. From this activity, students can individually choose two labels that the authors of *Presenting Avi* used to describe him. One student might choose to focus on Avi as magician and historian while another might choose risk taker and truth teller. These labels allow readers to appreciate Avi's writing from a different perspective than just reading the plot and appreciating the characters. A brief snippet of a student's notebook is shared in Figure 9.4.

Alternatively, students can consider Avi's work by focusing on word pictures, characters, plots, themes, and so on. Students can have personal charts similar to the one in Figure 9.5 to record their thoughts.

These charts can facilitate conversation among students reading the same book and comparisons across books. Students learn about the way Avi creates word pictures, similarities among characters, plot, and theme; and so on.

Avi's books are listed by category in Figure 9.6, starting with picturebooks. Importantly, many of these books cross category or genre, and some are multigenre. Students will be impressed with the breadth of genres that Avi works with.

Considering that the list in Figure 9.6 does not even include all of Avi's books it is clear that choosing a touchstone book will be very difficult. However, I chose *Crispin* because not only did it win the Newbery Medal but it also is historical fiction, a genre that Avi prefers. Avi notes that there are three issues when writing historical fiction: getting the language right; thinking the same way as people would have during that time period; and sharing clothing, home, and items from that time (*www.plumtv.com/videos/vail-avi/index.html*). To support understanding of Avi's insight, using a blank paper folded into three sections, while the story is being read, students note details that target

Avi as magician	**Avi as historian**
In Strange Happenings, Avi writes about transformations. A boy turns into a cat and a cat turns into a boy. There are magic mirrors too. Animals can talk.	In The True Confessions of Charlotte Doyle, Avi shares information about 1832. Women wore full skirts and high-buttoned shoes. Charlotte crossed the ocean from England to the U.S. in a ship. (There were no planes.)
In The Mayor of Central Park, a squirrel is the mayor and animals play baseball.	In Don't You Know There's a War On?, Avi shares headlines about the war and military draft from 1943. He talks about an old wagon called the Radio Flyer.

FIGURE 9.4. Notebook snippet.

Name of Book ______________________
Genre ______________________
Main characters and descriptions
Basic plot
Word pictures
Theme
Connections
I still wonder

FIGURE 9.5. Student chart for Avi books.

Name of Book (year)	Genre
The Bird, the Frog, and the Light (1994)	Fable
Things That Sometimes Happen (1970)	Short stories
What Do Fish Have to Do with Anything? (1997)	Short stories
Silent Movie (2003a)	A silent movie about immigration and adventure
City of Light, City of Dark (1993)	Comic book novel
The End of the Beginning (2004b)	Adventure featuring animals
A Beginning, a Muddle, and an End (2008a)	Adventure featuring animals
Ragweed (1999b)	Adventure featuring animals
Poppy (1995)	Adventure featuring animals
Poppy and Rye (1998)	Adventure featuring animals
Ereth's Birthday (2001b)	Adventure featuring animals
Poppy's Return (2005a)	Adventure featuring animals
Poppy and Ereth (2009b)	Adventure featuring animals
The Mayor of Central Park (2003c)	Adventure featuring animals
Prairie School (2001c)	Historical fiction
The Secret School (2001d)	Historical fiction
Iron Thunder (2007a)	Historical fiction and multigenre
Hard Gold (2008b)	Historical fiction and multigenre
Crispin: The Cross of Lead (2002)	Historical fiction
Crispin: At the Edge of the World (2006a)	Historical fiction
The Traitors' Gate (2007b)	Historical fiction
Midnight Magic (1999a)	Comedy
Murder at Midnight (2009a)	Mystery
Strange Happenings (2006b)	Mystery
The Book without Words (2005b)	Fantasy
True Confessions of Charlotte Doyle (1990)	Adventure
The Good Dog (2003b)	Adventure
Don't You Know There's a War On? (2001a)	Adventure, comedy, and multigenre
Never Mind (2004a)	Realistic fiction
Nothing But the Truth (1991)	Realistic fiction and multigenre

FIGURE 9.6. Avi's books.

Language	Thinking	Clothes and other details
A whipping or a clipping of the ear Long past the hour of Compline	Sought forgiveness for sinful life Being declared a Wolf's Head	Parchment Barley bread Watered ale

FIGURE 9.7. Historical fiction issues with details from *Crispin*.

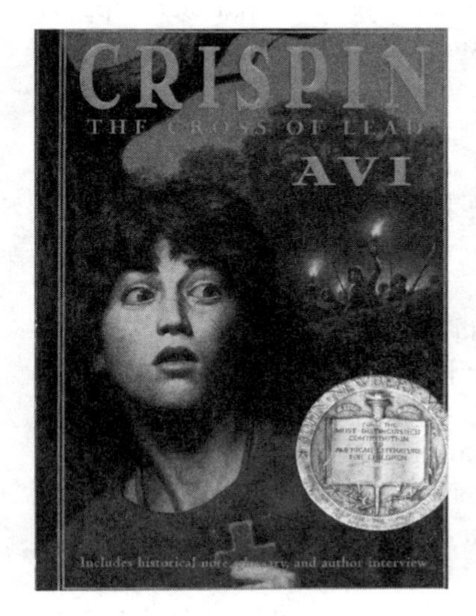

each of the issues (see Figure 9.7 for an example from the beginning of the book).

With this book as a read-aloud, small groups could read other historical fiction during independent reading and complete a similar chart either with a partner or alone. This close focus on historical fiction, through Avi's books, allows students to appreciate the research required and the writing expectations of this genre.

Teachers then have many other options for engaging students with other Avi books. They may have students choose a different genre or just an interesting book. Students will enjoy reading with a partner or small group so they can talk about their reading.

At the end of each week, students can synthesize their reflections about Avi's books, either orally or written. Teachers can place students into small groups to facilitate discussion, of the teacher-selected topic (e.g., genre, word pictures, characters). For instance, if teachers are focused on genre, the discussion would center on details of the genre that students learned from reading Avi's books. Importantly, teachers guide the topic for conversation by encouraging students to focus on this topic when reading. When students return to book club or independent reading, these contributions will enrich their understandings.

As a culminating activity, it would seem appropriate for students to create a multigenre project about Avi. Teachers can decide how many pieces should be included in the project, with an overall explanation of the pieces. Typically, three or four pieces are sufficient to create a well-crafted project. For example, for their genres, students might write an ad for a new Avi book, a brochure about a book, a death notice about a character, a drawing of a setting, or a short biography. These pieces would be compiled and organized (which should be read first, second, and so on), and then students would describe how they decided on each piece and how each piece shares information about Avi. Students could share these projects with each other, and perhaps parents might be invited to the classroom to learn about Avi as well.

Organization is critical to students' success when working on multigenre projects. Students can begin by brainstorming possible genres. Then they can select three or four they want to use. At this point, each student must decide which genre he or she will write first. It is important for teachers to confer with students as they write so they don't get stuck. Once one genre is complete, each student can move to the next, and so on, until the three or four pieces are complete.

Multigenre projects take more than a week, so teachers may want to engage students in these projects as they are learning about Avi and reading his books. An overlap in reading and writing is integral to the exploration of Avi. Teachers may want to create timelines for genre completion so that students stay on track. When finished, students benefit from working with a partner as they reflect on their writing to determine a presentation sequence and what they learned through this writing. This partner support allows students to move beyond a single genre and consider the grouping of genres and what they share about this author.

EXTENDED TEXT SETS

Exploring Mysteries

Mystery is a genre that is enjoyed by boys and girls alike. Moreover, there are a multitude of mysteries written for all ages and for all reading levels. To set the stage for this exploration, teachers can have a display in the classroom with multiple mystery choices and with a poster highlighting mystery and its essential characteristics. Students can brainstorm characteristics from their previous reading as a beginning. As students read mysteries, teachers can stop periodically to add to this list.

I went to the Scholastic website (*teacher.scholastic.com*) and found a detective dictionary. The dictionary included the following words: *alibi, clue, crime, detective, evidence, mystery, red herring, sleuth, suspect, victim*, and *witness*. Students will enjoy working with these words, identifying them when found during their reading. Most likely, teachers will need to help students learn what a red herring is and how to recognize one during reading. This website also has a suspect list for students to guide their reading. The suspect list includes three columns, with the suspect's name in the first, the reason this character is a suspect in the middle column, and a third column for checking if the character is no longer a suspect. Forms like these can help students pay careful attention to the characteristics of mysteries.

To begin this exploration, teachers need to locate many mysteries for reading aloud and for independent reading. Figure 9.8 shares mysteries that teachers might select.

Once the books are located, I would choose two touchstone books—one easy and one more complex—and begin with a book from the *Cam Jansen* mysteries or *A to Z Mysteries*. By beginning with a simple mystery, students can pay attention to the characteristics of mystery. The goal of this first touchstone book is to build knowledge of this genre. Then I would choose a more complex mystery that engages students in contemplating clues. Teachers can prepare an organizer to support students as they listen to this complex mystery. Figure 9.9 provides some ideas for this organizer. After daily

Name of Book	Author (publisher)
Cam Jansen mysteries	David Adler (Scholastic)
The Boxcar Children mysteries	Gertrude Warner and others (Albert Whitman and Company)
A to Z Mysteries	Ron Roy (Random House for Young Readers)
Jigsaw Jones mysteries	James Preller (Scholastic)
Nate the Great	Marjorie Sharmat and Marc Simont (Delacorte Books for Young Readers)
Maximum Ride mysteries	James Patterson (Little, Brown)
39 Clues	Various authors (Scholastic)
The Mysterious Benedict Society mysteries	Trenton Lee Stewart (Little, Brown)
The Evolution of Calpurnia Tate	Jacqueline Kelly (Henry Holt)
The Egypt Game	Zilpha Keatley Snyder (Yearling)
Scat	Carl Hiaasen (Knopf)
Chasing Vermeer, The Wright 3, and The Calder Game	Blue Balliett (Scholastic)
On the Run mystery series	Gordon Korman (Scholastic)
Inkheart, Inkspell, and *Inkdeath*	Cornellia Funke (Scholastic)
When You Reach Me	Rebecca Stead (Wendy Lamb Books)
Gregor the Overlander	Suzanne Collins (Scholastic)
Swindle and *Zoobreak*	Gordon Korman (Scholastic)
Murder at Midnight	Avi (Scholastic)

FIGURE 9.8. Mysteries.

reading, teachers would provide time for students to respond on an organizer so they can keep track of the story over several days of reading.

To complement the reading of mysteries, students can write their own. I asked students to plan their writing using the Mystery Cube at *readwritethink.org/materials/mystery_cube*. Although I used this cube for writing, students can also use it for reading mysteries, completing various sides of the cube during their reading. Once students sign in, all they need to do is write their first name; they see the numbers for each side of the cube. The first side of the cube is setting. If students are writing their own story, they would indicate the setting; for reading, they would describe the setting from their book. The second side of the cube asks the student to describe the detective. For the third side,

Mystery Characteristic	What I Noticed about this Characteristic
Characters Suspects Detective Witnesses	
Setting	
Plot Problem Secret The crime	
Clues	
Red herring	
Solution of the mystery	

FIGURE 9.9. Graphic organizer for mystery.

they describe the crime or mystery. On the fourth side, students focus on the victim. The fifth side asks students to identify their clues. The last side requires students to indicate the solution. Once completed, the cube sheet can be printed with the details added and can be folded into a cube.

When Josh, a fourth grader, completed his cube as a writing organizer for his mystery he wrote:

> Setting—an old house and his house
>
> Detective—Me
>
> Mystery—The light goes on in the old house. I go to investigate and I run into ghosts. How did the light go on?
>
> Victim—Me when I went to find out why the light went on
>
> Clues—the light, a noise, ghosts
>
> Solution—I ran out into the night

From this beginning, Josh drafted his story where a part of it is shared in Figure 9.10.

Although the whole of Josh's mystery is not shared, it is clear that he is building his mystery carefully and that he has placed himself as the victim and detective. This snippet of his writing shows that he has internalized the key characteristics of a mystery. Moreover, he draws readers in with his dialogue and his sharing of feelings.

To organize the reading of mysteries, teachers can let students choose a mystery that they want to read with their book club; this would require that multiple copies of some titles be available to students. Teachers can also suggest that each student reads a mystery of choice. Then groups can be convened where students share important characteristics of their book and note similarities and differences across books.

> The Old, Old House
>
> One night I was going to bed and then a light went on in the old, old house. I thought, "no one lives in it." So I went to investigate. When I got there I heard a noise. It said, "Come In." I just stared at the house like this 
>
> It said again, "Come In." So I went in. I was scared to death, but I still went in. I needed to know what was happening.
>
> At first, I was scared, but I wanted to know why the lights went on. What if there were thieves in the house? When I entered, I saw some old, old stairs. I started to go up, but half way up I heard a shriek. Maybe a murder was happening? I didn't care. I started up the steps again.

FIGURE 9.10. Josh's mystery.

Exploring Wolves and Dogs in Fiction and Informational Text

The next text sets are much larger, with one text set (wolves) transitioning to the text set about dogs. The idea for these text sets grew out of my reading *Beware of the Storybook Wolves* (Child, 2006). As I read this book, I thought that children would love to explore the wolves that are in storybooks—there are many. I then included real wolves because they are interesting too. I discovered the book *The Dog Who Cried Wolf* (Kasza, 2005), and the connections to dogs developed. This text set ties to science standards focused on mammals and those that are tame or wild. It supports language arts standards centered on comprehension of informational and fiction texts.

To begin the exploration centered on wolves, I would place students into groups of four or five depending on the number of students in a classroom. Each group would have several informational books about wolves to explore. Once children have had a chance to explore all of the books, they can build a chart that showcases facts about wolves. This process can repeat, perhaps on a second day, with groups exploring books from other groups. Once teachers feel that students have discovered sufficient facts about wolves, they can have students group the facts by description, food, natural enemies, and so on. Figure 9.11 highlights several informational books about wolves.

Once students have an understanding about real wolves, they are ready to add images of wolves in informational text. To enrich this inquiry, students can expand their chart of wolf facts where they add a check when a fact is confirmed in informational text or add a fictional detail about wolves in a final column (see Figure 9.12).

There is an amazing range of narrative with wolves as characters. For a touchstone book, I chose *Beware of the Storybook Wolves.* This book immediately informs students of

Parker, B. (1998). *North American Wolves.* New York: Scholastic.
Berger, M. (2002). *Howl!: A Book about Wolves.* New York: Cartwheel.
Simon, S. (1995). *Wolves.* New York: HarperCollins.
George, J. (1998). *Look to the North: A Wolf Pup Diary.* New York: HarperCollins.
Johnson, S. (1987). *Wolf Pack: Tracking Wolves in the Wild.* Minneapolis: Lerner.
Evert, L. (2000) *Wolves.* Lanham, MD: NorthWord Books for Young Readers.
Howker, J. (2002). *Walk with a Wolf: Read and Wonder.* New York: Candlewick.
Busch, R. (2007). *The Wolf Almanac, New and Revised: A Celebration of Wolves and Their World.* Guilford, CT: Lyons Press.
Patent, D. (1994). *Gray Wolf, Red Wolf.* San Anselmo, CA: Sandpiper Press.
Barry, S. (2007). *Wolf Empire: An Intimate Portrait of a Species.* Guilford, CT: Lyons Press.

FIGURE 9.11. Informational books about wolves.

Real Facts	Confirmed in Text	Fictional Details
Wolves live in packs	✓ *Wolves*	Wolves can talk
Wolves are predators	✓ *Little Red Riding Hood*	Wolves can read
The dominant wolf is the alpha male		Wolves fly in hot air balloons
Wolves howl to communicate		Wolves play video games
Whimpers show submission		Wolves wear clothes
Wolves live in dens		
Wolves were almost extinct		

FIGURE 9.12. Chart for wolf reading.

the shift from information to fiction. Herb loves to hear stories before he goes to bed, but he makes his mother take the book away if it has wolves in it because he is afraid. The wolf from *Little Red Riding Hood* proves to be a major character in this book.

From this book, teachers may want to share versions of *Little Red Riding Hood*, including *Lon Po Po* (Young, 1989). Although the storyline will be familiar across books, children will be enraptured by how various illustrators create their wolf. Some are definitely scarier than others. After reading multiple versions of this story, teachers may want to read *There's a Wolf at the Door* (Alley, 2008), which shares five fairytales with wolves in them: *The Three Little Pigs, The Boy Who Cried Wolf, Little Red Riding Hood, The Wolf in Sheep's Clothing*, and *The Wolf and the Seven Little Goslings*. This book is written in a comic book format, with one story merging into the next.

To round out the text set, I selected a few books that I found to be unique and knew would appeal to children. I start with books that are comfortable for teachers and then move to more complicated, dark ones.

The first book is *Nicky and the Big, Bad Wolves* (Gorbachev, 1998). A bunny, sleeping with four sisters or brothers, wakes up from a bad dream where wolves are chasing him. In one illustration, the wolves almost appear like crocodiles, because their mouths are enhanced. On other pages they drive motorcycles, ride in a boat, or ride in a hot air balloon. Finally, the bunny's mother chases off the wolves by sweeping them away.

A similar book is *Wolf's Coming!* (Kulka, 2007). The book shows animals afraid and running because Wolf is coming, apparently to eat them. The book ends with Wolf coming into their home for a surprise birthday party: his own! Observant readers will be full of questions after hearing and viewing this book. For instance, why were the animals afraid when they were throwing the party? Why does the illustrator make Wolf look so scary?

A must-read book for this inquiry is *Wolves* (Gravett, 2006). A rabbit goes to the library and checks out a book about wolves. As the rabbit is reading, the wolf emerges from the book, although the rabbit is so engrossed in the book he doesn't even notice.

The wolf gets larger throughout the book and the rabbit gets smaller, and it appears that the wolf may have eaten the rabbit. This situation is confirmed: The next page shows a partially eaten book cover and no rabbit. The next page has a message telling the reader that no rabbits were eaten because this is work of fiction and provides an alternative ending: The wolf is a vegetarian. I can't imagine the eyes of children when they discover that the wolf actually ate the rabbit. Shocking!

The next two books are unique in both illustration and text. *The Wolves in the Walls* (Gaiman, 2003) begins with Lucy telling her mother that she hears wolves in the walls. Her mother replies, "If the wolves come out of the walls, then it's all over" (unpaged). Readers/viewers should be thinking, "She didn't say there weren't wolves in the wall!" What does it mean it's all over?" Lucy goes to her father, who says there aren't wolves in the walls and then repeats what Lucy's mother said about them. As Lucy sleeps, the wolves come out of the wall and the book changes to gray tones. Lucy creeps into the walls and finds a wolf snoring. Then the whole family creeps into the walls and finds a pack of wolves partying. There is a satisfying resolution to this book, but the images stay with the viewers. *Woolvs in the Sitee* (Wild, 2006) is bizarre and filled with the invented spelling of the main character. The book begins with wolves coming for everyone, and the colors are somber and somewhat terrifying. Ben visits Mrs. Radinski and she tells him there aren't any wolves, but he tells her to listen more carefully. She disappears. The book ends with Ben alone, asking readers to join him.

As a culmination to this exploration about wolves, the class could be divided into two groups, each completing separate projects. One group will create a book that shares the 25 most interesting facts about wolves. Students will decide on the facts and provide sidebars, tables, charts, maps, and sketches to enrich their book project. The other group will create a book about narrative wolves. They will also decide on 25 interesting facts about wolves in narratives. However, rather than informational text graphics, they will illustrate each of their facts to enrich their meaning. Teachers can certainly manipulate how they want this project to be completed. For instance, those with smaller classes might consider reducing the number of facts.

The study of wolves would end with *The Dog Who Cried Wolf*, because it segues from wolves to dogs. In this book, a young girl reads to her dog, Moka, and tells him that he is like a wolf. Moka decides that being a wolf is much more fun than being a dog, until he meets real wolves, that is.

Once this shift in topic is made, the available books would focus on dogs, and classroom displays would change accordingly. Teachers have many choices in how they might engage students throughout this exploration or as a culminating activity. Next, I list several activities that might support student knowledge during their reading.

1. With notebook sections divided into two parts—fact and fiction—while they read, students record interesting pieces of fact and fiction.
2. Students choose a breed of dog and create a report filled with sketches and facts. They might share their report through PowerPoint.
3. Students create a podcast showcasing interesting information about dogs.

4. Students create an alphabet book and, for each letter, add information about fiction and nonfiction dogs.
5. Students create a multigenre project about dogs.
6. Students complete and share a chart on dogs similar to the one created for wolves.
7. Students focus on how dogs are illustrated in picturebooks and create a sketchbook of their own illustrations.
8. Students can create a book similar to *Once I Ate a Pie.*
9. Students can write about one event in a dog's life from the dog's perspective.

If these suggestions do not resonate, I know that you will have a plan to keep students involved during reading and for a culminating project.

There are tons of books about dogs. Figure 9.13 lists a sampling of these, categorized by genre, which ranges from wordless books to novels. I think these would all be appropriate for intermediate students. For younger students, I would provide fewer novels and focus more on picturebooks.

I chose two touchstone books for this exploration: a poetry picturebook—*Once I Ate a Pie*—and two novels—*A Dog's Life* and *Everything for a Dog.* Teachers can decide which one works better for them. I love these three books because they use dogs' voices.

Name of Book	Genre
Strother, R. (2008). *W is for Woof: A Dog Alphabet.* Chelsea, MI: Sleeping Bear Press.	Nonfiction, alphabet book
Beck, P. (2007). *Uncover a Dog.* San Diego: Silver Dolphin Books.	Nonfiction
Dewin, H. (2007). *The Dog: Dogs Rule and Cats Drool!* New York: Scholastic.	Nonfiction
Jordan, A. (2008). *The Dog: Best in Show.* New York: Scholastic.	Nonfiction
Dewin, H. (2006). *Nintendogs: Do you Know Your Dog?* New York: Scholastic.	Nonfiction
Jenkins, S. (2007). *Dogs and Cats.* Boston: Houghton Mifflin.	Nonfiction
Spinner, S. (2008). *Uno: Blue-Ribbon Beagle.* New York: Grosset & Dunlap.	Nonfiction
Newman, L. (2004). *Hachiko Waits.* New York: Scholastic.	Novel based on true story
Bix, D., & Hansen, A. (2006). *At the Dog Park.* Edina, MN: Gryphon Press.	Picturebook based on realistic situation
Blake, R. (2002). *Togo.* New York: Philomel Books.	Historical fiction

(cont.)

FIGURE 9.13. Books about dogs.

Name of Book	**Genre**
Day, A. (1989). *Carl Goes Shopping*. New York: Farrar Straus Giroux.	Wordless book
Bruel, N. (2007). *Poor Puppy.* New York: Roaring Brook Press.	Fiction and alphabet book
Wood, A. (2007). *A Dog Needs a Bone*. New York: Blue Sky Press.	Fiction
Page, G. (2006). *How to Be a Good Dog*. New York: Bloomsbury Children's Books.	Fiction
Hill, E. (1992). *Spot Goes to a Party.* New York: Putnam's.	Fiction with pop-ups
Lee, S., & Lee, T. (2005). *Please, Puppy, Please*. New York: Scholastic.	Fiction
Broach, E. (2005). *Wet Dog*. New York: Scholastic.	Fiction
Willems, M. (2008). *The Pigeon Wants a Puppy.* New York: Hyperion Books.	Fiction
Rathman, P. (1995). *Officer Buckle and Gloria*. New York: Putnam's.	Fiction
Teague, M. (2002). *Dear Mrs. LaRue: Letters from Obedience School.* New York: Scholastic.	Fiction
Pilkey, D. (1993). *Dogzilla*. New York: Harcourt.	Fiction
Pilkey, D. (1994). *Dog Breath*. New York: Scholastic.	Fiction
Stevens, J., & Crummel, S. (2008). *Help Me, Mr. Mutt!: Expert Answers for Dogs with People Problems*. New York: Harcourt.	Fiction, multigenre
Zion, G. (1988). *Harry and the Lady Next Door.* New York: HarperTrophy.	Fiction, simple novel
Schmidt. A. (2009). *Loose Leashes*. New York: Random House.	Poetry
MacLachlan, P., & Charest, E. (2006). *Once I Ate a Pie*. New York: Joanna Cotler Books.	Poetry
Creech, S. (2001). *Love That Dog*. New York: Joanna Cotler Books.	Novel in poetic form
DiCamillo, K. (2000). *Because of Winn-Dixie*. New York: Candlewick Press.	Novel, adventure
Appelt, K. (2008). *The Underneath*. New York: Atheneum Books for Young Children.	Novel, adventure
Paulsen, G. (1998). *My Life in Dog Years*. New York: Yearling.	Memoir
Martin, A. (2005). *A Dog's Life: The Autobiography of a Stray.* New York: Scholastic	Fiction, adventure
Martin, A. (2009). *Everything for a Dog*. New York: Feiwel & Friends.	Fiction, adventure

FIGURE 9.13. *(cont.)*

Rather than reading about them, readers who identify with character position themselves as the dog. How powerful to be able to write this way. While the poems in *Once I Ate a Pie* are humorous, *A Dog's Life* has many sad parts. Being a stray is not always easy, as Squirrel shows, and not always easy to read about. Teachers might follow up this book by sharing its sequel, *Everything for a Dog* (Martin, 2009), where readers find out what happened to Bone, Squirrel's brother. They also learn about Henry and how desperately he wants to own a dog. I enjoyed the chapter shifts, where each character becomes the narrator in various chapters. Eventually, the voices merge into a single chapter.

To support students in writing from the point of view of a dog, teachers might visit *www.guidedogs.com* where students learn about guide dogs for the blind and about the training they receive. Students can then organize their writing around four elements of a guide dog's life: Being a puppy; Growing up; Saying goodbye; and A new life. For each of these categories, they can identify events in the dog's life. Once they have completed this prewriting activity, they may be asked to focus on just one event from a time period in the dog's life. Then they would once again brainstorm on what the dog might feel or experience during this event. Once prepared, they write about this event from the perspective of the dog. Completed stories can be displayed according to the time period of the dog's life that they represent. This activity allows students to learn about guide dogs and then to respond by writing in the voice of the dog.

During the sharing of these books, small groups of students can be organized to support comprehension throughout the reading of informational and fiction books about dogs. Teachers may choose to have students read various titles and during some time periods allow small groups to read the same book. When students read the same book, they can move to thematic and personal connections conversations. When students read a variety of titles, they may focus on plot.

I hope this chapter and Chapter 8 leave you with many ways to group books for student learning and enjoyment. If you haven't thought about books in this way before, start with small sets, because it is the easiest and most comfortable way to begin. From this simple beginning, where groups of students are reading independently, you might develop social studies and science book sets based on units you are expected to teach. This expansion of a unit is a good stepping stone to add to your children's book library and increase reading. Once you are comfortable with the creation of these text sets, be brave and move to more extensive collections. Then once students are clear on expectations, step back and watch them enjoy reading, writing, drawing, and talking about books.

ENGAGING STUDENTS

There are so many ways to engage students through longer explorations of text. I share just a few ways that teachers might consider.

1. *Lessons from reading.* Once the exploration is nearing its end, have each student select his or her favorite book. Then read from *Everything I Need to Know I Learned from a Children's Book* (Silvey, 2009), in which famous people talk about a favorite book they read as a child and how it influenced their thinking. The book is organized around inspiration, understanding, principles, vocation, motivation, and storytelling. After students get a sense of how authors thought about a favorite children's book, they are ready to write their own. When complete, students can group their responses by the theme represented within. Their reports can be displayed for all students to read and reflect on.
2. *Quotes.* In *Today I Will* (Spinelli & Spinelli, 2009), the Spinellis chose interesting quotes from a variety of books and shared one for each day of the year. Following each quote, both authors responded with their thoughts and interpretations. As students participate in a text set exploration, they might be asked to copy quotes they find interesting, thought provoking, or funny. When a text set is coming to a close, they can choose one or two quotes and respond in the manner of the Spinellis. These quotes and responses can be collected in a class book to be shared with parents.
3. *Reviewing a book.* Using Peterson and Swartz's (2008) suggestion, students can act as a book reviewer. When an author study or larger text set is nearing completion, each student can choose one book to review. To maintain consistency across reviewers, they can respond to the following prompts.
   a. *Narrative*
      - "What did you like about this book?"
      - "What questions came to mind as you read?"
      - "What did you think about the way the characters were represented?"
      - "What was the theme of this book?"
      - "Was the plot exciting?"
      - "Was this book believable?"
      - "Was this book interesting?"
      - "Would you recommend this book?"

   b. *Informational text*
      - "What did you like about this book?"
      - "What questions came to mind as you read?"
      - "What did you think about the way the information was shared?"
      - "Did the visual support help you understand this topic?"
      - "Was the book organized to support your learning?"

- "Was the book interesting?"
- "Would you recommend this book?"

At the end of this chapter and book, it is once again time to take a few moments to reflect:

1. Think about an author whom you believe your students would love to read. Explore the full set of books this author has written. Determine whether there is website support to learn more about this author. Now think of activities and conversations to support your students as they explore this author.
2. Find three books listed within this chapter that you have not read, secure them, and just enjoy reading them. Which ones will you share with your students? Why?
3. Consider a recent social studies unit you have taught. How might you expand this unit with informational and narrative text?

RECOMMENDED READING

For readers who would like to know about creating text sets, the following resources should help.

Moss, J. (2000). *Teaching literature in the middle grades: A thematic approach* (2nd ed.). Norwood, MA: Christopher-Gordon.

Moss shows teachers how to organize text sets thematically. She provides models that focus on dilemmas and decisions, artists in fiction and nonfiction, and friendship.

Youngs, S., & Barone, D. (2007). *Writing without boundaries: What's possible when students combine genres.* Portsmouth, NH: Heinemann.

This book provides step-by-step directions on how to engage students in multigenre writing. There are numerous student examples throughout.

Zile, S., & Napoli, M. (2009). *Teaching literary elements with picture books.* New York: Scholastic.

This book helps teachers see how to make connections between books and writing. They provide specific planning sheets to help students bring theme, voice, and so on into their writing based on how these elements are used in picturebooks.

Epilogue

Okay, you are saying professional books don't have epilogues. You are right! But I learned from the creators of postmodern picturebooks to take some risks. The result? An epilogue. You see, I just can't stop reading children's books, and I found a few that are too good to miss. So here they are. Enjoy!!!

- *Smash! Crash!* (Scieszka, 2008b). This is a book within the *Trucktown* series. There are two featured trucks, Jack Truck and Dump Truck Dan, who are best friends. They love to crash all day long. Kids will giggle when the two friends crash the cement truck and get into trouble. There is a short scary part where a voice tells them to follow and one page folds out so the viewers can see a crane. This is just fun.
- *Truckery Rhymes* (Scieszka, 2009). Scieszka features the trucks from *Trucktown*. He has used traditional rhymes like *Jack Be Nimble*, replacing the traditional characters with trucks. Plus Scieszka adds some fun: In *Jack Be Nimble*, Jack the truck smashes through a brick wall. What a way to get kids to love rhymes and unleash a lot of giggles.
- *All God's Critters* (Staines, 2009). This book is a song that is performed by the most unlikely creatures: frogs, owls, and hippos, to name a few. You can't just read this book, you always wind up singing no matter how good or bad your voice is. Kadir Nelson's animal illustrations are beautiful. The book includes music sheets for the song for those who can play an instrument.
- *Down, Down, Down: A Journey to the Bottom of the Sea* (Jenkins, 2009). This book is beautiful and full of information about the ocean. On one page is an illustration of a gull, with side information about the deepest depth of the ocean.

• *The Lion and the Mouse* (Pinkney, 2009). Just looking at the cover, with a single lion's face glancing at a small mouse on the back cover, I knew I had to own this book. I spent hours just viewing the front and back pages and the title page. The pencil and watercolor artwork is magical in its detail and nuances. Although I have heard and read this fable many times, I have new appreciation of it through this version by Pinkney.

• *A Book* (Gerstein, 2009). In this postmodern picturebook, the character, a little girl, talks to the reader. The story is about a family where each member has a story to tell with the exception of the little girl. In developing her story, the little girl meets characters from fairytales and other stories and explores various possible genres. For text, there are speech bubbles throughout.

• *Crazy Hair* (Gaiman & McKean, 2009). *Crazy Hair*, written in rhyme, centers on a young girl exploring the crazy hair of a young man who has let his hair grow since he was 2. This much hair on a man can hold a lot of things, like animals and hot air balloons. The illustrations are quite amazing in their complexity and surrealistic qualities.

• *Long Shot* (Paul, 2009). This picturebook about basketball shares the personal story of Chris Paul, an NBA All-Star: how almost everyone thought Paul was too short to play basketball. His family supported him, and Paul succeeded. The amazing illustrations convey Paul's feelings beautifully.

• *Who Wants to Be a Poodle, I Don't* (Child, 2009d). I have three poodles, so there was no way I could resist this book. Child shares the story of Trixie Twinkle Toes Trot-a-Lot Delight, the poodle of Verity Brulée. Although Trixie is pampered and treated like a child, she is not happy. The way Trixie is treated causes readers to giggle and reflect on the way they treat dogs.

• *Dogs* (Gravett, 2010). In this book Gravett shares her love for all kinds of dogs, even ones that are naughty. Her book ends with a humorous twist in that she loves all dogs that don't chase her.

• *The Evolution of Calpurnia Tate* (Kelly, 2009). This is a historical fiction set in the late 1800s. Callie avoids the chores that are expected of girls at this time and instead studies nature with her grandfather. The book is laced with quotes from the book *The Origin of the Species*, which Callie's grandfather gave her to read. Callie's goal is to become a scientist, a very brave and bold ambition.

• *Scat* (Hiaasen, 2009). In this adventurous mystery, Nick and Marta's biology teacher is missing when a fire erupts during a field trip to a swamp. Within this mystery comes lessons on environmental awareness and sensitivity for others, in this case Nick's father, who was injured in the Iraq war. Readers will love the nuanced layers of meaning within this plot.

• *When You Reach Me* (Stead, 2009). This book is about friendship and the loss of it. Miranda reads a *Wrinkle in Time* and then receives notes predicting the future. Time travel is a part of this story in much the same way as in *Wrinkle in Time*. Miranda's story takes place in 1979 and touches on many themes, such as friendship and identity. This book is a fantasy that takes place in a real location, New York City.

- *Everything for a Dog* (Martin, 2009). In this sequel, to *A Dog's Life* (Martin, 2005; see Chapter 9), we learn what happened to Bone, the brother of Squirrel, both of whom were strays. This book entails more than just learning about a dog, however. It is essentially a book about relationships: between dogs and humans and between parents and children.

- *The Sixty-Eight Rooms* (Malone, 2010). This books takes place in the Art Institute of Chicago in the Thorne Room Collection The Thorne Rooms are miniature rooms filled with period furniture and accessories. Two children, Ruthie and Jack, are able to shrink in size and become visitors within the rooms. Once inside, they experience many adventures tied to the historical periods of the room they are within.

- *A Nest for Celeste: A Story about Art, Inspiration, and the Meaning of Home* (Cole, 2010). A young mouse, Celeste, lives in a home that Audubon visits as he is creating his images of birds. Readers learn about the sometimes not very pleasant ways that Audubon uses to secure the birds that he is recording. The artwork in the book reminds me of the blacktoned illustrations within *The Invention of Hugo Cabret* (Selznick, 2007).

This epilogue demonstrates that, once enamored with children's books, there is no end to reading and adding to the books you find that engage you and your students. Happy reading!

References

Allington, R., & McGill-Franzen, A. (2003). The impact of summer loss on the reading achievement gap. *Phi Delta Kappan, 85*(6), 68–75.

Anderson, N. (2002). *Elementary children's literature*. Boston: Allyn & Bacon.

Anderson, R., Hiebert, E., Scott, J., & Wilkinson, I. (1985). *Becoming a nation of readers*. Washington, DC: National Institute of Education.

Applebee, A. (1978). *The child's concept of story*. Chicago: University of Chicago Press.

Applegate, A., & Applegate, M. (2004). The Peter effect: Reading habits and attitudes of preservice teachers. *The Reading Teacher, 57*, 554–563.

Arizpe, E., & Styles, M. (2003). *Children reading pictures: Interpreting visual texts*. New York: Routledge.

Bandré, P., Colabucci, L., Parsons, L., & Son, E. (2007). Read-alouds worth remembering. *Language Arts, 84*, 293–299.

Bang, M. (2000). *Picture this: How pictures work*. New York: SeaStar.

Barone, D. (1989). Young children's written responses to literature: The relationship between written response and orthographic knowledge. In S. McCormick & J. Zutell (Eds.), *Cognitive and social perspectives for literacy research and instruction: Thirty-eighth yearbook of the National Reading Conference* (pp. 371–380). Chicago: National Reading Conference.

Barone, D. (1990). The written responses of young children: Beyond comprehension to story understanding. *The New Advocate, 3*(1), 49–56.

Barone, D. (2006). *Narrowing the literacy gap: What works in high-poverty schools*. New York: Guilford Press.

Barone, D., & Wright, T. E. (2008). Literacy instruction with digital and media technologies. *The Reading Teacher, 62*, 292–302.

Barone, D., & Xu, S. (2008). *Literacy instruction for English language learners pre-K–2*. New York: Guilford Press.

Barone, D., & Youngs, S. (2008a). *Your core reading program and children's literature: Effective strategies for using the best of both (K–3)*. New York: Scholastic.

Barone, D., & Youngs, S. (2008b). *Your core reading program and children's literature: Effective strategies for using the best of both (4–6)*. New York: Scholastic.

Bishop, R. (1992). Children's books in a multicultural world: A view from the USA. In E. Evans (Ed.), *Reading against racism* (pp. 19–38). Philadelphia: Open University Press.

Blackford, H. (2004). *Out of this world: Why literature matters to girls*. New York: Teachers College Press.

Brenner, D., Hiebert, E., & Tompkins, R. (2009). How much and what are third graders reading? Reading in core programs. In E. Hiebert (Ed.), *Reading more, reading better* (pp. 118–140). New York: Guilford Press.

Butler, D. (1975). *Cushla and her books*. Boston: Horn Book.

Calkins, L. (1994). *The art of teaching writing*. Portsmouth, NH: Heinemann.

Charles, Z. (2008). Tumbling into Wonderland. In L. Robinson & Z. Charles (Eds.), *Over rainbows and down rabbit holes: The art of children's books* (pp. 10–15). Santa Barbara, CA: Santa Barbara Museum of Art and Eric Carle Museum of Picture Book Art.

Children's Book Committee, Bank Street College of Education. (2009). *The best children's books of the year*. New York: Teacher's College Press.

Cochran-Smith, M. (1984). *The making of a reader*. Norwood, NJ: Ablex.

Cooper, P. (2009). Children's literature for reading strategy instruction: Innovation or interference? *Language Arts, 86*, 178–187.

Cunningham, A., & Stanovich, K. (1998). What reading does for the mind. *American Educator, 22*, 1–8.

Curtis, C. P. (2008). The literary worlds of Bud, Kenny, Luther, and Christopher: Finding books for me. In S. S. Lehr (Ed.), *Shattering the looking glass: Challenge, risk and controversy in children's literature* (pp. 155–159). Norwood, MA: Christopher-Gordon.

Daane, M., Campbell, J., Grigg, W., Goodman, M., Oranje, A., & Goldstein, A. (2005). *The nation's report card: Fourth-grade students reading aloud—NAEP 2002 special study of oral reading*. Washington, DC: U.S. Department of Education, Institute of Education Sciences, National Center for Education Statistics.

Doonan, J. (1992). *Looking at pictures in picture books*. Stroud, UK: Thimble Press.

Duke, N. (2004). What research says about reading: The case of informational text. *Educational Leadership, 61*(5), 40–44.

Duke, N., & Bennett-Armistead, V. (2003). *Reading and writing informational text in the primary grades: Research-based practices*. New York: Scholastic.

Esquith, R. (2007). *Teach like your hair's on fire*. New York: Penguin Books.

Fleener, C., Morrison, S., Linek, W., & Rasinski, T. (1997). Recreational reading choices: How do children select books? In W. Linek & E. Sturtevant (Eds.), *Exploring literacy* (pp. 75–84). Platteville, WI: College Reading Association.

Flint, A. (2008). *Literate lives: Teaching reading and writing in elementary classrooms*. Hoboken, NJ: Wiley.

Ford, P. (Ed.). (1897). *The New England primer: Its origin and development*. New York: Dodd, Mead.

Fox, M. (2008). *Reading magic: Why reading aloud to our children will change their lives forever*. New York: Harcourt.

Galda, L. (1988). Readers, texts, and contexts: A response-based view of literature in the classroom. *The New Advocate, 1*, 92–102.

Gamble, N., & Yates, S. (2008). *Exploring children's literature* (2nd ed.). Los Angeles: Sage.

Gambrell, L. (1984). How much time do children spend reading during teacher-directed reading instruction? In J. Niles & L. Harris (Eds.), *Changing perspectives on research in reading/language processing and instruction: Thirty-third yearbook of the National Reading Conference* (pp. 193–198). Chicago: National Reading Conference.

Gambrell, L. (1996). Creating classroom cultures that foster reading motivation. *The Reading Teacher, 50*, 14–25.

Gambrell, L. (2009). Creating opportunities to read more so that students read better. In E. Hiebert (Ed.), *Reading more, reading better* (pp. 251–266). New York: Guilford Press.

Genuard, M. (2005). *Focus on nonfiction literature: Students' reading preferences and teachers' beliefs and practices*. Unpublished master's thesis, Queens College, City University of New York.

Gill, S. (2009). What teachers need to know about the "new" nonfiction. *The Reading Teacher, 63*, 260–267.

Golden, J. (1990). *The narrative symbol in childhood literature: Explorations in the construction of text.* Berlin: Mouton.

Goldstone, B. (2001/2002). Whaz up with our books? Changing picture book codes and teaching implications. *The Reading Teacher, 55,* 362–371.

Gunning, T. G. (2008). *Creating literacy instruction for all students in grades 4–8* (2nd ed.). Boston: Allyn & Bacon.

Gunning, T. G. (2010). *Creating literacy instruction for all students* (7th ed.). Boston: Allyn & Bacon.

Guthrie, J. (2004). Teaching for literacy engagement. *Journal of Literacy Research, 36,* 1–28.

Guthrie, J., & Humenick, N. (2004). Motivating students to read: Evidence for classroom practices that increase motivation and achievement. In P. McCardle & V. Chhabra (Eds.), *The voice of evidence in reading research* (pp. 329–354). Baltimore: Brookes.

Guthrie, J., & Wigfield, A. (2000). Engagement and motivation in reading. In M. L. Kamil, P. B. Mosenthal, P. D. Pearson, & R. Barr (Eds.), *Handbook of reading research* (Vol. 3, pp. 403–422). Mahwah, NJ: Erlbaum.

Hancock, M. (2000). *A celebration of literature and response: Children, books, and teachers in K–8 classrooms.* Upper Saddle River, NJ: Pearson Prentice Hall.

Hartman, D., & Hartman, J. (1993). Reading across texts: Expanding the role of the reader. *The Reading Teacher, 47,* 202–211.

Harvey, S., & Goudvis, A. (2000). *Strategies that work: Teaching comprehension to enhance understanding.* Portland, ME: Stenhouse.

Hassett, D., & Curwood, J. (2009). Theories and practices of multimodal education: The instructional dynamics of picture books and primary classrooms. *The Reading Teacher, 63,* 270–282.

Heffernan, L. (2004). *Critical literacy and writer's workshop: Bringing purpose and passion to student writing.* Newark, DE: International Reading Association.

Hill, R. A. (2009). The gross and the gory: Making a reading connection with boys. *Book Links, 18*(5), 6–10.

Hunt, P. (2005). Introduction. In P. Hunt (Ed.), *Understanding children's literature* (2nd ed., pp. 1–14). New York: Routledge.

Iser, W. (1978). *The act of reading: A theory of aesthetic response.* Baltimore: Johns Hopkins University Press.

Johnson, N., & Giorgis, C. (2007). *The wonder of it all: When literature and literacy intersect.* Portsmouth, NH: Heinemann.

Kaiser Foundation. (2006). *The media family: Electronic media in the lives of infants, toddlers, preschoolers, and their parents.* Menlo Park, CA: Kaiser Family Foundation.

Keene, E., & Zimmermann, S. (2007). *Mosaic of thought* (2nd ed.). Portsmouth, NH: Heinemann.

Kelley, M., & Clausen-Grace, N. (2008). *R^5 in your classroom: A guide to differentiating independent reading and developing avid readers.* Newark, DE: International Reading Association.

Kelley, M., & Clausen-Grace, N. (2009). Facilitating engagement by differentiating independent reading. *The Reading Teacher, 63,* 313–318.

Kersten, J., Apol, L., & Pagtaray-Ching, J. (2007). Exploring the role of children's literature in the 21st-century classroom. *Language Arts, 84,* 286–292.

Kiefer, B. (1995). *The potential of picturebooks: From visual literacy to aesthetic understanding.* Columbus, OH: Merrill/Prentice-Hall.

Kiefer, B. (2007). *Charlotte Huck's children's literature* (9th ed.). Boston: McGraw-Hill.

Kiefer, B. (2008). Visual images in children's picture books. In S. S. Lehr (Ed.), *Shattering the looking glass: Challenge, risk and controversy in children's literature* (pp. 257–272). Norwood, MA: Christopher-Gordon.

Kiefer, B. Z. (2010). *Charlotte Huck's children's literature* (10th ed.). New York: McGraw-Hill.

Kress, G., & vanLeeuwen, T. (1996). *Reading images: The grammar of visual design.* London: Routledge.

Lehman, B. (2009). Children's literature in a testing time. *Language Arts, 86,* 196–200.

Lehr, S. S. (1991). *The child's developing sense of theme: Responses to literature.* New York: Teachers College Press.

Lehr, S. S. (2008). Introduction. In S. S. Lehr (Ed.), *Shattering the looking glass: Challenge, risk and controversy in children's literature* (pp. xi–xxvi). Norwood, MA: Christopher-Gordon.

Lerer, S. (2008). *Children's literature: A reader's history from Aesop to Harry Potter.* Chicago: University of Chicago Press.

Lewis, D. (2001). *Reading contemporary picturebooks: Picturing text.* New York: Routledge.

Lukens, R. (2007). *A critical handbook of children's literature* (8th ed.). Boston: Allyn & Bacon.

Lurie, A. (1990). *Don't tell the grown-ups: The subversive power of children's literature.* Boston: Little, Brown.

Mangelson, J., & Castek, J. (2009). Thinking outside the book: Pairing nonfiction books and web sites. *Book Links, 18*(3), 48–49.

Manning, M. (2005). Reading aloud. *Teaching K–8, 35*, 80–81.

Marcus, L. (2007a). *Golden legacy.* New York: Golden Books.

Marcus, L. (2007b). *Pass it down.* New York: Walker.

Marcus, L. (2008). *Minders of make-believe.* Boston: Houghton Mifflin.

Marcus, L., Curley, J., & Ward, C. (2007). *Children should be seen: The image of the child in American picture-book art.* Amherst, MA: Eric Carle Museum of Picture Book Art.

McCarty, T. (1995). What's wrong with *Ten Little Rabbits? The New Advocate, 8*(2), 97–98.

McGill-Franzen, A., & Botzakis, S. (2009). Series books, graphic novels, and magazines: Unauthorized texts, authorized literacy practices. In E. Hiebert (Ed.), *Reading more, reading better* (pp. 101–117). New York: Guilford Press.

McLaughlin, M., & Fisher, L. (2005). *Research-based reading lessons for K–3: Phonemic awareness, phonics, fluency, vocabulary, and comprehension.* New York: Scholastic.

Miller, D. (2009). *The book whisperer: Awakening the inner reading in every child.* San Francisco: Jossey-Bass.

Mitchell, D. (2003). *Children's literature: An invitation to the world.* Boston: Allyn & Bacon.

Mohr, K. (2003). Children's choices: A comparison of book preferences between Hispanic and non-Hispanic first graders. *Reading Psychology, 24*, 163–176.

Morrison, V., & Wlodarczyk, L. (2009). Revisiting read-aloud: Instructional strategies that encourage students' engagement with texts. *The Reading Teacher, 63*, 110–118.

Moss, B. (2003). *Exploring the literature of fact. Children's nonfiction trade books in the elementary classroom.* New York: Guilford Press.

Moss, J. (2000). *Teaching literature in the middle grades: A thematic approach* (2nd ed.). Norwood, MA: Christopher-Gordon.

National Endowment for the Arts. (2004). *Survey of literary reading in America* (Research Division Report 46). Washington, DC: Library of Congress.

National Endowment for the Arts. (2007). *To read or not to read: A question of national consequence* (Research Division Report 47). Washington, DC: Library of Congress.

National Reading Panel. (2001). *Teaching children to read: An evidence-based assessment of the scientific research literature on reading and its implications for reading instruction* [Online]. Available at *www.nichd.nih.gov/publications/nrp/smallbook.cfm.*

Nikolajeva, M. (1988). Exit children's literature? *The Lion and the Unicorn, 22*, 221–236.

Nikolajeva, M. (2005). *Aesthetic approaches to children's literature: An introduction.* Lanham, MD: Scarecrow Press.

Nikolajeva, M., & Scott, C. (2001). *How picturebooks work.* New York: Routledge.

Nodelman, P. (1988). *Words about pictures.* Athens: University of Georgia Press.

Nodelman, P. (2008). *The hidden adult: Defining children's literature.* Baltimore: Johns Hopkins University Press.

Nodelman, P., & Reimer, M. (2003). *The pleasure of children's literature* (3rd ed.). Boston: Allyn & Bacon.

Norton, D. (1995). *Through the eyes of a child: An introduction to children's literature* (4th ed.). Englewood Cliffs, NJ: Merrill.

Norton, D. (2007). *Literacy for life.* Boston: Pearson.

Nystrand, M. (1997). *Opening dialogue: Understanding the dynamics of language and learning in the English classroom.* New York: Teachers College Press.

Ogle, D. (1986). K-W-L: A teaching model that develops active reading of expository text. *The Reading Teacher, 59*, 564–570.

Pantaleo, S. (2004). Young children and radical change characteristics in picture books. *The Reading Teacher, 58*, 178–187.

Pantaleo, S. (2007). Scieszka's *The Stinky Cheese Man*: A tossed salad of parodic re-versions. *Children's Literature in Education, 38*, 277–295.

Pantaleo, S. (2008). *Exploring student response to contemporary picturebooks*. Toronto: University of Toronto Press.

Pantaleo, S., & Sipe, L. R. (2008). Introduction: Postmodernism and picturebooks. In L. R. Sipe & S. Pantaleo (Eds.), *Postmodern picturebooks: Play, parody, and self-referentiality* (pp. 1–8). New York: Routledge.

Pappas, C. (1991). Fostering full access to literacy by including informational books. *Language Arts, 68*, 449–461.

Pearson, P.D. (2008, February). *Teaching reading comprehension 24/7*. Paper presented at the Colorado Council International Reading Association 2008 Conference on Literacy, Denver, CO.

Peterson, R., & Eeds, M. (2007). *Grand conversations: Literature groups in action*. New York: Scholastic.

Peterson, S. S., & Swartz, L. (2008). *Good books matter: How to choose and use children's literature to help students grow as readers*. Portland, ME: Pembroke.

Pressley, M. (2006). Whole language. In M. Pressley (Ed.), *Reading instruction that works* (pp. 15–48). New York: Guilford Press.

Purcell-Gates, V., & Duke, N. (2003, May). *Learning to read and write information text in 2nd and 3rd grade science*. Paper presented at the 48th Annual Convention of the International Reading Association, Orlando, FL.

Ray, S. (2004). The world of children's literature: An introduction. In P. Hunt (Ed.), *International companion encyclopedia of children's literature* (2nd ed., pp. 849–857). New York: Routledge.

Read, S., Reutzel, D.R., & Fawson, P. (2008). Do you want to know what I learned? Using informational trade books as models to teach text structure. *Early Childhood Education Journal, 36*, 213–219.

Reutzel, D.R., & Cooter, Jr., R. (2008). *Teaching children to read* (5th ed.). Upper Saddle River, NJ: Pearson.

Reutzel, D.R., Jones, C., Fawson, P., & Smith, J. (2008). Scaffolded silent reading: A complement to guided repeated oral reading that works! *The Reading Teacher, 62*, 194–207.

Robb, L. (2002). Multiple texts: Multiple opportunities for teaching and learning. *Voices from the Middle, 9*(4), 28–32.

Robinson, L. (2008). Travels through time and genre. In L. Robinson & Z. Charles (Eds.), *Over rainbows and down rabbit holes* (pp. 16–34). Santa Barbara, CA: Santa Barbara Museum of Art and Eric Carle Museum of Picture Book Art.

Robinson, L., & Charles, Z. (2008). *Over rainbows and down rabbit holes*. Santa Barbara, CA: Santa Barbara Museum of Art and Eric Carle Museum of Picture Book Art.

Rosenblatt, L. (1938). *Literature as exploration*. New York: Appleton-Century-Crofts.

Rosenblatt, L. (2005). *Making meaning with texts: Selected essays*. Portsmouth, NH: Heinemann.

Ross, C. (1995). If they read *Nancy Drew*, so what? Series book readers talk back. *Library and Information Science Research, 17*, 210–236.

Serafini, F., & Giorgis, C. (2003). *Reading aloud and beyond: Fostering the intellectual life with older readers*. Portsmouth, NH: Heinemann.

Serafini, F., & Ladd, S. (2008). The challenge of moving beyond the literal in literature discussions. *Journal of Language and Literacy Education, 4*(2), 6–20.

Sipe, L. (2008). *Storytime: Young children's literary understanding in the classroom*. New York: Teachers College Press.

Sipe, L., & Brightman, A. (2009). Young children's interpretations of page breaks in contemporary picture books. *Journal of Literacy Research, 41*, 68–103.

Sipe, L., & McGuire, C. (2008). *The Stinky Cheese Man* and other fairly postmodern picture books for children. In S. Lehr (Ed.), *Shattering the looking glass: Challenge, risk and controversy in children's literature* (pp. 273–288). Norwood, MA: Christopher-Gordon.

Smith, M., & Wilhelm, J. (2002). *Reading don't fix no Chevys: Literacy in the lives of young men.* Portsmouth, NH: Heinemann.

Snow, C., Burns, M., & Griffin, P. (Eds.). (1998). *Preventing reading difficulties in young children.* Washington, DC: National Research Council.

Stead, T. (2006). *Reality checks: Teaching reading comprehension with nonfiction K–5.* Portland, ME: Stenhouse.

Sumara, D. (2002). *Why reading literature in school still matters.* Mahwah, NJ: Erlbaum.

Teale, W. (2008, May). *What it takes for read-alouds to make a difference with children in early literacy.* Paper presented at the 53rd Annual Convention of the International Reading Association, Atlanta.

Teale, W., Kim, J., & Boerman-Cornell, W. (2008). It's elementary! Graphic novels for the K–6 classroom. *Book Links, 17,* 6–13.

Temple, C., Martinez, M., & Yokota, J. (2006). *Children's books in children's hands: An introduction to their literature* (3rd ed.). Boston: Pearson.

Tomlinson, C., & Lynch-Brown, C. (2002). *Essentials of children's literature (4th ed.).* Boston: Allyn & Bacon.

Tompkins, G. (2010). *Literacy for the 21st century: A balanced approach* (5th ed.). Boston: Allyn & Bacon.

Trelease, J. (2006). *The read-aloud handbook.* New York: Penguin Books.

Tunnell, M., & Jacobs, J. (2008). *Children's literature, briefly* (4th ed.). New York: Pearson.

U.S. Department of Education. (2005). *NAEP 2004 trends in academic progress: Three decades of student performance in reading and mathematics.* Washington, DC: National Center for Education Statistics.

Vasquez, V. (2010). *Getting beyond "I like the book": Creating space for critical literacy in K–6 classrooms* (2nd ed.). Newark, DE: International Reading Association.

Weisman, K. (2009). Talking with Avi. *Book Links, 18*(6), 40–42.

Wharton-McDonald, R. (2006). The need for increased comprehension instruction. In M. Pressley (Ed.), *Reading instruction that works* (pp. 293–346). New York: Guilford Press.

White, D. (1956). *Books before five.* New York: Oxford University Press.

Wilhelm, J. (2008). *"You gotta be the book": Teaching engaged and reflective reading with adolescents.* New York: Teachers College Press and National Council of Teachers of English.

Wolf, M. (2007). *Proust and the squid.* New York: HarperCollins.

Wolf, S. (2004). *Interpreting literature with children.* Mahwah, NJ: Erlbaum.

Wolf, S., & Heath, S. (1992). *The braid of literature: Children's worlds of reading.* Cambridge, MA: Harvard University Press.

Wolfenbarger, C., & Sipe, L. (2007). A unique visual and literary art form: Recent research on picturebooks. *Language Arts, 84,* 273–280.

Wray, D., & Lewis, M. (1993). The reading experiences and interests of junior school children. *Children's Literature in Education, 24,* 251–263.

Xu, S. H., Perkins, R., & Zunich, L. (2005). *Trading cars to comic strips: Popular culture texts and literacy learning in grades K–8.* Newark, DE: International Reading Association.

Young, T. (2009, February). *Nonfiction read aloud strategies.* Paper presented at the Colorado Council State Reading 2009 Conference on Literacy, Denver, CO.

Youngs, S., & Barone, D. (2007). *Writing without boundaries: What's possible when students combine genres.* Portsmouth, NH: Heinemann.

Zambo, D., & Brozo, W. (2009). *Bright beginnings for boys: Engaging young boys in active literacy.* Newark, DE: International Reading Association.

Zipes, J. (2009). *Relentless progress: The reconfiguration of children's literature, fairy tales, and storytelling.* New York: Routledge.

Children's Literature

Adoff, A. (2004). *Black is brown is tan*. New York: Armistad.
Aguilar, D. (2008). *Planets: A new view of the solar system*. Washington, DC: National Geographic.
Ahlberg, J., & Ahlberg, A. (1986). *The jolly postman and other people's letters*. New York: L,B Kids.
Alcott, L. (1997). *Little women*. New York: Viking. (Original work published 1868)
Alfano, M. (2008). *How to draw the newest Pokémon*. New York: Scholastic.
Alley, Z. (2008). *There's a wolf at the door*. New York: Roaring Brook Press.
Amato, M. (2004). *Snarf attack, underfoodle, and the secret of life: The Riot brothers tell all*. New York: Holiday House.
Andersen, H. (1906). *The ugly duckling*. New York: A. L. Burt.
Angelou, M. (1993). *Life doesn't frighten me*. New York: Stewart, Tabori & Chang.
Anno, M. (1974). *Anno's alphabet*. New York: Harper & Row.
Anno, M. (1986). *Anno's counting book*. New York: Harper & Row.
Armstrong, W. (1969). *Sounder*. New York: Scholastic.
Arnosky, J. (2009). *Slither and crawl*. New York: Sterling.
Avi. (1970). *Things that sometimes happen*. New York: Doubleday.
Avi. (1990). *True confessions of Charlotte Doyle*. New York: Scholastic.
Avi. (1991). *Nothing but the truth*. New York: Avon.
Avi. (1993). *City of light, city of dark*. New York: Orchard Books.
Avi. (1994). *The bird, the frog, and the light*. New York: Orchard Books.
Avi. (1995). *Poppy*. New York: HarperTrophy.
Avi. (1997). *What do fish have to do with anything?* Cambridge, MA: Candlewick Press.
Avi. (1998). *Poppy and Rye*. New York: HarperCollins.
Avi. (1999a). *Midnight magic*. New York: Scholastic.
Avi. (1999b). *Ragweed*. New York: HarperTrophy.
Avi. (2001a). *Don't you know there's a war on?* New York HarperCollins.
Avi. (2001b). *Ereth's birthday*. New York: HarperCollins.
Avi. (2001c). *Prairie school*. New York: HarperCollins.
Avi. (2001d). *The secret school*. New York: Harcourt.
Avi. (2002). *Crispin: The cross of lead*. New York: Hyperion Books.
Avi. (2003a). *Silent movie*. New York: Atheneum Books for Young Readers.
Avi. (2003b). *The good dog*. New York: Aladdin.

Avi. (2003c). *The mayor of Central Park.* New York: HarperCollins.
Avi. (2004a). *Never mind.* New York: HarperCollins.
Avi. (2004b). *The end of the beginning.* New York: Harcourt.
Avi. (2005a). *Poppy's return.* New York: HarperCollins.
Avi. (2005b). *The book without words.* New York: Hyperion Books.
Avi. (2006a). *Crispin: At the edge of the world.* New York: Hyperion Books.
Avi. (2006b). *Strange happenings.* New York: Harcourt.
Avi. (2007a). *Iron thunder.* New York: Hyperion Books.
Avi. (2007b). *The traitor's gate.* New York: Atheneum Books for Young Readers.
Avi. (2008a). *A beginning, a muddle, and an end.* Orlando, FL: Harcourt.
Avi. (2008b). *Hard gold: The Colorado gold rush of 1859.* New York: Hyperion Books.
Avi. (2009a). *Murder at midnight.* New York: Scholastic.
Avi. (2009b). *Poppy and Ereth.* New York: HarperCollins.
Balliett, B. (2004). *Chasing Vermeer.* New York: Scholastic.
Balliett, B. (2008). *The Calder game.* New York: Scholastic.
Bang, M. (1980). *The grey lady and the strawberry snatcher.* New York: Four Winds Press.
Bang, M. (1988). *Delphine.* New York: Morrow.
Bang, M. (1990). *The paper crane.* New York: Greenwillow Books.
Bang, M. (1991). *Ten, nine, eight.* New York: Greenwillow Books.
Bang, M. (1996). *Goose.* New York: Blue Sky Press.
Bang, M. (1997). *Common ground: The water, earth, and air we share.* New York: Blue Sky Press.
Bang, M. (1999). *When Sophie gets angry—Really, really angry.* New York: Scholastic.
Bang, M. (2002). *Dawn.* New York: SeaStar Books.
Bang, M. (2004). *My light.* New York: Blue Sky Press.
Bang, M. (2006). *In my heart.* Boston: Little, Brown.
Bang, M. (2009). *Living sunlight: How plants bring the earth to life.* New York: Blue Sky Press.
Base, G. (2008). *Enigma: A magical mystery.* New York: Abrams Books for Young Readers.
Bataille, M. (2008). *ABC3D.* New York: Roaring Brook Press.
Baum, F. (1900). *The wonderful Wizard of Oz.* New York: Holt.
Baum, F. (1957). *The wonderful Wizard of Oz.* Racine, WI: Whitman.
Bemelmans, L. (1967). *Madeline.* New York: Viking. (Original work published 1939)
Berger, S., & Chanko, P. (1999). *School.* New York: Scholastic.
Bildner, P. (2002). *Shoeless Joe & Black Betsy.* New York: Aladdin.
Bishop, C. (1938). *The five Chinese brothers.* New York: Coward, McCann & Geoghegan.
Bloom, B. (1999). *Wolf!* New York: Orchard Books.
Bloom, S., & Mercier, C. (1997). *Presenting Avi.* New York: Twayne.
Blume, J. (1972). *Tales of a fourth grade nothing.* New York: Dutton.
Bonner, H. (2003). *When bugs were big, plants were strange, and tetrapods stalked the earth.* Washington, DC: National Geographic.
Borgenicht, D., & Pyle, H. (1996). *The legend of King Arthur.* Philadelphia: Running Press.
Bouchard, D. (1999). *The dragon new year: A Chinese legend.* Atlanta, GA: Peachtree.
Bredeson, C. (2003). *Astronauts.* New York: Scholastic.
Brett, J. (1989). *The mitten.* New York: Putnam.
Brown, I. (1992). *Skitterbrain.* Portland, OR: Blue Heron.
Brown, M. (1939). *Goodnight moon.* New York: Harper.
Brown, M. (2002). *The good little bad little pig.* New York: Hyperion Books.
Browne, A. (1986). *Piggybook.* New York: Alfred A. Knopf.
Browne, A. (1989). *The tunnel.* New York: Walker Books.
Browne, A. (1994). *Zoo.* Somerville, MA: Candlewick Press.
Browne, A. (1997). *Willy the dreamer.* London: Walker Books.
Browne, A. (1998). *Voices in the park.* New York: DK.
Browne, A. (2000a). *My dad.* New York: Farrar Straus Giroux.
Browne, A. (2000b). *Willy and Hugh.* Somerville, MA: Candlewick Press.
Browne, A. (2000c). *Willy's pictures.* Cambridge, MA: Candlewick Press.

Browne, A. (2003a). *The shape game*. New York: Farrar, Strauss, and Giroux.
Browne, A. (2003b). *Willy the wizard*. London: Corgi Children.
Browne, A. (2004). *Into the forest*. Cambridge, MA: Candlewick Press.
Browne, A. (2005a). *King Kong*. London: Picture Corgi
Browne, A. (2005b). *My mom*. New York: Farrar, Strauss, and Giroux.
Browne, A. (2007). *Silly Billy*. New York: Walker Books.
Browne, A. (2008a). *Changes*. New York: Walker Books.
Browne, A. (2008b). *Hansel and Gretel*. New York: Walker Books.
Browne, A. (2008c). *Little beauty*. Cambridge, MA: Candlewick Press.
Browne, A. (2008d). *Willy the champ*. New York: Walker Books.
Browne, A. (2008e). *Willy the wimp*. New York: Walker Books.
Bruel, N. (2005). *Bad kitty*. New Milford, CT: Roaring Brook Press.
Buehner, C. (2002). *The snowmen*. New York: Dial Books for Young Readers.
Buehner, C., & Buehner, M. (1999). *The escape of Marvin the ape*. New York: Puffin Books.
Bunting, E. (1994). *Night of the gargoyles*. New York: Houghton Mifflin.
Bunting, E. (2007). *S is for shamrock: An Ireland alphabet*. Chelsea, MI: Sleeping Bear Press.
Burleigh, R. (1998). *Home run*. San Diego; Voyager Books.
Burleigh, R. (2008). *Abraham Lincoln comes home*. New York: Holt.
Burnie, D. (2007). *Amazing animals Q&A: Everything you never knew about the animal kingdom*. New York: DK.
Burningham, J. (1977). *Come away from the water, Shirley*. New York: Crowell.
Burns, L. (2007). *Tracking trash: Flotsam, jetsam, and the science of ocean movement*. Boston: Houghton Mifflin.
Cannon, J. (1997). *Stellaluna*. San Diego: Harcourt.
Carle, E. (1968). *1, 2, 3, to the zoo*. New York: Philomel.
Carroll, L. (1941). *Alice's adventures in Wonderland*. New York: Heritage Press.
Carroll, L. (2008). *Alice's adventures in Wonderland*. Seattle, WA: CreateSpace. (Original work published 1865)
Carter, D. (2007). *600 black spots*. New York: Simon & Schuster.
Cave, K. (2003). *One child, one seed*. New York: Holt.
Cech, J. (2009). *Aesop's fables*. New York: Sterling.
Chaikin, A. (2009). *Mission control, this is Apollo: The story of the first voyages to the moon*. New York: Viking.
Child, L. (2002). *Who's afraid of the big bad book?* New York: Hyperion Books.
Child, L. (2006). *Beware of the storybook wolves*. London: Hodder Children's Books.
Child, L. (2009a). *Goldilocks and the three bears*. New York: Hyperion Books.
Child, L. (2009b). *Help! I really mean it!* New York: Grosset & Dunlap.
Child, L. (2009c). *I am extremely absolutely boiling*. New York: Grosset & Dunlap.
Child, L. (2009d). *Who wants to be a poodle, I don't*. Somerville, MA: Candlewick Press.
Child, L. (2009e). *You won't like this present as much as I do!* New York: Grosset & Dunlap.
Cleary, B. (1988). *A girl from Yamhill*. New York: Morrow.
Clements, A. (1996). *Frindle*. New York: Scholastic.
Cole, H. (2010). *A nest for Celeste: A story about art, inspiration, and the meaning of home*. New York: HarperCollins.
Collard, S. (2008). *Reign of the sea dragons*. Watertown, MA: Charlesbridge.
Collins, S. (2008). *The hunger games*. New York: Scholastic.
Collins, S. (2009). *Catching fire*. New York: Scholastic.
Converse. (1996). *Converse all star football: How to play like a pro*. New York: Wiley.
Cooper, F. (2008). *Willie and the all-stars*. New York: Philomel Books.
Covill, B. (1991). *Jeremy Thatcher, dragon hatcher*. New York: Scholastic.
Crampton, G. (1973). *Tootle*. New York: Golden Books.
Creech, S. (2001). *Love that dog*. New York: Joanna Cotler Books.
Crews, D. (1978). *Freight train*. New York: HarperCollins.
Crews, D. (1991). *Bigmama's*. New York: Greenwillow Books.

Cronin, D. (2000). *Click, clack, moo cows that type.* New York: Simon & Schuster Books for Young Readers.
Cronin, D., & Lewin, B. (2006). *Dooby dooby moo.* New York: Atheneum Books for Young Readers.
Cronin, D., & Lewin, B. (2008). *Thump, quack, moo: A whacky adventure.* New York: Atheneum Books for Young Readers.
Curtis, C. (1995). *The Watsons go to Birmingham—1963.* New York: Scholastic.
Curtis, C. (1999). *Bud, not Buddy.* New York: Dell.
Curtis, J., & Cornell, L. (2004). *It's hard to be five: Learning how to work my control panel.* New York: Joanna Cotler Books.
Cushman, K. (1996). *The midwife's apprentice.* New York: HarperCollins.
D'Amico, C., & D'Amico, S. (2004). *Ella the elegant elephant.* New York: Arthur A. Levine Books.
D'Aulaire, I., & D'Aulaire, E. (1992). *D'Aulaires' book of Greek myths.* New York: Delacorte Books for Young Readers. (Original work published 1962)
Dahl, R. (1975). *Danny the champion of the world.* New York: Bantam Skylark.
Dahl, R. (1983a). *Revolting rhymes.* New York: Bantam Books.
Dahl, R. (1983b). *The witches.* New York: Puffin Books.
Dahl, R. (1988). *Matilda.* New York: Puffin Books.
Dahl, R. (1999). *Boy.* New York: Puffin Books.
Dahl, R. (2001). *Charlie and the chocolate factory.* New York: Puffin Books.
Dahl, R. (2008). *More about boy.* New York: Penguin.
Davies, A. (2007). *Super-size bugs.* New York: Sterling.
Day, A. (1997). *Good dog, Carl.* New York: Aladdin.
Deary, T. (2006). *The wicked history of the world.* New York: Scholastic.
Defoe, D. (1719). *The life and strange surprising adventures of Robinson Crusoe, of York, Mariner.* London: W. Taylor.
dePaola, T. (1978). *Pancakes for breakfast.* San Diego: Harcourt Brace Jovanovich.
dePaola, T. (1989). *The art lesson.* New York: Putnam.
dePaola, T. (1991). *Bonjour, Mr. Satie.* New York: Putnam.
dePaola, T. (1993). *Tom.* New York: Putnam.
dePaola, T. (1997). *The art lesson.* New York: Putnam.
dePaola, T. (1998). *The knight and the dragon.* New York: Putnam Juvenile.
dePaola, T. (2007). *Big book of favorite legends.* New York: Putnam.
DiCamillo, K. (2000). *Because of Winn-Dixie.* Somerville, MA: Candlewick Press.
DK Publishing. (1999). *My big alphabet book.* New York: Author.
DK Publishing. (2008). *Encyclopedia of dinosaurs and prehistoric life.* New York: Author.
Doeden, M. (2008). *Real-life dragons.* Mankato, MN: Capstone Press.
Downard, B. (2004). *The little red hen.* New York: Simon & Schuster.
Dr. Seuss. (1937). *And to think that I saw it on Mulberry Street.* New York: Random House.
Dr. Seuss. (1957a). *Go, dog. Go!* New York: Random House.
Dr. Seuss. (1957b). *How the Grinch stole Christmas.* New York: Random House.
Dr. Seuss. (1957c). *The cat in the hat.* New York: Random House.
Dr. Seuss. (1960). *Green eggs and ham.* New York: Random House.
Dr. Seuss. (1961). *The sneetches and other stories.* New York: Random House.
Dr. Seuss. (1968). *The foot book.* New York: Random House.
Dr. Seuss. (1970). *Mr. Brown can moo! Can you?* New York: Random House.
Dr. Seuss. (1984). *The butter battle book.* New York: Random House.
Dr. Seuss. (1988). *Green eggs and ham.* New York: Random House.
Editors of Phaidon Press. (2007). *The art book for children, book two.* London: Phaidon Press.
Editors of *TIME for Kids.* (2005). *Benjamin Franklin.* New York: HarperCollins.
Elliott, D. (2004). *Evangeline Mudd and the golden-haired apes of the Ikkinasti jungle.* Cambridge, MA: Candlewick Press.
Elting, M., & Folsom, M. (2005). *Q is for duck: An alphabet guessing game.* Boston: Sandpiper.
Emberly, R. (1990). *My house/mi casa.* Boston: Little, Brown.

Falconer, I. (2001). *Olivia saves the circus*. New York: Atheneum Books for Young Readers.
Fanelli, S. (1995). *My map book*. New York: HarperCollins.
Ferris, J. (2002). *Once upon a marigold*. Orlando, FL: Harcourt.
Fish, H. (1937). *Animals of the bible: A picture book*. New York: HarperCollins.
Fitzhugh, L. (1964). *Harriet the spy*. New York: Yearling.
Fleischman, P. (2007). *Glass slipper gold sandal*. New York: Holt.
Fox, M. (1991). *Possum magic*. New York: Voyager Books.
Friedman, I. (1984). *How my parents learned to eat*. Boston: Houghton Mifflin.
Fritz, J. (1976). *What's the big idea, Ben Franklin?* New York: Putnam & Grosset.
Fritz, J. (2001). *Leonardo's horse*. New York: Putnam.
Funke, C. (2003). *Inkheart*. New York: Scholastic.
Gág, W. (1928). *Millions of cats*. New York: Putnam & Grosset.
Gaiman, N. (2003). *The wolves in the walls*. New York: HarperTrophy.
Gaiman, N. (2008a). *The dangerous alphabet*. New York: HarperCollins.
Gaiman, N. (2008b). *The graveyard book*. New York: HarperCollins.
Gaiman, N., & McKean, D. (2009). *Crazy hair*. New York: HarperCollins.
Galdone, P. (1973). *The little red hen*. New York: Scholastic.
Gardiner, J. R. (1992). *Stone fox*. New York: HarperCollins.
Gerstein, M. (2003). *The man who walked between the towers*. New York: Square Fish.
Gerstein, M. (2009). *A book*. New York: Roaring Brook Press.
Gibbons, G. (1999). *Behold... the dragons*. New York: HarperCollins.
Gibbons, G. (2000). *My football book*. New York: HarperCollins.
Gifford, P. (2008). *Moxy Maxwell does not love Stuart Little*. New York: Yearling.
Gorbachev, V. (1998). *Nicky and the big, bad wolves*. New York: North-South Books.
Gravett, E. (2006). *Wolves*. London: Macmillan Children's Books.
Gravett, E. (2010). *Dogs*. New York: Simon & Schuster Books for Young Readers.
Greenfield, E. (1988). *Nathaniel talking*. Washington, DC: Black Butterfly.
Greenfield, E., & Little, L. (1979). *Childtimes: A three-generation memoir*. New York: Thomas Y. Crowell.
Greger, M. (2006). *Kites for everyone: How to make and fly them*. Mineola, NY: Dover.
Grossman, V., & Long, S. (1991). *Ten little rabbits*. New York: Chronicle Books.
Haddix, M. (1999). *Just Ella*. New York: Aladdin.
Hague, M. (2005). *The book of dragons*. New York: HarperCollins.
Hall, K. (2006). *Animal hearing*. Milwaukee, WI: Gareth Stevens.
Halvorsen, L. (2000). *Letters home from Italy*. Woodbridge, CT: Blackbirch Press.
Hamilton, V. (1992). *Cousins*. New York: Scholastic.
Heide, F., & Smith, L. (2009). *Princess Hyacinth: The surprising tale of a girl who floated*. New York: Schwartz & Wade Books.
Henkes, K. (2004). *Kitten's first full moon*. New York: Greenwillow Books.
Hermes, P. (2002). *A perfect place: Joshua's Oregon Trail diary*. New York: Scholastic.
Herzog, B. (2004). *H is for home run: A baseball alphabet*. Chelsea, MI: Sleeping Bear Press.
Hesse, K. (1997). *Out of the dust*. New York: Scholastic.
Hiaasen, C. (2009). *Scat*. New York: Knopf Books for Young Readers.
Hill, E. (1981). *Spot's first walk*. New York: Putnam.
Hinton, S. (1997). *The outsiders*. New York: Puffin Books.
Hosler, J. (2000). *Clan apis*. Columbus, OH: Active Synapse.
Hutchins, P. (1971). *Rosie's walk*. New York: Aladdin.
Hyman, T. S. (1983). *Little Red Riding Hood*. Boston: Houghton Mifflin.
Irvine, J. (1991). *How to make pop-ups*. Surrey, UK: Beech Tree Books.
Isadora, R. (1983). *City seen from A to Z*. New York: Greenwillow Books.
Jacques, B. (2007). *Redwall: The graphic novel*. New York: Philomel.
Jay, A. (2007). *1-2-3: A child's first counting book*. New York: Dutton.
Jenkins, M. (2007). *Ape*. Cambridge, MA: Candlewick Press.

Jenkins, S. (2003). *What do you do with a tail like this?* Boston: Houghton Mifflin.
Jenkins, S. (2004). *Actual size*. Boston: Houghton Mifflin.
Jenkins, S. (2007). *Living color*. Boston: Houghton Mifflin.
Jenkins, S. (2009). *Down, down, down: A journey to the bottom of the sea*. Boston: Houghton Mifflin.
Jerome, K. (2004). *Science at the aquarium*. Washington, DC: National Geographic Society.
Jeunesse, G., & Peyrols, S. (1989). *Ladybugs and other insects*. New York: Scholastic.
Jonas, A. (1990). *Aardvarks, disembark!* New York: Greenwillow Books.
Jordan, H. (1992). *How a seed grows*. New York: HarperCollins.
Juster, N. (2005). *The hello, goodbye window*. New York: Hyperion Books.
Kadohata, C. (2004). *Kira-kira*. New York: Aladdin.
Kasza, K. (2005). *The dog who cried wolf*. New York: Puffin Books.
Keating, F. (2006). *Theodore*. New York: Simon & Schuster.
Keats, E. (1976). *The snowy day*. New York: Puffin Books. (Original work published 1962)
Keller, L. (1998). *The scrambled states of America*. New York: Holt.
Keller, L. (2008). *The scrambled states of America talent show*. New York: Holt.
Kellogg, S. (1985). *Chicken Little*. Boston: Houghton Mifflin.
Kellogg, S. (1986). *Pecos Bill*. New York: Scholastic.
Kellogg, S. (1988). *Johnny Appleseed*. New York: Scholastic.
Kelly, J. (2009). *The evolution of Calpurnia Tate*. New York: Holt.
Kinney, J. (2007). *Diary of a wimpy kid*. New York: Amulet.
Kipling, R. (1950). *The jungle book*. New York: Grosset & Dunlap. (Original work published 1894)
Kloske, G., & Blitt, B. (2005). *Once upon a time, the end*. New York: Atheneum Books.
Konigsburg, E.L. (1996). *The view from Saturday*. New York: Aladdin.
Korman, G. (1998). *The 6th grade nickname game*. New York: Hyperion Books.
Korman, G. (2000). *No more dead dogs*. New York: Scholastic.
Korman, G. (2005). Guy things. In J. Scieszka (Ed.), *Guys write for guys read* (pp. 137–140). New York: Viking.
Korman, G. (2006). *Kidnapped: Book three: The rescue*. New York: Scholastic.
Korman, G. (2007). *Schooled*. New York: Hyperion Books.
Korman, G. (2008). *Swindle*. New York: Scholastic.
Korman, G. (2009). *Zoobreak*. New York: Scholastic.
Kudlinski, K. (2005). *Dr. Seuss*. New York: Aladdin.
Kulka, J. (2007). *Wolf's coming!* Minneapolis, MN: Carolrhoda Books.
Kunhardt, D. (1940). *Pat the bunny*. New York: Golden Books.
Kuskin, K. (1986). *The Philharmonic gets dressed*. New York: HarperCollins.
Lach, W. (2006). *Can you hear it?* London: Abrams Books for Young Readers.
Lachtman, O. (1995). *Pepita talks twice*. Houston, TX: Piñata Books.
Leaf, M. (2001). *The story of Ferdinand*. Jaffrey, NH: Godine. (Original work published 1936)
Lear, E. (1983). *An Edward Lear alphabet*. New York: Mulberry Books.
Lee, S., & Lee, T. (2005). *Please, puppy, please*. New York: Scholastic.
L'Engle, M. (1962). *A wrinkle in time*. New York: Dell.
Lester, J. (1994). *John Henry*. New York: Puffin Books.
Levine, E. (1989). *I hate English!* New York: Scholastic.
Levine, E., & Nelson, K. (2007). *Henry's freedom box*. New York: Scholastic.
Lewis, C. S. (2005). *The lion, the witch and the wardrobe*. New York: HarperCollins. (Original work published 1950)
Lies, B. (2008). *Bats at the library*. Boston: Houghton Mifflin.
Lobel, A. (1976). *Frog and Toad all year*. New York: HarperCollins.
Lobel, A. (1983). *Fables*. New York: HarperCollins.
Long, M., & Shannon, D. (2003). *How I became a pirate*. New York: Harcourt.
Lovett, S. (1991). *Extremely weird spiders*. Santa Fe, NM: John Muir.
Lowrey, J. (1996). *The poky little puppy*. New York: Golden Books. (Original work published 1942)
Lowry, L. (1993). *The giver*. Boston: Houghton Mifflin.
Lowry, L. (1998). *Looking back: A book of memories*. Boston: Houghton Mifflin.

Macaulay, D. (1990). *Black and white*. Boston: Houghton Mifflin.
MacLachlan, P. (1994). *All the places to love*. New York: HarperCollins.
MacLachlan, P., & Charest, E. (2006). *Once I ate a pie*. New York: Joanna Cottler.
Malone, M. (2010). *The sixty-eight rooms*. New York: Random House.
Marchetti, V. (2001). *Orangutans*. Bothell, WA: Wright Group.
Markham, L. (1996). *Avi*. Santa Barbara, CA: Learning Works.
Marsalis, W. (2005). *Jazz A.B.Z*. Cambridge, MA: Candlewick Press.
Martin, A. (2005). *A dog's life: The autobiography of a stray*. New York: Scholastic.
Martin, A. (2009). *Everything for a dog*. New York: Feiwel and Friends.
Martin, J. B. (1998). *Snowflake Bentley*. Boston: Houghton Mifflin.
Martin, Jr., B. (1970). *Brown bear, brown bear, what do you see?* New York: Holt, Rinehart, and Winston.
Martin, Jr., B., & Archambault, J. (1989). *Chicka chicka boom boom*. New York: Simon & Schuster.
Martin, R. (1989). *Will's mammoth*. New York: Dell.
Marzolla, J. (2000). *I spy little letters*. New York: Cartwheel.
Masoff, J. (2006). *Oh yikes! History's grossest, wackiest moments*. New York: Workman.
Mayer, M. (1976). *Hiccup*. New York: Dial Books for Young Readers.
McCarty, P. (2002). *Hondo & Fabian*. New York: Holt.
McClafferty, C. (2006). *Something out of nothing: Marie Curie and radium*. New York: Farrar, Straus and Giroux.
McCloskey, R. (1941). *Make way for ducklings*. New York: Penguin.
McCloskey, R. (1976). *Blueberries for Sal*. New York: Puffin Books.
McDermott, G. (1997). *Arrow to the sun*. New York: Puffin Books.
McDermott, G. (2001). *Raven*. New York: Sandpiper.
McDermott, G. (2003). *Creation*. New York: Dutton.
Micklethwait, L. (1996). *I spy: An alphabet in art*. New York: HarperCollins.
Micklethwait, L. (2008). *Children: A first art book*. London: Frances Lincoln Children's Books.
Miles, V. (2007). *Old mother bear*. San Francisco: Chronicle Books.
Morley, J. (1995). *How would you survive as an ancient Egyptian?* New York: Franklin Watts.
Munsch, R. (1996). *Stephanie's ponytail*. Buffalo, NY: Annick Press.
Muntean, M. (2006). *Do not open this book!* New York: Scholastic.
Myers, C. (2007). *Jabberwocky*. New York: Hyperion Books.
Nagda, A., & Bickle, C. (2000). *Tiger math*. New York: Holt.
Nagda, A., & Bickel, C. (2004). *Polar bear math*. New York: Holt.
Naylor, P. (1994). *The fear place*. New York: Aladdin.
Naylor, P. (1999). *Saving Shiloh*. New York: Aladdin.
Naylor, P. (2000). *Shiloh*. New York: Aladdin.
Nelson, K. (2008). We *are the ship: The story of Negro league baseball*. New York: Hyperion Books.
Newbery, J. (1744). *A little pretty pocket-book*. New York: Harcourt, Brace & World.
Neye, E. (2000). *Butterflies*. New York: Scholastic.
Niepold, M., & Verdu, J. (2007). *Oooh! Matisse*. Berkeley, CA: Tricycle Press.
Niepold, M., & Verdu, J. (2009). *Oooh! Picasso*. Berkeley, CA: Tricycle Press.
O'Dell, S. (1971). *Island of the blue dolphins*. New York: Dell.
O'Dell, S. (1996). *The black pearl*. New York: Yearling.
Osborne, M. P. (1995). *Afternoon on the Amazon*. New York: Random House.
Osborne, M. P. (1998). *Day of the dragon king*. New York: Random House.
Osborne, M. (1999). *Buffalo before breakfast*. New York: Scholastic.
Otway, H. (2008). *1001 unbelievable facts*. Singapore: Arcturus.
Page, G. (2006). *How to be a good dog*. New York: Bloomsbury Children's Books.
Pak, S. (1999). *Dear Juno*. New York: Puffin Books.
Pallotta, J. (1993). *The extinct alphabet book*. New York: Dell.
Pallotta, J. (2005). *Ocean counting odd numbers*. Watertown, MA: Charlesbridge.
Pang, E., & Louie, H. (2008). *Good dog! Kids teach kids about dog behavior and training*. Wenatchee, WA: Dogwise.

Park, L. (2001). *A single shard*. New York: Yearling.
Paterson, K. (1978). *The great Gilly Hopkins*. New York: HarperTrophy.
Paterson, K. (2004). *Bridge to Terabithia*. New York: HarperTeen.
Patron, S. (2006). *The higher power of Lucky*. New York: Atheneum Books for Young Children.
Paul, C. (2009). *Long shot: Never too small to dream big*. New York: Simon & Schuster.
Paulsen, G. (1987). *Hatchet*. New York: Aladdin.
Paulsen, G. (1998). *My life in dog years*. New York: Yearling.
Paulsen, G. (2001). *Guts*. New York: Dell.
Pelham, D. (2007). *Trail*. New York: Simon & Schuster.
Pelletier, D. (1996). *The graphic alphabet*. New York: Scholastic.
Phelan, G. (2004). *Extreme weather*. Washington, DC: National Geographic.
Pinkney, D. (2000). *Aesop's fables*. New York: Chronicle Books.
Pinkney, J. (2009). *The lion and the mouse*. New York: Little, Brown Books for Young Readers.
Polacco, P. (1998). *Thank you, Mr. Falker*. New York: Philomel.
Polacco, P. (2001). *The keeping quilt*. New York: Aladdin.
Polacco, P. (2007). *The lemonade club*. New York: Philomel.
Potter, B. (1940). *The tale of Peter Rabbit*. London: Ladybird Books.
Potter, B. (2002). *The tale of Peter Rabbit*. New York: Warne. (Original work published 1902)
Prelutsky, J. (1993). *The dragons are singing tonight*. New York: Greenwillow Books.
Rathmann, P. (1995). *Officer Buckle and Gloria*. New York: Putnam.
Recorvits, H. (2003). *My name is Yoon*. New York: Farrar, Straus and Giroux.
Reeder, T. (2005). *Komodo dragons*. Washington, DC: National Geographic.
Reibstein, M. (2008). *Wabi Sabi*. New York: Little, Brown.
Reschke, T. (2005). *A dragon's birth*. Charleston, SC: BookSurge.
Rex, D. (2007). *Pssst!* New York: Harcourt.
Reynolds, P. (2003). *The dot*. Cambridge, MA: Candlewick Press.
Riordan, R. (2005). *The lightning thief*. New York: Miramax Books.
Riordan, R. (2008). *The 39 clues: The maze of bones*. New York: Scholastic.
Rockwell, T. (1975). *How to eat fried worms*. New York: Dell Yearling.
Rohmann, E. (2002). *My friend rabbit*. New York: Roaring Brook Press.
Rose, D. (2003). *One nighttime sea*. New York: Scholastic.
Rosen, M. (Ed.) (1992). *Home*. New York: Charlotte Zolotow.
Ross, K. (1998). *Crafts from your favorite fairy tales*. Minneapolis, MN: Millbrook Press.
Rowling, J. K. (2002). *Harry Potter and the goblet of fire*. New York: Scholastic.
Rowling, J. K. (2007). *Harry Potter and the deathly hallows*. New York: Scholastic.
Rubin, S. (2007). *Counting with Wayne Thiebaud*. San Francisco: Chronicle Books.
Ryan, P. (2004). *Becoming Naomi León*. New York: Scholastic.
Rylant, C. (1982). *When I was young in the mountains*. New York: Dutton.
Sachar, L. (1998). *Holes*. New York: Farrar, Straus and Giroux.
Sandler, M. (2008). *Lincoln through the lens*. New York: Scholastic.
Say, A. (1993). *Grandfather's journey*. Boston: Houghton Mifflin.
Say, A. (2009). *Ericka-San*. Boston: Houghton Mifflin.
Scarry, R. (1968). *What do people do all day?* New York: Random House for Young Readers.
Schachner, J. (2003). *Skippyjon Jones*. New York: Puffin Books.
Scholastic. (2009). *How to draw Bakugan*. New York: Author.
Schwartz, D. (1985). *How much is a million?* New York: Scholastic.
Scieszka, J. (1998). *Summer reading is killing me!* New York: Puffin Books.
Scieszka, J. (Ed.). (2005). *Guys write for guys read*. New York: Viking.
Scieszka, J. (2008a). *Knucklehead*. New York: Viking.
Scieszka, J. (2008b). *Smash! Crash!* New York: Simon & Schuster.
Scieszka, J. (2009). *Truckery rhymes*. New York: Simon & Schuster.
Scieszka, J., & Smith, L. (1992). *The stinky cheese man and other fairly stupid tales*. New York: Viking.
Scieszka, J., & Smith, L. (1998). *Squids will be squids*. New York: Scholastic.

Scieszka, J., & Smith, L. (2005). *Seen art?* New York: Museum of Modern Art and Viking.
Scott, W. (2000). *Ivanhoe.* New York: Penguin Classics. (Original work published 1820)
Seeger, P. (2001). *Abiyoyo.* New York: Simon & Schuster.
Selznick, B. (2007). *The invention of Hugo Cabret.* New York: Scholastic.
Sendak, M. (1988). *Where the wild things are.* New York: HarperCollins. (Original work published 1963)
Shannon, D. (1998). *No, David!* New York: Blue Sky Press.
Shannon, D. (2004). *A bad case of stripes.* New York: Scholastic.
Shannon, G. (1999). *Tomorrow's alphabet.* New York: HarperCollins.
Shetterly, R. (2005). *Americans who tell the truth.* New York: Dutton Children's Books.
Siegel, S. (2006). *To dance: A ballerina's graphic novel.* New York: Simon & Schuster.
Sierra, J. (2004). *Wild about books.* New York: Knopf.
Silvey, A. (Ed.). (2009). *Everything I need to know I learned from a children's book.* New York: Roaring Brook Press.
Simon, S. (1990). *Deserts.* New York: Morrow Junior Books.
Simon, S. (2002). *Super storms.* New York: Scholastic.
Simon, S. (2006). *Earthquakes.* New York: HarperCollins.
Sis, P. (1998). *Fire truck.* New York: Greenwillow Books.
Smith, D. (2004). *Taste of blackberries.* New York: HarperCollins.
Snicket, L. (2009). *The composer is dead.* New York: HarperCollins.
Solheim, J. (1998). *It's disgusting and we ate it! True food facts from around the world and throughout history.* New York: Aladdin.
Soloff-Levy, B. (2002). *How to draw sea creatures.* New York: Troll Communications.
Spinelli, E., & Spinelli, J. (2009). *Today I will.* New York: Knopf.
Spinelli, J. (1990). *Maniac Magee.* Boston: Little, Brown.
Spinelli, J. (1996). *Crash.* New York: Dell.
Spinelli, J. (1997). *Wringer.* New York: Scholastic.
Spinelli, J. (1998). *Knots in my yo-yo string: The autobiography of a kid.* New York: Knopf.
Spinelli, J. (2000). *Stargirl.* New York: Knopf.
St. George, J., & Small, D. (2000). *So you want to be president?* New York: Philomel.
Staines, B. (2009). *All God's critters.* New York: Simon & Schuster.
Stead, R. (2009). *When you reach me.* Bel Air, CA: Wendy Lamb Books.
Steer, D. (2006). *The dragon's eye.* Cambridge, MA: Candlewick Press.
Stevenson, J. (1986). *When I was nine.* New York: Greenwillow Books.
Stevenson, R. (1985). *A child's garden of verses.* New York: Delacorte. (Original work published 1885)
Stewart, T. (2008). *The mysterious Benedict Society.* New York: Little, Brown.
Stewart, W. (2009). *Who was Walt Disney?* New York: Grosset & Dunlap.
Surat, M. (1989). *Angel child, dragon child.* New York: Scholastic.
Swanson, S. (2008). *The house in the night.* Boston: Houghton Mifflin.
Taback, S. (1999). *Joseph had a little overcoat.* New York: Viking.
Teague, M. (2002). *Dear Mrs. LaRue: Letters from obedience school.* New York: Scholastic.
Thompson, J. (1997). *Scary godmother.* New York: Sirius Entertainment.
Turkle, B. (1976). *Deep in the forest.* New York: Dutton.
Twain, M. (1876). *The adventures of Tom Sawyer.* Hartford, CT: American.
Twain, M. (1884). *The adventures of Huckleberry Finn.* New York: Charles Webster.
Van Allsburg, C. (1979). *The garden of Abdul Gasazi.* Boston: Houghton Mifflin.
Van Allsburg, C. (1987). *The Z was zapped.* Boston: Houghton Mifflin.
Van Allsburg, C. (1990). *Just a dream.* Boston: Houghton Mifflin.
Van Allsburg, C. (1995). *Bad day at Riverbend.* Boston: Houghton Mifflin.
Van Loon, H. (2007). *The story of mankind.* Chapel Hill, NC: Yesterday's Classics. (Original work published 1921)
Verne, J. (2005). *Twenty thousand leagues under the sea.* New York: Pocket Books. (Original work published 1869)

Viorst, J. (1972). *Alexander and the terrible, horrible, no good, very bad day.* New York: Aladdin.
VIZ Media. (2008). *The complete Pokémon pocket guide, Vol. 1.* San Francisco: VIZ Media.
Watt, M. (2007). *Chester.* Toronto: Kids Can Press.
Watt, M. (2008). *Chester's back.* Toronto: Kids Can Press.
Welch, C. A. (2008). *Benjamin Banneker.* New York: Lerner.
Werner, S., & Forss, S. (2009). *Alphabeasties and other amazing types.* Maplewood, NJ: Blue Apple Books.
White, D. (2005). *Your safari dragons: In search of the real komodo dragon.* Livermore, CA: WingSpan.
White, E. B. (2001). *Charlotte's web.* New York: HarperCollins. (Original work published 1952)
Wiesner, D. (1990). *Hurricane.* Boston: Clarion Books.
Wiesner, D. (1992). *June 29, 1999.* New York: Houghton Mifflin.
Wiesner, D. (1997). *Tuesday.* Boston: Sandpiper.
Wiesner, D. (1999). *Sector 7.* Boston: Clarion Books.
Wiesner, D. (2001). *The three pigs.* Boston: Clarion Books.
Wiesner, D. (2004). *Gonna roll the bones.* New York: Houghton Mifflin.
Wiesner, D. (2006). *Flotsam.* Boston: Clarion Books.
Wiesner, D. (2008). *Free fall.* New York: HarperCollins Publishers. (Original work published 1988)
Wild, M. (2006). *Woolvs in the sitee.* Asheville, NC: Front Street.
Wilks, M. (1986). *The ultimate alphabet.* New York: Holt.
Willems, M. (2003). *Don't let the pigeon drive the bus!* New York: Hyperion Books.
Willems, M. (2004). *Knuffle bunny.* New York: Hyperion Books.
Willems, M. (2005). *Leonardo the terrible monster.* New York: Hyperion Books.
Willems, M. (2006). *Edwina: The dinosaur who didn't know she was extinct.* New York: Hyperion Books.
Willems, M. (2007). *Knuffle Bunny too.* New York: Hyperion Books.
Wilson, J. (1989). *Oh, brother.* New York: Scholastic.
Wisniewski, D. (1996). *Golem.* New York: Clarion Books.
Yep, L. (2008). *The dragon's child: A story of Angel Island.* New York: HarperCollins.
Yolen, J. (2007). *How do dinosaurs go to school?* New York: Blue Sky Press.
Young, E. (1989). *Lon Po Po.* New York: Philomel.
Young, E. (2009). *Hook.* New York: Roaring Brook Press.

Index

f following a page number indicates a figure

D

E

F

Q

R

S